# CHILD POVERTY IN AMERICA TODAY

# CHILD POVERTY IN AMERICA TODAY

## Volume 1: Families and Children

*Edited by Barbara A. Arrighi and David J. Maume*

*Introduction by Diana Pearce*

**Praeger Perspectives**

**Westport, Connecticut
London**

**Library of Congress Cataloging-in-Publication Data**

Child poverty in America today / edited by Barbara A. Arrighi and David J. Maume.
    p.  cm.
    Includes bibliographical references and index.
    ISBN 978–0–275–98926–2 (set : alk. paper)—ISBN 978–0–275–98927–9 (v. 1 : alk. paper)—
    ISBN 978–0–275–98928–6 (v. 2 : alk. paper)—ISBN 978–0–275–98929–3 (v. 3 : alk. paper)—
    ISBN 978–0–275–98930–9 (v. 4 : alk. paper)
    1. Poor children—United States.   2. Poor families—United States.   3. Poverty—United States.
    4. Child welfare—United States.   5. Children—United States—Social conditions.
    6. Children—Government policy—United States.   I. Arrighi, Barbara A.   II. Maume, David J.
    HV741.C4875   2007
    362.7086′9420973–dc22        2007003046

British Library Cataloguing in Publication Data is available.

Library of Congress Catalog Card Number: 2007003046
ISBN-10: 0–275–98926–7 (set)      ISBN-13: 978–0–275–98926–2 (set)
          0–275–98927–5 (vol. 1)          978–0–275–98927–9 (vol. 1)
          0–275–98928–3 (vol. 2)          978–0–275–98928–6 (vol. 2)
          0–275–98929–1 (vol. 3)          978–0–275–98929–3 (vol. 3)
          0–275–98930–5 (vol. 4)          978–0–275–98930–9 (vol. 4)

First published in 2007

Praeger Publishers, 88 Post Road West, Westport, CT 06881
An imprint of Greenwood Publishing Group, Inc.
www.praeger.com

Printed in the United States of America

The paper used in this book complies with the
Permanent Paper Standard issued by the National
Information Standards Organization (Z39.48–1984).

10 9 8 7 6 5 4 3 2 1

*To our children*
*Eiler, Elena, and Megan*
*and*
*Meghan and Allison*
*Our concern for their welfare piqued our interest in the*
*welfare of all children*

# CONTENTS

# ACKNOWLEDGMENTS

First, we wish to thank all the contributors to the four volumes for the exceptional caliber of their research. Their dedication and commitment to understanding the causes of child and family poverty is remarkable. It has been a pleasure to work with such a fine group of scholars. It is noteworthy, too, that more than a few of the contributors endured family emergencies and/or experienced personal crises during the research and writing phase, yet remained committed to the project. For that, we are grateful.

We are honored that Diana Pearce is the author of the Introduction for Volume 1: Families and Children. Professor Pearce has written a thoughtful essay weaving common threads among diverse chapters. She is a tireless researcher who has been a pioneer in examining the causes and effects of poverty in the lives of women and children. Not only has Professor Pearce illuminated the way for other researchers in explaining the complex factors influencing women's poverty, she has been an ardent advocate for ending the feminization of poverty.

Thanks to Rachel Sebastian, graduate student at the University of Cincinnati, who assisted with the project. We appreciate, too, the guidance of Elizabeth Potenza, editor at Praeger, throughout the editorial process, Anne Rehill who assisted early on in the project, Nicole Azze, production manager, Vivek Sood and Saloni Jain who oversaw the copyediting. Finally, thanks to Marie Ellen Larcada, who first approached Barbara about editing the four-volume set.

# Introduction

## *Diana Pearce*

"A child in the United States is born into poverty every 40 seconds."[1]

Child poverty in the world's richest nation continues to be a confounding paradox. No one is "for" child poverty, yet it persists, and continues to increase: over the last five years, an additional approximately 1.5 million children in America became poor, with the total now over 13 million.[2] Comparative studies have found that it is worse to be a poor child in America than in any other developed country.[3]

While none would doubt that it is harmful, the numbers are still quite sobering:

- At birth, a poor child is 1.8 times as likely to be premature, 1.9 times to be low birth weight, and 2.8 times as likely to have had inadequate prenatal care as the nonpoor child.
- A poor child is 1.6 times more likely to die as an infant, and 8 times as likely to live in a family that has had too little food in the last four months.
- A poor child is twice as likely to repeat a grade, about 3.5 times as likely to be expelled or drop out of school, and only half as likely to finish college as a nonpoor child.[4]
- The impacts do not end with childhood, as various studies have documented that childhood poverty is associated with higher rates of teenage childbearing, juvenile delinquency, and adult poverty.[5]

Yet simply describing childhood poverty and its effects on children, does not advance our understanding of this phenomenon, and why it persists. So the task undertaken by this volume is to present new perspectives on why and how childhood poverty persists. We begin with the contexts of child poverty in early twenty-first century America, starting with the demographic and historical context.

## THE CHANGING DEMOGRAPHIC CONTEXT OF CHILD POVERTY

The demographic context in which children experience poverty has been changing dramatically. At the same time that the number of poor children is increasing, children and their families are becoming more and more a minority of households, and those households are changing. Once the norm was that most households were headed by married couples, and most of them had children; for example, in 1940, three-fourths of households were headed by married couples, and even as late as 1980, over half of families had children.[6] However, as of 2004, only 32 percent of households have children in them, less than one-third.[7] At the same time, the living circumstances of children have become more diverse, with more children living in families with less economic security. As recently as 1960, seven out of eight children lived with two parents. However, by 2005 only two-thirds of children lived with two parents, while almost one in four lived with his/her mother, only one in 20 with father only and about the same number with other relatives (grandmother, aunts, uncles, etc.) or non-relatives.[8] Likewise, the proportion of households with children that are not white increased from 20 percent to 38 percent between 1975 and 2005, with Hispanics increasing their proportion the most over the last three decades, from 6 percent to 17 percent of families with children.[9]

Poverty trends are similar, but the even more dramatic demographic shifts have had a differential impact on children. Because children have become, with the decrease in birth rates and increased longevity, a smaller proportion of the population, children are a smaller proportion of the poor, falling from 44 percent of all poor persons in 1975 to 35 percent in 2005.[10] At the same time, poor *families* with children increased their proportion of all poor *families*, from about two-thirds of all poor families in 1960 to about three-fourths in 2005. This trend reflects the increased diversity of race-ethnicity and living arrangements described above, so that more of the burden of child poverty is now found among families who are either maintained by women alone, or are African American or Hispanic, or both. Thus in 1975, more than half of poor families with children were white (non-Hispanic) (53%) but by 2005, that proportion had fallen to less than two in five (38%). Conversely, the proportion who are non-Hispanic African American fell slightly over these three decades (from 31% to 28%) while the proportion who are Hispanic increased dramatically over this period from 13 percent to 29 percent. Likewise, the percentage of poor families with children who are maintained by women alone has increased dramatically, from 28 percent of all poor families in 1960 to 61 percent in 2005.[11]

Finally, it is worth noting the differential and disturbing trends in poverty rates. On the one hand, the poverty rates for all families, and for all persons fell dramatically between 1960 and 2005, from 18 percent to 10 percent for families, and from 22 percent to 13 percent for all persons. Poverty rates also fell for some of the most economically disadvantaged groups as well: for example, the poverty rate for black families fell from 39 percent in 1967 (the earliest year for which there is this data by race) to 28 percent in 2005, while the poverty rate for women-maintained families fell from 49 percent in 1960 to 31 percent in 2005. However, while the poverty rate for children under 18 initially also fell—from 27 percent in 1960 to a low of 14 percent in 1969—it rose again, reaching 17 percent by1975, and has stayed at approximately this level, rising and falling by a few percentage points, for the next 30 years, and is now at 18 percent.[12] Thus, alone, among all demographic groups, children's poverty has remained stubbornly high for three decades.

In sum, then, the demographic trends are such that:

- Children and families with children are a smaller proportion of the population as a whole, and of the poverty population as well. There are fewer children per family, and fewer families with children.

- While other demographic groups (characterized by age, gender of head, and/or race-ethnicity) have experienced declining poverty rates, that has been much less true of children.

- Children in the United States, especially poor children, reflect greater diversity than in the past in terms of race-ethnicity and living arrangements.

- The continuing high poverty rates of children reflect the high numbers of children in single mother and/or African American, Hispanic, and Native American families.

This demographic context provides the serious challenge of disentangling and understanding the dynamics of children's poverty, even as it is becoming more complex and diversified. Children's poverty in the United States has become in a real sense, a series of different poverties, overlapping to some extent but also differing in essential and important ways. For this reason, these chapters can be seen as analogous to the proverbial blind men and the elephant, each describing a different aspect of children's poverty, with their differences not reflecting inconsistency, but a real diversity of the reality of American childhood poverty.

## THE POLITICAL/POLICY, ECONOMIC, AND SOCIAL CONTEXT

This growing diversity exists in a societal context that shapes the choices and options for all entities, whether individual, institutional, or societal. There are three trends that should be mentioned in particular, but in brief:

1. *A Decreased "Safety Net"/Benefit Programs.* Welfare reform, enacted in 1996, ended the entitlement to cash assistance. Combined with time limits and an emphasis on "work first" (rather than addressing health problems or deficits in educational preparation or English language), this has greatly reduced the availability of a "safety net" for poor single mother families. In addition, beginning in the 1980s, there has been an erosion of a range of other transfer programs, in terms of both benefit levels and coverage, from unemployment insurance to food stamps, from disability benefits to health insurance.

2. *Increased Reliance on Market/Wage Income.* At the same time, a rapidly expanding economy in the late 1990s increased employment opportunities, resulting in an increased proportion of single mothers in the workforce. Even though the sluggish economy in the early years of the twenty-first century has resulted in some loss of these employment gains, the curve has shifted, so that a substantially larger proportion of poor families,

particularly single mother families, are reliant to a larger degree on earnings rather than transfers (both cash and noncash). This means, as will be seen in more detail, both higher living costs (with the addition of employment-related costs such as child care) and greater instability of income.

3. *Increased Economic Inequality.* Although beginning several decades ago, by the early 2000s, several economic trends have coalesced to create an income (and resources) distribution that is increasingly unequal, with particular consequences for those at the lower end. These trends include: the shift in employment from higher-paying manufacturing to lower-waged service sector jobs; the decline in unions—with the attendant decrease in the union-associated premium on wages; the shrinking of the public sector; the decrease in health insurance and other benefits through employers; the erosion of the federal minimum wage "floor" under the wage structure (only partially offset by recent state minimum wage increases).

## NEW PERSPECTIVES ON CHILD POVERTY

Given the changing demographic, political, and economic context in American society, these chapters break important new ground by offering new perspectives on children's poverty. They do so through a number of themes that recur across these chapters that together provide the reader with new understandings on childhood poverty. These themes are:

1. An emphasis on structural factors in explaining children's poverty such as racial and ethnic residential segregation or gender-based occupational segregation, rather than individual characteristics such as age or educational level.

2. The necessity of addressing the fact that the measurement of poverty is problematic, and thus alternative definitions or approaches must be used to define poverty, and who is poor.

3. The need to more directly measure economic hardship, reflecting another weakness of the poverty measure, through examination of the "costs" side of the poverty "equation."

4. Poverty among children is concentrated in certain racial and ethnic groups, particularly African American and Hispanic families, as well as Native American, and thus childhood poverty analyses must take into account how race and ethnicity impact the experience and dynamics of children and their poverties in each of these groups.

5. Childhood poverty occurs within a neighborhood context, with race-ethnic and household composition characteristics that interact to create impacts on children that reflect neighborhoods levels of poverty concentration.

6. Poverty among children is today very strongly related to women's poverty, and thus understanding children's poverty must include a gender analysis

### Theme #1: Emphasis on Structural Factors

While it is almost a truism, it bears repeating that because children are by definition dependent, understanding their poverty must involve analysis of the sources of poverty for the adults on which they are economically (as well as emotionally)

dependent. The reason for the need for this emphasis is that too often, children who are poor are characterized as "innocent victims." While one would hardly disagree with this particular characterization, it contains an implicit syllogism that if children are innocent victims, their parents must be "guilty" perpetrators. Thus, it is but one step from this characterization of children to one that blames the parents, the responsible and supporting adults, for the poverty experienced by their children. Such analysis then can easily become a classic "blame the victim" analysis, in which the characteristics of the adult parents who are poor are used to explain their individual poverty.[13] An example of this would be to blame parental poverty on the number of children in the family, or on being a single parent.

In contrast, all the chapters in this volume avoid this trap, looking instead at a range of structural factors to explain parental poverty. For example, several authors— Barnes and Bynum, Kelly, Firestone, and McDonough—explore the child-care issues faced by low-income parents, demonstrating how the lack of a system of affordable quality child care forces parents to make Hobbesian choices between taking care of their children themselves, or using problematic child care so that they can work for a minimally adequate income at best. Child-care difficulties are both cause and effect of poverty, and are part of the structure and context that must be understood to address children's poverty.

A second analytical bias that a "children as innocent victims" perspective may lead to is that of mistaking "correlation" for causation, sometimes even missing that the causal links go in the other direction. For example, alcohol abuse may be the result of poverty, rather than the cause; neighborhoods may have high levels of teen parenting because they are high poverty neighborhoods. Thus, even though at the individual level, teen parenting has a high probability of resulting in subsequent lifelong low income, understanding how the neighborhood context plays a role in this reveals an important dynamic of poverty.

At the same time, structural analysis does not mean that the responsible adults, parents, and guardians, are but passive victims themselves, but are agents in their own lives, both positive and negative. Indeed, it is clear from all the chapters here, as well as many other analyses, that poor parents struggle greatly to make ends meet, to meet the material needs but also the child care, health care, and other needs of their children, against very great odds. As Friedman points out, it is important to empower, rather than blame parents for their poverty/homelessness. To understand these efforts better, however, requires the kind of analysis presented here that disentangles the various structural factors that contribute to children's poverty.

## Theme #2: A Flawed Measure of Poverty

Up to this point, the discussion has taken for granted that the readers and authors are in agreement as to what is meant by "poverty." While most would agree on a general conception that encompasses the idea of "not having enough resources to meet basic needs" (with perhaps some debate about how to define "enough"), U.S. researchers face a very basic measurement problem. That is, there is broad agreement that the widely used official federal poverty measure no longer accurately measures what most people mean by poverty.[14] Indeed, this is one of those rare topics in social science where one can, with reasonable confidence, assert that there is a consensus. One indicator is that the calls for changes in the early nineteen-nineties resulted in a Congressionally mandated multiyear study with dozens of research projects, culminating in the National Academy of Sciences publishing a massive study, *Measuring Poverty*, in 1995, including findings and recommendations.[15] What is lacking, however, is a political consensus, for no political entity wants to pay the political cost of overhauling the poverty measure, for it would undoubtedly increase the count of the poor substantially. Thus more than a decade later, the measure remains unchanged (see below.)

Given this stalemate, the researcher is faced with a federal poverty measure that is seriously out of date, no longer reflecting the reality of the costs faced by the poor, nor their variation by place, family type, and work status. Developed over four decades ago by Molly Orshansky, the federal poverty measure was based on a food budget that provided enough for a minimally adequate diet nutritionally. On the basis of expenditure surveys that showed families spent about a third of their income on food, this food budget was multiplied by three to cover all necessities. This froze the relationship between food and other expenses, building in the assumption that all expenses would increase at the same rate, and allowed for no new costs, such as child care. As workforce participation patterns and family composition changed, and as some costs such as housing and health care rose much faster than food, this measure has become increasingly out of kilter with the actual expenses faced by families. Even the Census Bureau acknowledges this: "The poverty measure . . . use as a historical measure, not as a yardstick of what families and individuals need to meet their needs. . . ."[16]

As a result of its outdated and "frozen" methodology, the federal poverty measure has a number of flaws, but first and foremost, it is too low, and therefore seriously underestimates the poverty population, which in turn means it does not "capture" the true nature and diversity of the poverty population, or of the poverty problem. For example, there is no variation in the federal poverty measure between places, even though major costs such as housing and child care vary as much as 5:1 from the most to least expensive place.[17] Finally, it should be noted that as the "count" of the poor in the United States is based on a household survey, it does not include the poorest of the poor, those who are homeless, including homeless families. Thus, analyses of the homeless, such as those of Friedman and Jasinski et al., and others elsewhere, are focused on a poverty population, a substantial number of whom are children, who are not even "counted" as poor in official statistics. This is not an insubstantial number: estimates of the number of homeless children range from 1.2 million[18] to 1.35 million among 600,000 families.[19]

Every analyst and every policy or program has had to address these issues, implicitly or explicitly, and the chapters in this volume are no exception. Indeed, they illustrate the two very different approaches taken to reconcile a flawed measure with the need for finding a way to analyze poverty. On the one hand, several chapters take a substantially qualitative approach, and use an ecological, or self-defined definition of poverty. This is the approach taken by Jasinski et al., for example, in her study of homeless women. Alternatively, those who are undertaking more quantitative analyses often use multiples of the poverty line, such as 125 percent (Davidson) or 200 percent of the poverty line (Kelly), designating households that fall beneath this line as "low income," "working poor," or "near poor." A variation of this approach which is an equivalent of multiples of the poverty line, used by Timberlake in this volume to measure poverty at the neighborhood level, is to designate a neighborhood as "high poverty" when 40 percent or more of residents have incomes below the official federal poverty measure. Using such a measure—which is common and widely accepted[20]—is based on the assumption that one can designate a neighborhood as "high poverty" when only a minority of residents are officially poor, because many of those whose incomes are above the poverty threshold nevertheless lack enough resources to adequately meet their needs. That is, as with using 125 percent or 200 percent of the federal poverty measure, if we had a more adequate measure, they would be designated as poor. There is a third alternative, which is to more directly assess the ability of families to meet the costs of specific basic needs, such as housing, which we will discuss in the next section in more detail.

To sum up, a common theme across these chapters is that the analysis of poverty is complicated greatly by the lack of an accurate, credible measure of who is poor, requiring researchers to find alternative measures to define the population they are studying. Of course, whenever the measures being used are not "standardized," this makes comparison and generalization somewhat more difficult and hazardous, for it may be the measure, rather than the findings that differ between studies. Nevertheless, by addressing this issue, and more accurately drawing the line around who is poor in a real sense, the poverty analysis is much more accurate and comprehensive in all these chapters.

## Theme #3: Making Ends Meet: The High Cost of Housing and Child Care

All too often, analyses of poverty emphasize the "income" side of the poverty "equation," and ignore the "cost" side. Yet it is the costs side, and the problems and distortions that are occurring in this area that often are key to understanding poverty dynamics today. This is in part the result of another inadequacy of the poverty measure, which is based on a single need, that of food, so that one cannot use this measure to explain, much less measure, poverty that is *cost*-related. If instead, the poverty measure was built up from the cost of *each* major basic need, then its analysis could begin with a discussion of how, for example, the substantial increase in poverty thresholds has been driven by rising housing prices, and therefore, this additional group of people, in these particular places, are experiencing increased poverty (including homelessness). Lacking such a measure, which would be a tool to analyze such issues, requires using another definition of poverty, explicitly or implicitly. For example, it seems obvious that those who become homeless lack sufficient income to meet this basic need, regardless of whether that income is above or below the official poverty threshold, and therefore are "poor." Thus, to understand the issues facing the poor, it is necessary to look in detail at these basic needs, and the problems inherent in meeting these needs, both in terms of price and availability. In short, understanding poverty cannot be reduced to just a question of income, as not all problems or needs are "fungible" in a market.

The official poverty measure not only does not directly reflect what it costs to "make ends meet," it is built on implicit assumptions that are now long out of date—such as that "low income people do not pay taxes," or that "there is no need to allow for child-care costs because either one parent stays home or if a single parent, that single parent would not be in the workforce." This results in conclusions such as the frequent assertion that welfare reform has successfully reduced "poverty," for employment rates and incomes have risen for single mothers, taking some out of official poverty. If, however, analysis were to measure the increases in *costs* (such as taxes, child care, and transportation) associated with employment and not just the increases in *income*, one would undoubtedly get a very different, and more mixed view of the outcome of welfare reform.

Chapters in this volume address the costs side of poverty in two ways, by examining in detail how families in fact manage to meet the costs of their basic needs, and by developing alternative estimates of income adequacy to measure economic hardship.

Of these costs, the chapters in this volume particularly focus on two, housing and child care. As Friedman demonstrates, the cost of housing has risen so much, relative to incomes, particularly in some metropolitan areas, that many families end up losing their housing, and become homeless, resulting in a whole different set of issues beyond the poverty experienced by the housed. Thus, to see this just as a "market" problem, or just another one of the basic needs to be purchased, misunderstands the nature of poverty as it is now experienced. As is pointed out by Friedman, and in a different way by Jasiniski et al, the very existence of the family unit, as a functioning entity, is threatened by the inadequacies of the shelter system. What begins as an affordability/availability problem must be solved by much more global efforts to empower families to make their way in a frayed safety net of services as well as the housing market. Yet for poor families, particularly those maintained by women alone, the resources available such as welfare and child welfare, often "blame" them, rather than provide support to meet this need. This is particularly the case for women—and children as well—who are experiencing domestic violence. As pointed out by Brandwein, when the housing is "owned" by the abuser, or the woman must flee for her and her children's safety, meeting the need of housing is key to addressing poverty. Clearly, the issues of housing and children's poverty are not just ones that are market, or economic, but reflect larger welfare and other policies that reflect sexism, racism, and classism, as argued by Brandwein and others. And, as pointed out by Jasinski et al., the poverty that is highly correlated with abuse in one generation, becomes both cause and effect of poverty and abuse in the next generation.

Child care is another "cost" issue that is much more than cost. As Firestone, Scott, Barnes and Barnum, Kelly, and McDonough all point out, child care involves a complex of issues—not only cost/affordability, but availability of child care (particularly for Latina mothers), low child-care salaries that affect availability and cost, lack of child care for evening and weekend in an economy in which service jobs are rapidly expanding, issues with relative care, lack of services for children with disabilities and special needs, the difficult logistics (especially for single mothers) of combining work and child care (without being tardy/absent), inconsistent/unstable child-care provision (especially in rural areas and for low-income parents), and the inadequate, highly rationed availability of public child-care subsidies to parents and providers. Clearly, child care is a poverty issue that is about cost—and much more.

Another way to highlight the costs issue is to assess the ability of a family's income, regardless of the poverty level, to meet the costs of a set of major basic needs. Davidson developed such a measure to assess income adequacy, or economic hardship (using four major basic needs). This is a version of the basic needs budgets and other measures developed by the critics of the poverty measure, including the Self-Sufficiency Standard. These measures use an empirical approach to build an income adequacy measure from the costs of all basic needs (not just food), and vary it by family composition (number of adults, and number and age of children), as well as by place (usually county.)[21]

## Theme #4: The Neighborhood Context of Children's Poverty

An important theme in these chapters that advances our understanding of children's poverty is that of the neighborhood or community context of that poverty. Rather than the individualistic paradigm described above, several authors explore how poverty is experienced, as well as created/perpetuated within communities with high levels of poverty. This is a major focus of the Timberlake and Michael, and Wagmiller chapters that develop a detailed picture of the kind of communities in which poor children grow up, whether urban or nonmetropolitan. As pointed out by Timberlake and Michael, interest in this phenomenon was sparked by William Julius Wilson's work, but it has rarely been applied to analyses of children's poverty. Interestingly, Jasinski et al.'s chapter on childhood exposure to violence as a predictor of adult homelessness and poverty, although focused on this phenomenon as individual/intergenerational, also includes discussions of the community experience and exposure to violence. The community context clearly impacted on, and reinforced the impact of childhood victimization on their subsequent adult lives. Likewise, Firestone's discussion of child-care issues for Latina mothers in San Antonio, references the community context.

## Theme #5: Poverty and Diversity: Race-Ethnicity and Disability

Not all poverties are experienced in the same way, nor do they have the same causes, or cures, yet too often analyses of poverty make, at best, a passing reference to race and/or ethnicity, or disability. Commonly, it is noted that children's poverty, as with people of all ages, is experienced at much higher levels among most nonwhite races and ethnic groups, except Asian Americans (with exceptions for certain subgroups of Asian Americans, such as Hmong.) The analysis here provides new insight into how these higher poverty rates affect children of color, and how these effects differ by group. Thus both Timberlake and Michael, and Wagmiller describe how racial and ethnic segregation has reinforced the segregation of the poor, creating doubly disadvantaged communities, exposing children particularly in those communities to economic disadvantage at the community level, even if their own families are not poor. This combination of racial segregation and poverty segregation led Wagmiller to conclude that black children occupy a unique, and unfortunate, "ecological niche" of highly disadvantaged neighborhoods. At the same time, both authors note that while these segregation levels (both racial and economic) rose during the 1970s and 1980s, they have started to fall significantly in the 1990s, as they and other others have documented.[22]

Other chapters contribute greater understanding of how the strategies used to deal with poverty differ between various ethnic and racial groups. For example, Firestone documents how low income Latina mothers bridge the gap between their low incomes and their need for child care, through a higher rate of usage of relative care (less expensive, though often not free). Similarly, Davidson's analysis of the variety of living arrangements found in single mother households differentiates these, and their impact on poverty and economic hardship, by ethnicity and race, finding that because different living arrangements are associated with different race-ethnic groups, and thus with poverty levels, a focus on race-ethnicity rather than marriage may be a more effective antidote to poverty. Finally, Scott's chapter analyzes in depth how disability interacts with often quite rigid institutions of school and work, resulting in further impoverishing families with children with disabilities (particularly socio-emotional difficulties.) Altogether, across these chapters, there is a recurring theme that suggests that calls for renewed attention to how race and ethnic segregation and discrimination are contributing to child poverty.

### Theme #6: Gender and Children's Poverty

While none of these articles takes an explicitly gendered approach, or uses a gender analysis exclusively (except it is one of the explicit frames used by Brandwein, with sexism, racism, and classism informing her analysis throughout), gender is the subtext virtually throughout this volume. That is, one cannot discuss children's poverty from almost any perspective, without acknowledging that children in women-maintained families, especially those maintained by African American and Latina mothers, experience substantially higher rates of poverty and related disadvantage and economic hardship.

Women's poverty is qualitatively different from that experienced by men, and in the context of children's poverty, single mother's poverty is distinctly different from that experienced by families maintained by married couples or men alone. There are three aspects of single mother's poverty that are particularly salient.

- First, women tend to bear the economic as well as emotional burden of childrearing, alone or mostly alone. This is so much accepted, almost as a truism, that it may seem odd to mention it. But it is striking that across all of these chapters, child support is hardly mentioned (and then only as a less than dependable or substantial income source).

- Second, single mothers in the workforce, although often the primary or sole source of income for their families, nevertheless face all the disadvantages of all women in the workforce. As with all women, single mothers experience unequal pay (74 cents compared to the dollar earned by male workers), occupational segregation patterns in which predominantly female occupations are consistently and significantly lower in pay, jobs in the service sector with hours (evening, weekends, swing shift) that are difficult to combine with family responsibilities, and sexual and gender harassment (particularly if they seek higher paying jobs that are nontraditional for women) that result in lost wages, promotions, and jobs.

- Third, single mothers needing work supports (such as child care) or cash assistance when they cannot work, face a social welfare system that either does not acknowledge their particular circumstances as women, or the opposite, conditions services and benefits on sexist assumptions and requirements. Examples of programs that ignore the particular circumstances of women are unemployment compensation programs that do not recognize sexual harassment as a valid reason for leaving a job, or welfare programs that do not recognize the particular needs of women who have experienced domestic violence (Brandwein and Jasinski et al.) or childhood abuse (with impacts on the next generation as well, as pointed out by Jasinski et al. and McDonough). The opposite problem is that of social welfare programs which impose gender-based and gender-biased requirements as conditions for receiving assistance, such as those that encourage or even require marriage ("wedfare"), encourage or require the use of contraceptives, or require certain parental behavior such as guaranteeing school attendance by their children.

The distinctive character of women's poverty is a theme found in almost every chapter. Thus Kelly, Scott, Firestone, and Barnes and Bynum particularly focus on the interrelationship between the first and second aspects of women's poverty described above, that is, how single mothers seek to balance the competing demands of work and family. As shown in almost every chapter, it is the combination of the low wages that women receive, and the burden (borne almost uniformly by mothers alone) of trying to arrange child care against its high costs and limited availability—especially for children with special needs or children of color—plus the extremely limited and highly contingent support from the public sector (in the form of benefits such as child-care assistance, etc.) that make for such high levels of economic hardship for their children. Without these gendered aspects of their poverty, children's poverty would be more easily addressed. But certainly acknowledging and specifying these issues is a very important step to better understanding, and thus addressing children's poverty.

Altogether, these chapters provide insights that build a new perspective on children's poverty, one that acknowledges the many diversities of poverties experienced by children who differ by where they live (urban, suburban, or rural; high, moderate or low poverty neighborhoods, areas of high or low racial/ethnic segregation), and by their living arrangements (particularly, if they live in a single-mother household).

They finesse the problems of an inadequate poverty measure in imaginative ways. Finally, they provide new insights into two key issues that are major costs, but also shape the lives and futures for families with children, and those issues are housing (including homelessness) and child care. All these perspectives emphasize how the ecological, social, and welfare structures impact on the lives of poor children, and point the way to alternative futures, ones in which the poverty of children is addressed and reduced.

## NOTES

1. "Children in the United States," Children's Defense Fund, n.d. Available at http://www.childrensdefense.org/site/DocServer/us-2.pdf?docID=958

2. DeNavas-Walt, Carmen, Bernadette D. Proctor, and Cheryl Hill Lee, U.S. Census Bureau. *Income, Poverty and Health Insurance Coverage in the United States: 2005.* Current Population Reports, p60–231, U.S. Government Printing Office, Washington, D.C., 2006.

3. Lee Rainwater and Timothy Smeeding, *Poor Kids in a Rich Country: America's Children in a Comparative Perspective.* New York: Russell Sage, 2003. UNICEF, *Child Poverty in Rich Countries, 2005.* Innocenti Report Card No. 6. UNICEF Innocenti Research Centre, Florence. 2005. Bruce Bradbury and Marcus Jantti, "Child Poverty Across Industrialized Nations." Innocent Occasional Papers, Economic and Social Policy Series No. 71, UNICEF International Child Development Centre, Florence.

4. Arloc Sherman, *Poverty Matters: The Cost of Child Poverty in America* (Children's Defense Fund, 1997), 4.

5. Greg J. Duncan and J. Brooks-Gunn (Eds.), *Consequences of Growing Up Poor.* New York: Russell Sage Foundation, 1997; Kristin Anderson Moore and Zakia Redd, "Children in Poverty: Trends, Consequences and Policy Options," Child Trends Research Brief, Publication #2002-54, Child Trends: Washington, DC, 2002.

6. U.S. Census Bureau, The 2006 Statistical Abstract: The National Data Book, Table 53. Households, Families, Subfamilies, and Married Couples: 1980 to 2004. Available at http://www.census.gov/compendia/statab/population/

7. Ibid.

8. U.S. Census Bureau, Table CH-1. Living Arrangements of Children Under 18 Years Old: 1960 to Present, Internet Release Date, September 21, 2006. Available at http://www.census.gov/population/www/socdemo/hh-fam.html

9. U.S. Census Bureau, Table 4. Poverty Status of Families, by Type of Family, Presence of Related Children, Race, and Hispanic Origin: 1959 to 2005. Available at http://www.census.gov/hhes/www/poverty/histpov/hstpov4.html

10. U.S. Census Bureau, Table 15. Age Distribution of the Poor: 1966 to 2005. Available at www.census.gov/hhes/www/poverty/histpov/hstpov15.html

11. Table 4. Poverty Status Status of Families, by Type of Family, Presence of Related Children, Race, and Hispanic Origin: 1959 to 2005. Available at http://www.census.gov/hhes/www/poverty/histpov/hstpov4.html

12. The poverty rate for children varied over this period, rising to 22% in 1982, then again to 23% in 1993, and falling to a low of 16% in 2000. Table 3. Poverty Status of People, by Age, Race, and Hispanic Origin: 1959 to 2005. Available at http://www.census.gov/hhes/www/poverty/histpov/hstpov3.html

13. William Ryan, *Blaming the Victim* (New York: Vintage, 1971).

14. NPR Online. NPR/Kaiser/Kennedy School Poll. (2001). *Poverty in America.* Retrieved September 25, 2005 from http:///www.npr.org/programs/specials/poll/poverty.

15. Robert Michael and Constance Citro (eds.). 1995. *Measuring Poverty: A New Approach.* Washington, D.C.: National Academy Press.

16. DeNavas-Walt, Carmen, Bernadette D. Proctor, and Cheryl Hill Lee, U.S. Census Bureau. *Income, Poverty and Health Insurance Coverage in the United States: 2004.* Current Population Reports, p60–231, U.S. Government Printing Office, Washington, D.C., 2005.

17. Using the Fair Market Rents (for two-bedroom units), which are the rental costs at the 40th Percentile, the most expensive place to live in the United States is Stamford, Connecticut, where the cost is $2074, almost five times the cost in the least expensive place, which is a group of parishes in Louisiana (Acadia, Franklin, Jefferson, etc.) where housing costs $438 per month. See www.huduser.org/datasets/fmr.html.

18. National Mental Health Association, available at http://www.nmha.org/homeless/childrenhomelessnessfacts.cfm

19. National Alliance to End Homelessness, available at http://www.endhomelessness.org/section/policy/focusareas/families Scott J. South, Kyle Crowder, and Erick Chavez, "Exiting and Entering High-Poverty Neighborhoods: Latinos, Blacks and Anglos Compared," *Social Forces* 84, 2 (December, 2005), p. 873–900.

20. [Use of 40% for high poverty neighborhood measure]

21. The Self-Sufficiency Standard has been developed for 36 states; reports can be found at www.sixstrategies.org, and the actual measures are available from the state partners named in the reports and/or Diana Pearce at pearce@u.washington.edu. See also Renwick, Trudi and Barbara Bergman, "A Budget-Based definition of poverty: with an application to single-parent families." *The Journal of Human Resources,* 28, 1, (1993) p. 1–24.

22. Paul A. Jargowsky, *Urban Poverty, Race and the Inner City: The Bitter Fruit of Thirty Years of Neglect,* p. 79–94 in Harris, Fred and Lynn Curtis (Eds.), *Locked in the Poorhouse: Cities, Race, and Poverty in the United States,* Lanham, MD: Rowman and Littlefield, 1998.

# CHAPTER 1

# THE EFFECT OF CHILD CARE ON EMPLOYMENT TARDINESS AND ABSENCES FOR MOTHERS: DOES MARITAL STATUS MATTER?*

## *Sandra L. Barnes and Mia Smith Bynum*

Employment provides minority women with economic as well as personal satisfaction and is particularly important for women who are poor, single mothers, and those from racial/ethnic groups.[1] The disproportionate percentage of U.S. children who are poor is directly correlated with the employment and marital statuses of their mothers.[2] And mothers, even those who are employed, continue to be responsible for the majority of childrearing responsibilities.[3] One of the most pressing problems facing them is locating accessible, acceptable, affordable child care.[4] Earlier studies show that as many as one-forth of mothers are either unemployed or face constrained job opportunities because of child-care problems.[5] Child-related events such as unexpected illnesses, medical appointments, and school-related activities may result in absences from work.[6] Employed mothers who are frequently tardy or absent can face direct or indirect sanctions in terms of meaningful work, promotions, and lost wages.[7] And because employment is central for many poor and near poor mothers, child-care problems can exacerbate impoverished circumstances for them and their children.[8]

However, the literature on employment obstacles for mothers is incomplete for several reasons. Much of the research focuses on the problem of absences and does not consider chronic tardiness.[9] This study considers both tardiness and absences and mothers' human capital that may help minimize these problems. Next, research on this topic for non-White mothers is sparse or cursory. Few studies are based on a large, national sample of African Americans, Hispanics, whites, and Asians with varying marital statuses. Literature would also benefit from research on possible ways traditional (i.e., education, spouse's income) and nontraditional (i.e., self-esteem) forms of human capital affect absences and tardiness. Lastly, this research topic is important because of the continued challenges poor mothers have in balancing employment and childrearing, the disproportionate percentage of minority mothers who face this dilemma, and how such employment problems can be linked to the juvenilization of poverty.

## THEORETICAL FRAMEWORK AND BACKGROUND LITERATURE

According to human capital theory, a person's selection for employment and subsequent pay reflect their skills and employers' requirements. Individual "assets" or human capital such as education, experience, commitment, initiative, and personal knowledge make certain candidates more competitive than others. In addition to these traits, human capital also reflects having the time to commit, in an employer's estimation, to the job.[10] Historically, women of childbearing age were expected to exit the employment arena periodically in order to bear and rear children. For these reasons, many employers consider women to be less committed employees.[11] And poor mothers are often at a disadvantage because of varied employment-related human capital, the tendency to work in lower-paying jobs, residence in poor areas, and constrained child-care needs.[12] Because the human capital of mothers is often considered less viable than that of their male counterparts, they may find themselves "mommy tracked" into less demanding, less interesting, lower paying positions.[13] In such cases, the presence of dependents becomes a "liability" with economic consequences for mothers and their children. Thus, real and perceived human capital—assets needed to locate and maintain gainful employment—directly affect mother's opportunities. This theory has been used largely to explain pay inequities; it can also be applied to study factors that enable mothers to address child-care needs such that they can be employed. Applying this theory, the types of tangible and intangible assets (or human capital) mothers may have that minimize child-care-related employment issues are examined and whether variations exist based on marital status.

Applying this theory, mothers who have human assets that enable them to better balance child care and employment tend to fare better.[14] Thus mothers who have been able to balance work inside and outside the home can reap benefits in the form of enhanced identity, social status, self-esteem, privilege, stimulation, *and* economic support.[15] In addition to accessible, acceptable, affordable child care,[16] possible assets include a spouse, partner, or helper in the home[17] or assistance from extended family to help pay for child care or provide low-cost or free child care.[18] Several studies link the ability of mothers to balance multiple roles to age or education as well as previous childrearing experience that engenders confidence and self-efficacy.[19] In contrast, mothers who cannot afford child care or those without these types of resources are at a disadvantage. This analysis examines the influence of human capital such as marital status and education as deterrents to child-care-related employment problems.

### Marital Status/Household Structure

Although not considered a woman's personal asset, marital status and household type can be considered forms of human capital that can greatly influence the ability to balance child care and employment. For example, African American single parents, like female single parents in general, are often employed to stave off poverty[20] and may receive child care from extended family.[21] It has also been suggested that white female heads-of-households often have greater difficulty balancing employment and child care than some non-white mothers.[22] Unmarried mothers who are employed generally face a different set of economic and logistical obstacles.[23] Married mothers may benefit from spouses who assist in child care and other domestic tasks.[24] However, other studies suggest that married mothers, those who are white in particular, bear the brunt of child-care decisions and may have problems balancing employment and domestic responsibilities.[25] Furthermore, married mothers are more likely to be absent from work than their spouses.[26] More fluid gender roles and shared family responsibilities for married couples facilitate employment for some African American wives with children and often enable such families to maintain their economic status.[27] A spouse's income also enables some married mothers to more easily fund child care or to choose whether or not to seek employment.[28] Therefore employment problems such as tardiness or absences due to child care would be expected to be a greater challenge for single mothers, in general, and the disproportionate percentage of single parent African American and Hispanic mothers, in particular.[29] But the economic necessity of employment for single mothers may provide a stronger motivator for punctuality and attendance among those who are poor or working class. However, the added responsibilities as single parents may prevent punctuality and consistent attendance.[30]

## Spouse's Income and Child-Care Costs

Household incomes as well as expenses such as child-care costs influence mothers' employment.[31] These factors are also confounded with race/ethnicity. For many African American and Hispanic mothers, child care via extended family is an asset that facilitates employment.[32] Studies also show that Hispanic mothers rely on kin contact for economic and social support as much as African Americans[33] or more than whites and African Americans.[34] Furthermore, research posits a direct relationship between household income and the ability to afford child care.[35] In this context, the additional income from a spouse or partner would be expected to help mothers pay for child care as compared to mothers without these additional finances. Yet higher household income does not guarantee access to needed child care, for unlike poor and near poor families that may receive subsidized child care and wealthy families who can afford child care, "middle class" families often have difficulty finding appropriate child care that they can afford.[36] In this analysis, household economics as captured by spouse's income are expected to be inversely related to tardiness and absences. This measure (rather than household income in general) provides a parsimonious assessment of household income, marital status, contributors, and may uncover effects for mothers with this additional income as compared to those without it. Findings may also inform studies that are inconclusive about the influence of spouse's contributions.[37] In addition, one would expect more costly child care to be more dependable[38] and expect that child-care costs will be inversely related to tardiness and absences.

### Race/Ethnicity

Economic restructuring resulting in low-wage pink color jobs; lack of affordable housing and child care; absentee fathers; and, divorce have all been associated with the feminization and juvenilization of poverty. For example, 2000 census data show that about 34.3–46.4 percent of female-headed households with children under 18 and 5 years old, respectively, are poor; substantially greater representation occurs for racial/ethnic groups.[39] African American mothers (and those who are single mothers are more apt to be poor) are more likely than white mothers to be in the labor force. However, Hispanic mothers are the least likely to do so. Studies show that the income provided by African American mothers, married or single, is often more central to maintain household economic stability as compared to white mothers.[40] And such mothers (and many of Hispanic descent) are also more likely to be employed in the secondary labor market with lower wages and less favorable hours and conditions.[41]

Mothers who are economically able are more likely to forgo employment, at least temporarily, when they have children—especially when their children are young. This pattern appears to be more common among white and Hispanic mothers.[42] Other scholars[43] contend that, due to more traditional gender roles, labor force participation has little affect on the domestic responsibilities most Asian women have as wives and mothers. Other studies show similar findings for Taiwanese working-class wives[44] and Korean women.[45] Furthermore, poverty often requires married Puerto Rican and Filipino mothers to work outside the home and care for their children.[46] The above research suggests that the socioeconomic status of many African American, and to a lesser degree, Hispanic mothers, often necessitate balancing employment and child care. Extending these studies, tardiness, and absences due to child care are expected to vary by race/ethnicity. And for reasons presented above, African American mothers are expected to be less tardy or absent than non-African American mothers. However, limited research on this topic for Hispanic and Asian mothers precludes exact predictions about how they will be affected—hence the need to explore these issues.

### Children Age and Number of Children

Balancing employment and child care can be challenging based on the age and number of children[47] and can be particularly problematic for poor and working-class mothers who are employed.[48] Child care for younger children often requires mothers to be late or absent due to emergencies.[49] Studies also suggest that mothers with younger children and multiple children face additional child care problems due to both increased costs of child care and increased time constraints to care for their children.[50] Yet older siblings may represent "human capital" for mothers if they assist with child care for younger siblings and thereby reduce child-care-related employment problems.[51] In general, the presence of younger children and more children is expected to increase tardiness and absences.

## Formal and Informal Experiences (Education, Age, Self-Esteem, and Job Type)

Formal education results in positive labor market returns for many women[52] and can mediate potentially lower labor force involvement for mothers when their children are young.[53] More education can also translate into higher earnings and the ability to purchase substitute care for children. Thus, better educated mothers would be expected to reconcile employment and child care somewhat more easily than less educated mothers.[54] In addition, white and nonpoor women tend to be better educated—a form of human capital that can help balance employment and child care if they become mothers.[55] In addition, older, employed mothers are more likely to have childrearing experience and more experience balancing the two roles, as well as adolescent offspring who can assist with child care.[56]

Although not as commonly studied, sociopsychological variables play an important role in how mothers view their ability to balance work inside and outside the home. Self-esteem, defined as a level of personal acceptance that is associated with one's abilities and achievements and acceptance of one's limitations, has been directly correlated with self-efficacy.[57] Some studies show that working mother's self-efficacy mediates the relationship between greater levels of child care responsibility and psychological distress and lower personal well-being.[58] Self-esteem may help explain why some mothers decide to seek employment. For example, mothers who have higher levels of self-esteem may be more inclined to take on the demands of employment and parenthood simultaneously and may view child care concerns as surmountable. In contrast, those with lower levels of self-esteem may foresee child-care challenges and be less likely to pursue employment. When type of employment is considered, studies show that[59] dual-earner couples are more apt to "scale back" in order to balance work–family dynamics. Using one of the strategies (limiting the number of hours worked), mothers who are able to do so may opt to work part-time to reduce child-care-related issues. Four types of human capital are considered here, formal education, age (which may proxy for childrearing experience), self-esteem, and part-time employment. Older mothers are expected to be less likely to experience child-care-related employment problems; both education and self-esteem are predicted to be inversely related to absences and tardiness; and, part-time employment will result in fewer such incidents.

### Summary of Hypotheses

This project raises the following broad research question—are child-care-related employment tardiness and absences variable based on marital status? When considered simultaneously, will "human capital" such as marital status, age, spouse's income, or education influence punctuality and attendance? The topic is particularly important for poor and near poor mothers given the potential for lost employment and wages, reduced quality of life—both professional and personal—and the subsequent effects on their children. Informed by the above noted literature, six hypotheses will be considered. Married mothers will be less likely to be tardy or absent as compared to mothers who are single, separated, divorced, or cohabitating (Hypothesis 1). African Americans will be less likely to be tardy or absent as compared to Hispanic, Asian, and white mothers (Hypothesis 2). The presence of a young child and more children will increase tardiness and absences (Hypothesis 3). Part-time employment will result in less tardiness and fewer absences (Hypothesis 4). I also include the following five control variables and posit that they will be inversely related to tardiness and absences: child-care costs, spouse's income, respondent's age, years of education, and self-esteem (Hypothesis 5). Lastly (Hypothesis 6), the effects of not being married will be less severe for African Americans as compared to the three other groups [race/ethnicity and marital status interactions].

## DATA AND METHODS

The study is based on a subsample from the Multi-City Study of Urban Inequality (1992–1994).[60] The secondary database is a national sample of households developed to broaden the understanding of how changing labor markets, racial attitudes and stereotypes, and residential segregation foster urban inequality. The multistage probability sample includes four metropolitan areas: Atlanta, Boston, Detroit, and Los Angeles. In addition, the sampling frame was designed to include: poor and nonpoor households, five racial/ethnic groups, and male and female respondents between the ages of 18 and 65. Attitudinal and behavioral data were collected during face-to-face interviews that lasted 50–95 minutes. Interviews were conducted in English, Spanish, Korean, Mandarin Chinese, or Cantonese, based on the needs of the respondent. Response rates range from 68 percent (in Los Angeles) to 78 percent (in Detroit). Data were only collected for the child-care questions studied here in the Los Angeles, Atlanta, and Boston areas. These data are weighted to reflect population percentages for each racial/ethnic group. This study focuses on married, single, cohabitating, separated, and divorced mothers from four racial/ethnic groups who are employed full-time or part-time and who have dependent children 18 years old or younger. Based on these criteria, there are 550 married, 147 single, 59 cohabitating, and 295 separated/divorced mothers for a total sample of 1,051. Although the data are 10 years old and thus traditional generalizability is cautioned, it is important because of its detailed information on the experiences of diverse marital statuses and racial/ethnic subgroups.

### Study Variables

The dependent variable, *Tardy-Absent* measures whether a respondent's work punctuality and attendance have been negatively affected by child-care responsibilities. The variable is based on the following question: "In the past twelve months, has a concern about your child-care needs caused you: to be late for work or to be absent from work? Yes or no?" Bivariate results from these data suggest that tardiness and absences reflect degrees of a related problem. Therefore responses are coded as ordered possibilities;

"0" for neither tardiness nor absences, "1" if either occurred, and "2" if both occurred. The reader should note the strengths as well as limitations of use of a single-item question. This variable is broad in its reference to "child-care needs" (i.e., are the needs due to lack of affordable child care, inconsistent extended family child care, a young mother's concerns about a newborn, or some other issue). However, the specific child-care issues faced by the sample mothers cannot be ascertained in this secondary data source. The dependent variable is also not determined for mothers who may have had child-care problems prior to 12 months before the survey and those who do not need traditional child care (i.e., who may only have older adolescent children). However, the strength of the variable lies in its ability to directly link employment absences and tardiness to child-care issues as reported by mothers in the sample.

A total of 16 independent variables are considered based on demographic, social, and sociopsychological factors. Four 0–1 indicators identify whether respondents are married, separated/divorced, never married, or living with a partner; married serves as the reference. In the interest of preserving statistical power, separated and divorced are combined into a single variable. Four race/ethnicity variables are included to identify white, African American, Hispanic, and Asian mothers and white is the reference group. Years of education (0–17 or more years) is a continuous variable as is respondent's chronological age (21–69 years) and the amount paid in child care per week for the respondent's youngest child ($0–$500). The reader should note that, in the datafile, the child-care cost variable was developed such that it captures only costs for the youngest child. Based on the fact that most mothers in the sample have, on average, two children, this indicator should be considered a lower bound on child-care costs they incur. A question was not posed to capture total child-care costs. In order to examine the influence of children, two variables are included to determine the number of children in two contexts. This includes the total number of children 18 years old or younger (continuous, 1–8 children) and a dummy variable to identify employed mothers with a child 6 years old or younger. Although it would be ideal to consider the ages of the respondents' children, the latter variable reflects another limitation of the database and represents a lower bound on age-related problems employed mothers might face. Spouse's annual income ($0–$400,000) is included where zero captures both cases of spouses without incomes and respondents without spouses and a dummy variable is included to identify part-time employment.

A construct based on responses to four Likert-type items to gauge self-esteem is used: (a) I feel I do not have much to be proud of; (b) On the whole, I am satisfied with myself; (c) All in all, I am inclined to feel that I am a failure; and (d) I take a positive attitude toward myself. Responses are coded such that "0" corresponds to "strongly disagree," "1" to "moderately disagree," "2" to somewhat agree, and "3" to "strongly agree." Questions (a) and (c) are reverse scored such that the overall construct scores range from 0 to 12 where higher scores represent a greater sense of self-esteem. The indicators that make up this construct are theoretically related in the social psychology literature and are also correlated at the bivariate level. A rotated Principle Components Factor Analysis suggests unidimensionality (eigenvalue = 1.92) and Cronbach's alpha (0.62) supports construct reliability. While other ranges are feasible

Table 1.1

**Means and Proportions for Study Variables by Marital Status from Multi-City Study of Urban Inequality [1992–1994]**

| Variable | Marital Status | | | |
| --- | --- | --- | --- | --- |
| | Married (M) | Single (S) | Div./Sep. (D) | Cohab. (C) |
| 1. Tardy & absent (0–2) | 0.77 | 1.06 | .67 | .93 |
|    % Neither | 53.60$^C$ | 40.71 | 60.36$^C$ | 29.78$^{MD}$ |
|    % Tardy or absent | 46.40$^C$ | 59.30 | 39.64$^C$ | 70.22$^{MD}$ |
|    % Tardy & absent | 30.71 | 47.14 | 27.10 | 22.87 |
| 2. % African American | 10.31$^{SD}$ | 39.97$^{MC}$ | 23.46$^M$ | 16.02$^S$ |
| 3. % White | 63.03$^{SD}$ | 35.43$^M$ | 49.75$^M$ | 37.81 |
| 4. % Asian | 5.56$^{SC}$ | 0.51$^M$ | 1.59 | 0.55$^M$ |
| 5. % Hispanic | 21.03$^C$ | 23.95 | 25.18 | 45.55$^M$ |
| 6. % Work w/child ≤ 6 yrs | 40.32$^D$ | 57.86$^D$ | 26.19$^{MS}$ | 45.75 |
| 7. % Employed Part-time | 37.32$^{DC}$ | 42.71$^C$ | 24.62$^M$ | 16.26$^{MS}$ |
| 8. # Children ≤ 18 yrs | 1.91$^{SD}$ | 1.25$^{MDC}$ | 1.57$^{MS}$ | 1.73$^S$ |
| 9. Mean years of education | 13.22$^{SC}$ | 12.19$^{MD}$ | 13.33$^{SC}$ | 11.70$^{MD}$ |
| 10. Mean weekly child care | $25.51$^D$ | $22.71 | $13.44$^M$ | $22.72 |
| 11. Mean age | 35.64$^{SD}$ | 29.20$^{MDC}$ | 38.34$^{MS}$ | 34.86$^S$ |
| 12. Mean spouse's income | $30,965.25$^{SDC}$ | $0$^{MC}$ | $0$^{MC}$ | $18,108.90$^{MSD}$ [a] |
| 13. Mean self-esteem score | 14.52 | 14.47 | 14.32 | 14.23 |
| $n$ | 550 | 147 | 295 | 59 |

*Note:* Superscripts identify between-group mean differences that are significantly different: $p < 0.05$ based on $t$-tests: Div./Sep. = divorced or separated and Cohab. = cohabitating.

[a] Fifty cohabitating mothers identified a spouse's income. However, the data file does not indicate whether the mothers were referring to a live-in partner as a common-law spouse or an estranged spouse from whom they receive economic support. Including these amounts did not alter the modeling response patterns or levels of significance for predictive variables and were thus retained. $N = 1,051$.

based on assigning different values to the possible categories, it is the relative rankings of overall scores for each respondent that are important here.

## Methods

A two-part analysis examines the relationship between child-care issues and employment tardiness and absences. First, demographic variables, including the dependent variable, are compared across marital status using $t$-tests (Table 1.1). Next, tardiness and absences are studied across marital status (Table 1.2). During the modeling phase, the dependent variable, *Tardy-Absent*, is regressed on marital status dummy variables (Model 1) as well as marital status and the other demographic controls such as race/ethnicity, number of children, child-care costs, age, education, and self-esteem (Model 2). The final model considers the aforementioned variables and possible marital status and race/ethnicity interactions by including eight 0–1 dummy variables

**Table 1.2**
**Ordered Logit Regression Models for Mothers Employment Problems**

| | $b$ (std. error) | | |
|---|---|---|---|
| Variable | Model 1: Marital Status | Model 2: Marital Status & Controls | Model 3: Marital Status, Controls, & Interactions |
| Marital Status | | | |
| Single | .65 (.54) | .88 (.55)† | 2.46 (.97)** |
| Separated/divorced | −.23 (.32) | .91 (.51)† | .91 (.84) |
| Cohabitating | .39 (.31) | 1.07 (.47)* | 1.39 (1.01) |
| Race/Ethnicity and Controls | | | |
| African American | | −.64 (.43) | −.71 (.58) |
| Asian | .06 (.51) | .20 (.57) | |
| Hispanic | | −.72 (.46) | −.52 (.60) |
| Work w/ child ≤ 6 yrs | | .22 (.46) | .25 (.48) |
| Employed part-time | .53 (.36) | .50 (.36) | |
| # Children ≤ 18 yrs (1–8) | .35 (.18)† | .34 (.18)† | |
| Years of education (0–17) | −.04 (.06) | −.04 (.06) | |
| Child-care costs ($0–500 wk) | −.00 (.00) | −.00 (.00) | |
| Age (21–69 yrs) | −.09 (.03)** | −.09 (.03)** | |
| Spouse's income ($0–400K yr) | | .00 (.00) | .00 (.00) |
| Self-esteem (0–12) | | .05 (.09) | .04 (.09) |
| Race/Ethnicity Interactions | | | |
| AA*Single | | | −1.60 (1.05) |
| AA*Sep/Div | | | 60 (.95) |
| AA*Cohab. | | | −1.04 (1.27) |
| Asian*Sep/Div | −.86 (1.10) | | |
| Asian*Cohab. | −1.01 (1.16) | | |
| Hispanic*Single | | | −2.31 (1.08)* |
| Hispanic*Sep/Div | | | −.14 (.98) |
| Hispanic*Cohab. | | | −.41 (1.20) |
| $X^2$ (Pseudo $R^2$) | 4.25 (0.01) | 34.28 (0.08) | 47.88 (0.09) |
| $n$ | 871 | 641 | 641 |

*Note:* ***$p < .001$. **$p < .01$. *$p < .05$. †$p < .10$: Log odds provided first; std. error in parentheses. Asian*Single omitted in Mo.

that reflect interactions between African American, Asian, and Hispanic single, separated/divorced, and cohabitating mothers as compared to their white counterparts (Model 3) [the interaction variable representing single Asian mothers is omitted due to small sample counts, $n = 2$]. Because the dependent variable has ordered categorical measures, estimates are obtained using ordered logit models. This approach is used because more than two outcomes were possible and the method does not assume equal distance between outcome categories. Similar to binary regression models, the ordered logit is nonlinear and the magnitude of change in the outcome probability for a specific change in the independent variables is dependent on the levels of all independent variables.[61]

## FINDINGS

### Profiles of Employed Mothers: Bivariate Results

Table 1.1 presents demographic summaries of the employed mothers by marital status. First, scores from the *Tardy-Absent* construct are similar (between 0.67 and 1.06) and not statistically different from each other. However, when percentage representations are considered, cohabitating mothers are most apt to note that they are *either* tardy or absent (70.22%) and their experiences differ significantly from those of married, separated, and divorced mothers. Furthermore, regardless of marital status, at least 23 percent of mothers note being tardy *and* absent as a result of child-care-related issues. Differences in marital status are apparent based on race/ethnicity. Asian and white sample mothers are more likely to be married; African American mothers are more apt to be single. Furthermore, single mothers (57.86%) are more likely to be employed with young children, while cohabitating and divorced mothers are less likely (26.19%) to do so; these differences are statistically significant. Demographic diversity is also apparent for indicators such as number of children, years of education, and average age. Furthermore, cohabitating mothers in the sample are the least likely of the four marital groups to be employed part-time (16.26%) and their experiences differ statistically from those of single and married mothers and child-care costs only differ between married and divorced/separated mothers. And regardless of marital status, patterns are similar in terms of self-esteem score. Preliminary results illustrate different profiles and experiences based on marital status; further analyses will explore nuances when variables are examined simultaneously.

### Modeling Employment Tardiness and Absences

Review of ordered logit regression findings when marital status is considered alone (Table 1.2, Model 1) do not show significant differences across the groups. Single, divorced, cohabitating, and separated mothers are not more likely than married mothers to experience employment tardiness and absences due to child-care problems. Model 2 examines the possible effects of marital status after other demographic indicators are controlled. And the influence of marital status becomes evident in this test. Findings suggest that mothers without a spouse in residence are generally more apt to report tardiness and absences as compared to married mothers. In addition, the likelihood of such problems increases from mothers who have never been married ($b = 0.88$, $p < .10$), to those who *previously* had partners in residence ($b = 0.91$, $p < .10$), and is greatest for cohabitators ($b = 1.07$, $p < .05$). Although race/ethnicity is insignificant, age minimizes tardiness and absences. And mothers with more children report more tardiness and absences. Next, Model 3 includes possible differences in the effects of marital status for each racial/ethnic group using eight interaction variables. The model's predictive ability improves ($X^2 = 47.88$) and one of the interaction variables is predictive. These data show that Hispanic single mothers are less likely ($b = -2.31, p < .05$) to report tardiness and absences as compared to white mothers, regardless of the latter group's marital status. As in Model 2, mother's age tends to minimize employment problems and number of children exacerbates such problems. And although most of the remaining interaction variables imply lower incidences of tardiness and absences as compared to the white reference groups, no significant differences are apparent.[62]

## DISCUSSION

Hypothesis 1 is supported by these findings and parallel earlier studies because, after considering controls, married mothers are less likely to be tardy or absent than single, cohabitating, separated, or divorced mothers. Contrary to Hypothesis 2, the race/ethnicity variables are not directly significant in these tests. And contrary to existing literature,[63] these results only partially support Hypothesis 3 because the experiences of employed mothers with a young child do not differ from their employed counterparts with older children. However, as the number of children increases, so do instances of tardiness and absences. In addition, part-time employed mothers are no more or less likely to report these situations than their full-time counterparts—Hypothesis 4 is not supported by these findings. Furthermore, child-care costs, spouse's income, number of children, years of education, or self-esteem are not significant in these tests. However, older mothers appear to be able to balance employment and child-care issues more than their younger counterparts (Hypothesis 5). When interactions are compared, mediating effects are only apparent for Hispanic single mothers. Thus these data support Hypothesis 6—but for Hispanic rather than African American single mothers. Lastly, a more detailed review of the results in Table 1.1 help better understand the tendency for nonmarried mothers, especially those who cohabitate, toward more absences and tardiness in the modeling phase. Given the absence and/or relatively lower levels of spouse's income, similar child-care costs, the number of children, and need to work full-time, employment is central to nonmarried sample mothers, yet they are less likely to have certain forms of human capital required to minimize employment tardiness and absences. Although one can only postulate specific reasons for the child-care-related employment issues studied here, economic necessity appears to be a strong motivator in negotiating around such problems and in the inability to do so.

## CONCLUSION

Employment, especially for poor, working-class, and single-parent mothers, is crucial to sustain their families. However, the very children they seek to provide for are often associated with reasons for their constrained and challenging employment experiences. Furthermore, child poverty in the United States is indelibly linked to economic instability for mothers—many of whom are employed, unmarried, and face child-care issues. This research informs existing literature about child-care issues and tardiness and absences for mothers. This topic is important because problems that prevent employed mothers from working undermine their ability to provide for their children. Several findings here parallel previous studies; others require further inquiry. These results suggest that these employment problems were similar for almost 25 percent of sample mothers and slightly more problematic for cohabitating mothers. Controlling for variables such as race/ethnicity, income, and education, diminishes the effects of marital status, yet nonmarried mothers continued to be more apt to face such challenges. In addition, an interaction test only uncovered decreased chances of tardiness and absences for single Hispanic mothers. This is an important result that begs further study of ways in which mothers believed to embrace more traditional gender roles and who have entered the labor force less readily in the past may now have different employment experiences.[64] The profiles of the nonmarried mothers in this sample show that some may have to balance employment and child care to stave off poverty.

Paralleling others studies, findings suggest that mothers without a spouse tend to be at a disadvantage as compared to married mothers.[65] It is important to note that, although race/ethnicity is not directly significant, its affects are indirectly evident through marital status because a disproportionate percentage of African American and Hispanic mothers are unmarried.[66] Child-care challenges persist despite varying incomes. This finding also adds credence to the continued domestic role for mothers, regardless of their marital status, spouse's income, education, and age.[67] In addition, given that the cost of child care is not significant here suggests possible nonfinancial problems such as logistics or inconsistent care may be just as pressing as the need for low-cost child care. It may be the case that other nontraditional forms of human capital (i.e., fluid gender roles, coping strategies, or extended family, according to other studies) associated with marital status and economic needs emerge to minimize employment tardiness and absences. Future studies will be important to examine whether and how such dynamics may enable mothers to be adaptive and resilient such that employment and childrearing are more tenable.

## NOTES

* This is a secondary data analysis. For more information, note the following bibliographical citation: Lawrence Bobo, James Johnson, Melvin Oliver, Reynolds Farley, Barry Bluestone, Irene Brown, Sheldon Danziger, Gary Green, Harry Holzer, Maria Krysan, Michael Massagli, and Camille Zubrinsky Charles. Multi-City Study Of Urban Inequality, 1992–1994: [Atlanta, Boston, Detroit, and Los Angeles] [Household Survey Data] [Computer File]. 3rd ICPSR version. Atlanta, GA: Mathematics/Boston, MA: University of Massachusetts, Survey Research Laboratory/Ann Arbor, MI: University of Michigan, Detroit Area Study and Institute for Social Research, Survey Research Center/Los Angeles, CA: University of California, Survey Research Program [producers], 1998. Inter-university Consortium for Political and Social Research [distributor], 2000.

1. Robin Jarrett, 1994. "Living poor: Family life among single parent, African-American women," *Social Problems* 41(1): 30–49; Katherine Newman, 1999. *No shame in my game: The working poor in the inner city.* New York: Alfred A. Knopf and The Russell Sage Foundation.

2. Sandra Barnes, 2005. *The cost of being poor: A comparative study of life in poor urban neighborhoods in Gary, Indiana.* New York: State University Press of New York; Kathryn Edin and Laura Lein, 1996. "Work, welfare, and single mothers' economic survival strategies." *American Sociological Review* 61: 253–266.

3. Phyllis Moen, 1992. *Women's two roles: A contemporary dilemma.* New York: Auburn House.

4. R. Connelly, 1992. "The effect of child care costs on married women's labor force participation." *Review of Economics and Statistics* 74: 83–92; Jarrett, "Living poor"; Marion H. Wijnberg, and S. Weinger, 1998. "When dreams wither and resources fail: The social-support systems of poor single mothers." *Families in Society: The Journal of Contemporary Human Services* 79: 212–219.

5. Research News, 1988. "Childcare, work, and fertility." The University of Michigan Division of Research Development and Administration 391: 14–15.

6. Arne Mastekaasa, 2000. "Parenthood, gender and sickness absence." *Social Science & Medicine* 50: 1827–1842; J.P. Vistnes, 1997. "Gender differences in days lost from work due to illness." *Industrial and Labor Relations Review* 50: 304–323.

7. Moen, *Women's two roles.*

8. Sandra Barnes, 2003. "Determinants of individual neighborhood ties and social resources in poor urban neighborhoods." *Sociological Spectrum* 23(4): 463–497; Sandra Barnes, 2001. "Welfare and women in poor urban neighborhoods: The effect of dependency on attitudinal indicators." *Journal of Children and Poverty* 7(1): 63–84.

9. J.P. Leigh, 1983. "Sex differences in absenteeism." *Industrial Relations* 22: 349–361; Mastekaasa, "Parenthood, gender and sickness absence"; D.K. Scott, and E.L. McClellan, 1990. "Gender differences in absenteeism." *Public Personnel Management* 19: 229–252; Vistnes, "Gender differences in days lost from work due to illness."

10. Ruth A. Wallace and Alison Wolf, 1995. *Contemporary sociological theory: Continuing the classical tradition.* Englewood Cliffs, NJ: Prentice Hall.

11. G.S. Becker, 1985. "Human capital, effort, and the sexual division of labor." *Journal of Labor Economics* 3: S33–S58; Janet Saltzman Chafetz, 1989. "Gender equality: Toward a theory of change," in *Feminism and social theory*, edited by Ruth A. Wallace, 21–68. Newbury Park: Sage.

12. Barnes, *The cost of being poor*; Barnes, "Determinants of individual neighborhood ties and social resources in poor urban neighborhoods"; Mark Granovetter, 1993. "The strength of weak ties: A network theory revisited." *Sociology Theory.* Stony Brook: State University of New York; Newman, *No shame in my game*; William Julius Wilson, 1996. *When work disappears: The world of the new urban poor.* New York: Alfred A. Knopf.

13. Chafetz, *Feminism and social theory.*

14. Moen, *Women's two roles.*

15. J. Glass, and T. Fujimoto, 1994. "Housework, paid work, and depression among husbands and wives." *Journal of Health and Social Behavior* 35: 179–191; Peggy McDonough, 1996. "The social production of housework disability." *Women & Health* 24(4): 1–25.

16. Connelly, "The effect of child care costs on married women's labor force participation."

17. Julie Brines, 1992. "Economic dependency, gender, and the division of labor at home." *American Journal of Sociology* 100 (3): 652–688. Moen, *Women's two roles.*

18. Dennis P. Hogan, Ling-Xin Hao, and William L. Parish, 1990. "Race, kin networks, and assistance to mother-headed families." *Social Forces* 68(3): 797–812.

19. Becker, "Human capital, effort, and the sexual division of labor"; Moen, *Women's two roles*.

20. B.H. Burris, 1991. "Employed mothers: The impact of class and marital status on the prioritizing of family and work." *Social Science Quarterly* 72: 50–66; Elizabeth Pungello, and Beth Kurtz-Costes. 1999. "Why and how working women choose child care: A review with a focus on infancy." *Developmental Review* 19: 31–96.

21. Andrew Billingsley, 1992. *Climbing Jacob's ladder: The enduring legacy of African-American families*. New York: A Touchstone Book; Rukmalie Jayakody, Linda M. Chatters, and Robert J. Taylor, 1993. "Family support to single and married African American mothers: The provision of financial, emotional, and childcare assistance." *Journal of Marriage and Family* 55: 261–276.

22. Jarrett, "Living poor".

23. Francine D. Blau, M.A. Ferber, and A. Winkler. 1998. *The economics of women, men, and work*, 3rd ed. Upper Saddle River, NJ: Prentice Hall.

24. John F. Toth, and Xiaohe Xu, 1999. "Ethnic and cultural diversity in fathers' involvement." *Youth & Society* 31: 76–99.

25. Moen, *Women's two roles*; Phyllis Moen, and Donna I. Dempster-McClain, 1987. "Employed parents: Role strain, work time, and preferences for working less." *Journal of Marriage and Family* 49: 579–590.

26. Moen, *Women's two roles*.

27. Billingsley, *Climbing Jacob's ladder*; Robert Hill, 1997. *The strengths of African American families: Twenty-five years later*. Washington, DC: R & B Publishers.

28. Moen, *Women's two roles*; Penny Edgell Becker and Phyllis Moen, 1999. "Scaling back: Dual-earner couples' work-family strategies." *Journal of Marriage & Family* 614: 995–1007.

29. Nijole Benokraitis (ed.), 2002. *Contemporary ethnic families in the US*. Upper Saddle River, NJ: Prentice Hall; Billingsley, *Climbing Jacob's ladder*.

30. Jarrett, "Living poor"; Wijnberg and Weinger, "When dreams wither and resources fail."

31. J.D. Angrist and W.N. Evans, 1998. "Children and their parent's labor supply: Evidence from exogenous variation in family size." *American Economic Review* 88: 450–477; Connelly, "The effect of child care costs on married women's labor force participation"; Edin and Lein, "Work, welfare, and single mothers' economic survival strategies"; Moen, *Women's two roles*.

32. Billingsley, *Climbing Jacob's ladder*; Jarrett, "Living poor."

33. William Parish, Lingxin Hao, and Dennis P. Hogan, 1991. "Family support networks, welfare, and work among young mothers." *Journal of Marriage and Family* 53: 203–215.

34. Marta Tienda and Jennifer Glass, 1985. "Household structure and labor force participation of black, Hispanic, and white mothers." *Demography* 22: 381–394.

35. Becker and Moen, "Scaling back"; Wijnberg and Weinger, "When dreams wither and resources fail."

36. Pungello and Kurtz-Cortes, "Why and how working women choose child care."

37. C. Goldin, 1990. *Understanding the gender gap: An economic history of American women*. New York: Oxford University Press; Chinhui Juhn and Kevin Murphy, 1997. "Wage inequality and family labor supply." *Journal of Labor Economics* January: 72–97.

38. S. Kontos, C. Howes, M. Shinn, and E. Galinsky, 1995. *Quality in family child care and relative child care*. New York: Teachers College Press.

39. Barnes, *The cost of being poor*; Diana M. Pearce, 1983. "The feminization of ghetto poverty." *Society* 72(Nov–Dec): 70–74.

40. Billingsley, *Climbing Jacob's ladder*; Hill, *The strengths of African American families*.

41. Edin and Lein, "Work, welfare, and single mothers' economic survival strategies"; Newman, *No shame in my game*.

42. Benokraitis, *Contemporary ethnic families in the US*.

43. M.G. Wong, 1995. "Chinese America," in *Asian Americans: Contemporary trends and issues*, edited by P.G. Min. Thousand Oaks, CA: Sage.

44. Franklin Ng, 1998. *The Taiwanese Americans*. Westport, CT: Greenwood Press.

45. Moon H. Jo, 1999. *Korean immigrants and the challenge of adjustment*. Westport, CT: Greenwood Press; Pyong Gap Min, 1998. *Changes and conflicts: Korean immigrant families in New York*. Boston: Allyn and Bacon.

46. Melvin Delgado, 2002. *Community social work practice in and urban context: The potential of a capacity-enhancement perspective*. New York: Oxford University Press; Melvin Delgado, 1997. "Puerto Rican natural support systems: Impact on families, communities, and schools." *Urban Education* 32(1): 81–97; Melvin Delgado, Kay Jones, and Mojdeh Rohani, 2005. *Social work practice with refugee and immigrant youth in the United States*. Boston, MA: Pearson; R. Gardner, W. Robey, and C. Smith, 1985. "Asian Americans: Growth, change, and diversity." *Population Bulletin* 40(4): 1–43; Maura Toro-Morn, 2002. "Puerto Rican migrants: Juggling family and work roles," in *Contemporary ethnic families in the US*, edited by Nijole Benokraitis, 232–239.Upper Saddle River, NJ: Prentice Hall.

47. Elizabeth Menaghan and Toby Parcel 1990. "Parental employment and family life: Research in the 1980's." *Journal of Marriage and the Family* 52: 1079–1098; Moen and Dempster-McClain 1987.

48. Barnes, *The cost of being poor*.

49. D. Spain, 1996. *Balancing act: Motherhood, marriage, and employment among American women*. New York: Russell Sage; Wijnberg and Weinger, "When dreams wither and resources fail."

50. Angrist and Evans, "Children and their parent's labor supply"; Phillip Cohen and Suzanne M. Bianchi, 1999. "Marriage, children, and women's employment: What do we know?" *Monthly Labor Review* December: 22–31; C. Kagan, S. Lewis, P. Heaton, and M. Cranshaw.1999. "Enabled or disabled: Working parents of disabled children and the provision of child-care." *Journal of Community and Applied Social Psychology* 9: 369–381; M. Milkie and P. Peltola, 1999. "Playing all the roles: Gender and the work–family balancing act." *Journal of Marriage and Family* 61: 476–490.

51. Hill, *The strengths of African American families*.

52. Becker, "Human capital, effort, and the sexual division of labor."

53. Connelly, "The effect of child care costs on married women's labor force participation."

54. Angrist and Evans, "Children and their parent's labor supply"; Connelly, "The effect of child care costs on married women's labor force participation."

55. Granovetter, "The strength of weak ties"; Moen, *Women's two roles*.

56. Hill, *The strengths of African American families*.

57. Sandra Godman Brown and Gail Barbosa, 2001. "Nothing is going to stop me now: Obstacles perceived by low-income women as they become self-sufficient." *Public Health Nursing* 18(5): 364–372; Carr, Deborah, 2002. "The psychological consequences of work-family tradeoffs for three cohorts of men and women." *Social Psychology Quarterly* 65(2): 103–124; Arthur H. Goldsmith, Jonathan R Veum, and William Darity Jr., 1997. "Unemployment, joblessness, psychological well-being and self-esteem: Theory and evidence." *Journal of Socio-Economics* 26(2): 133–158.

58. E.M. Ozer, 1995. "The impact of childcare responsibility and self-efficacy on the psychological health of professional working mothers." *Psychology of Women Quarterly* 19: 315–335; H. Tingey, G. Kiger, and P.J. Riley, 1996. "Juggling multiple roles: Perceptions of working mothers." *Social Science Journal* 33: 183–191.

59. Becker and Moen, "Scaling back."

60. Multi-City Study of Urban Inequality 1992–1994. 1998. 3rd ICPSR version. Atlanta, GA: Mathematics/Boston, MA: University of Massachusetts, Survey Research Laboratory/Ann Arbor, MI: University of Michigan, Detroit Area Study and Institute for Social Research, Survey Research Center/Los Angeles, CA: University of California, Survey Research Program [producers]. Inter - university Consortium for Political and Social Research [distributor].

61. J. Scott Long, 1997. *Regression models for categorical and limited dependent variables.* Thousand Oaks, CA: Sage Publications. Given the importance of type of childcare on the ability to work for many mothers, an attempt was made to examine the effects of childcare via extended family. However, because over 50 percent of respondents did not identify childcare type, use of this variable in the analysis has been limited to preliminary models (provided upon request).

62. Although the number of missing responses for the type of childcare variable precludes its use in the primary research here, preliminary models were developed to examine its possible influence. A dummy variable to identify childcare via extended family was included in Models 2–3. In each case, the variable was statistically significant and reduced the likelihood of tardiness and absences. This speaks to the need for additional empirical research on this issue.

63. Menaghan and Parcel, "Parental employment and family life."

64. Parish, Hao, and Hogan, "Family support networks, welfare, and work among young mothers"; Toro-Morn, *Contemporary ethnic families in the US.*

65. Becker, "Human capital, effort, and the sexual division of labor"; Moen, *Women's two roles*; Toth and Xu, "Ethnic and cultural diversity in fathers' involvement."

66. Benokraitis, *Contemporary ethnic families in the US*; Edin and Lein, "Work, welfare, and single mothers' economic survival strategies."

67. Jo, *Korean immigrants and the challenge of adjustment*; Pat M. Keith, and Robert B. Schafer, 1994. "They hate to cook: Patterns of distress in an ordinary role." *Sociological Focus* 27(4): 289–301; Min, *Changes and conflicts: Korean immigrant families in New York*; Ng, *The Taiwanese Americans.*

# CHAPTER 2

# THE NOT-SO-TENDER TRAP: FAMILY VIOLENCE AND CHILD POVERTY

## *Ruth A. Brandwein*

In this chapter we will examine the many links between family violence, including both partner and child abuse, and child poverty. Because most children in poverty live in female-headed families, those families will be our focus. All too often discussions of both poverty and family violence tend to focus on individual "pathology," unhealthy family dynamics and cultural mores that are seen as the targets for change. In this chapter we will focus instead on the sociopolitical, economic, and larger societal forces that impact on poor children and their families.

We begin with an overview of the scope and demographics of family violence and of poverty, with special emphasis on female-headed families and families of color. Although family violence is ubiquitous in all socioeconomic classes, we will consider the particular ways in which it manifests in poor families. The term "family violence" includes violence among any family members including spouses, other intimate partners and children. (This term may even include related elders, but this group will not be a focus of this chapter.) Domestic violence, a form of family violence, refers to intimate partner abuse.

Specifically, we will consider the role that welfare plays in the lives of poor children and their abused mothers. We will address such issues as why abused women stay or leave and what effects these difficult choices have on their children. Following this discussion of how partner abuse affects children, we will present the dynamics of how child abuse is also linked to child poverty. Again, a Hobson's choice will be presented: removing the abuser from the home, leaving the home and risking homelessness, or risking the loss of one's child to foster care. Both short- and long-term consequences of these choices will be explored. The chapter will conclude with an exploration of policy alternatives that could make a difference in the lives of these families. The broader themes of patriarchy, racism, and classism will infuse the entire chapter but will be directly addressed in the conclusion.

## INTIMATE PARTNER VIOLENCE

Intimate partner violence, a subset of family violence, is a problem for all women. It transcends race, ethnicity, and socioeconomic status. It is estimated that between 2 and 4 million women in the United States are battered each year by husbands, partners, or boyfriends.[1-3] In their lifetimes, one out of every four women will have experienced abuse at least once during her lifetime.[4]

Perhaps we need to digress here to define what interpersonal, or domestic violence includes. We most readily think of physical violence: pushing, slapping, hitting, punching, choking, or attacking with a weapon. These are criminal acts and are most likely to be included in official police and U.S. Department of Justice statistics. Other types of abuse can be as damaging, though less evident. Sexual abuse often accompanies other types of abuse, but until recently, forced sexual activity by a spouse was not considered to be rape in most states.[5]

A third, most ubiquitous form of abuse, yet least likely to be documented, is psychological or emotional abuse. Most commonly this precedes physical abuse, but even if it does not escalate to physical violence, it takes a heavy toll. It includes isolating, demeaning, threatening, intimidating, terrorizing, and other forms of harassing the victim. It often results in her losing her sense of self, autonomy, and human dignity. Isolation, a very common strategy employed by abusers, may leave the woman bereft of friends or family to whom to turn, making her completely dependent on him.

How does domestic violence get played out? The abuser (in 85 percent of incidents men are the abusers, so we will employ the male pronoun throughout this chapter[6]) is often jealous, so he prevents her from working or going to school where she might meet other men. He may also do this in order to isolate her so she has no one but him for emotional or economic support. He does not want her to get an education or have an income that might make her more independent. Raphael documents cases of men beating their wives before a job interview so they were ashamed to be seen with bruises; harassing them the night before an important test, so they would fail; even hiding their car keys or destroying their coat so they would be unable to leave the house.[7,8] There are exceptions, of course. In some situations male partners instead push the women to work, but they still maintain control of the finances.[9,10]

Women who are prevented by their abusers from gaining work experience or pursuing education or training opportunities are doomed to poverty. Numerous studies have documented the relationship between income and education levels. Every year of post high school education can increase women's earnings by 4–12 percent, and earning a 2-year associates degree can mean earning 19–23 percent more than those with a high school degree. One study found 65 percent higher earnings for those with a college degree. The difference in earnings is most pronounced for women of color.[11-16]

## PARTNER VIOLENCE AND CHILDREN

Intimate partner abuse has secondary victims. These are the children. Children are not present in all cases of such violence, but when there are children in the family, they are likely to suffer as well. In about half of all domestic violence situations, the children are also being physically abused.[17–21] In many cases the abuser will beat the children and when the mother intervenes, he beats her too—or the reverse—when the mother is being beaten the children may try to intervene and also endure his blows.

Even if the children are not physically assaulted, they may experience emotional abuse by witnessing the abuse.[22] Witnessing does not mean necessarily being physically present at the time of the abuse. Children pick up cues—from seeing their mother's black eye, to just feeling the unremitting tension in the home.

When advocates first began to explore the impact of domestic abuse on children, they hoped that such findings would result in further protection of women and their children. However, such findings are now sometimes used to remove the children from the home so they will not experience the effects of the mother's abuse, rather than protecting the mother and her children from the abuse. Because of the increasing awareness that children who are in a home where domestic abuse has occurred may be negatively affected, Child Protective Services (CPS) may be brought in to determine whether the children are at risk. The mission of CPS is to protect children. Because of societal acceptance of traditionally gendered sex roles, the mother is seen as the parent who has responsibility to protect the children. If the mother does not—or cannot—remove the abuser from the household, CPS may determine that the mother is guilty of "failure to protect," may remove her children and place them in foster care. Thus, a woman victim of partner violence who does not have the power to get rid of the abuser may be doubly victimized—first by her intimate partner and then by the system.

## POOR FAMILIES AND VIOLENCE

Although all women are potential victims of abuse, there are additional issues for women who are poor. According to some studies, violence among poor families is more frequent and more violent.[23–24] It has been hypothesized that economic stress, and among poor families of color also the stress of racism, may exacerbate the violence. One study of homeless or poorly housed mothers found that over 60 percent had experienced severe abuse by their partner.[25] While poverty may be a factor in causing violence, domestic violence victims who leave their spouses may also become poor. Separation and divorce often lead to women's loss of income. As the activist lawyer Flo Kennedy once said, somewhat hyperbolically, "Every woman is one man away from welfare." And once a woman goes on welfare, her family is guaranteed to be poor. In no state does the welfare grant even come close to the federal poverty level (currently $19,350 for a family of four, $16,090 for a family of three[26]). In 2001, the average monthly welfare grant was $351 with another $228 in Food Stamps, for a combined annual income of just under $7,000.[27]

In 2004, the latest year for which statistics are available, nearly 13 percent of all families lived in poverty but almost 18 percent of all children under 18 and 20 percent of those under 6 lived in poverty. These figures are higher than any year since 1998. For female-headed families in 2000, the figure is almost triple—35.9 percent. For black and Hispanic women the 2004 figure is even more alarming: 43.4 percent and 45.9 percent, respectively.[28] Although the actual figures for all categories decreased from the mid-1990s and then began to increase after 2000, the relative difference for female-headed families and female-headed families of color remained consistently higher in approximately the same ratios. Although figures are not available for poor children by family head, almost 42 percent of all poor children under 18 lived in families below half the poverty line. This is exacerbated for African American children, of whom over 49 percent live in such families.[29]

For all full-time, full-year workers, women's annual median earnings in 2004 were $31,223 in comparison to $40,798 for men. Women's wages actually fell by one percent between 2003 and 2004.[30] For those earning minimum wage—$5.15 per hour— and fortunate enough to have a full-time, full-year job, they can expect to earn only $10,712 annually.

Poor women do not have the same resources to deal with the violence as other women. They may leave the abuser temporarily to stay with family or friends, but more likely these people are also poor and may not have the room to house them for any length of time. With child care ranging in cost from a minimum of $4,000 annually, and with decreased federal funding for subsidized child care, they are less likely to be able to afford care for their children if they try to work. This is exacerbated if they have more than one child. They may be forced to leave the children unsupervised or with informal care, which may be unsafe or be of low quality. In 1996, when the Personal Responsibility and Work Opportunity Reconciliation Act (PRWORA) was passed, requiring women on welfare to be involved in work activities, the Congressional Budget Office estimated if states all met their work requirement targets the funding it provided for child care would fall $1.4 billion short of need.[31]

The question is often asked about abused women, "Why does she stay?" Poor women are less likely to afford to stay in a motel or hotel, to buy an airplane ticket or to have access to credit. In an overwhelming number of situations they do not even own a vehicle or have a driver's license, so they have fewer means to escape a violent situation—or even to get to work or to the supermarket. They may end up in a homeless shelter, or if they are lucky, a domestic violence shelter. But these are only temporary solutions. There are time limits, after which they are required to leave the shelter. The federal McKinney Act provides funding only for temporary housing for the homeless, not for permanent housing. The lack of affordable permanent housing is a national concern, finally gaining some visibility. Many women with children cannot afford housing—they do not have the first and last month's rent and security deposit often required. The average rental for a two-bedroom home varies in this country from about $700 to over $1500/month. What housing that may be available is often in neighborhoods with poor schools and high crime. The National Low Income Housing Coalition has reported that the hourly wage, nationally, needed to rent a 2-bedroom unit is $15.78.[32] This is clearly a problem for poor women, but even those who were formerly middle class are likely to experience these problems with housing.

In many jurisdictions judges are reluctant to remove the violent offender, especially if he owns his home. The woman may be afraid that if he is forced to leave, he will stop providing support. She may also fear that by pursuing an order of support, the violence will escalate.[33-34] Even when the court orders child support, only about 50 percent of orders are complied with either fully or partially. Although the abused mother may have an Order of Protection for herself, her abusive partner, if he is the father, is likely to be allowed child visitation by the court. After all, it is said, he is the child's father and if there is abuse only against her and not the children, most judges are loath to deprive fathers of their children. These visits may be fraught with danger for the mother, unless some kind of supervised visitation is ordered.

The cost of housing, the lack of transportation, other economic pressures already discussed and fear are often the reasons the abused mother may stay. She may also choose to bear his abuse rather than subject her children to leaving their home, their school and their friends. Moreover, evidence is mounting that women may be in the most danger when they leave their abusers. Because abuse is about power and control, her leaving is a direct threat to his power over her. Divorced and separated women are 14 times more likely to be abused as women who remain with their partners, according to statistics from the U.S. Department of Justice.[35] Stalking and murder are more likely to occur soon after the woman leaves. For some women, it is prudent for them to stay. In fact, the women this author and others have interviewed have reported that it was only when they believed their children were in danger or were being emotionally harmed by the abuse, that they finally gained the courage to leave.[36-37]

## CHILD POVERTY AND WELFARE

If the abused mother leaves and she does not have other financial means, she can apply for public assistance. Even some women who were not poor prior to leaving, and who had an education, may decide that their children need them at home. In a focus group this author conducted one woman reported, when I asked her about getting a job, "My children don't have a father now, they need a mother."[38]

Public assistance for poor mothers began in the early twentieth century with some states providing a Widow's Pension. During the New Deal, Aid to Dependent Children (which later became Aid to Families with Dependent Children—AFDC) was incorporated in the Social Security Act of 1935. Its purpose was to enable single mothers to care for their children at home rather than having to send them to an orphanage because they could not support them.

In 1996 AFDC was abolished and replaced by Temporary Assistance to Needy Families (TANF). TANF, part of the Personal Responsibility and Work Opportunity Reconciliation Act (PRWORA), limits lifetime assistance to a total of 60 months (5 years) and requires recipients to be in some kind of work activity. This can be community service, workfare or paid jobs for a total of 30 hours per week, or 20 hours if the youngest child is under 6 years of age. TANF requires mothers with children older than 3 months (with state option of 1 month) to be engaged in these programs or face partial or full sanctions (partial sanction removes the mother from the grant; full sanction removes the entire family).[39]

In the original Act, higher education or training was explicitly excluded as a work activity. Now it is allowed by statute for no more than one year, however that is at the discretion of the local welfare office to approve and most, like New York State, have a "Work First" emphasis. That means the mother can go to school to improve her financial potential, but only after putting in her 20–30 hours in some dead-end job or make-work activity, and with no subsidized child care for those educational activities.

Numerous studies have shown the correlation between increased level of education, higher income, and lower use of welfare.[40] Between 1995 and 1997, 41 percent of welfare recipients lacked a high school diploma, in contrast, to 29 percent of those who left welfare during that period.[41] Women who had some post-high school education were 41 percent less likely to return to welfare than women who did not finish high school.[42] A national longitudinal study of high school graduates, tracked over 14 years, found that each year of college increased earnings by 4–9 percent.[43] Gruber[44] found that in 1995 the gap in earnings between women with high school and college degrees was 68 percent. It is no surprise then, that women with less education are less likely to leave welfare and more likely to return. In Maine, the innovative Parents as Scholars program found that welfare mothers who were allowed to pursue a college education earned an average of almost $12 an hour after completion.[45]

States also have the option of imposing a "family cap," which means that no additional grant is given for any child born after the woman is receiving TANF. So even if she has been forced to have sex by an abusive spouse, gets pregnant and does not have an abortion (which is exceedingly difficult to obtain in some states and is not covered by federal Medicaid), there will be no additional funds provided to support this additional child.

A poor mother who needs financial assistance may be placed in a double, or even triple jeopardy.[46] TANF requires that she be involved in a work activity. If she cannot find accessible, affordable child care she has the "choice" of not working, in which case she will lose all or part of her family's grant. If she does work and the children are not properly cared for, Child Protective Services may find her to have neglected her children. This situation is exacerbated if the father has been abusive. If she succeeds in getting him to leave the home, she may need TANF for financial support. However, if she is working she is unable to supervise her children and she may be found guilty of "failure to protect." Brandwein[47] describes an actual case of a Utah mother who required her husband to leave because he was sexually abusing their children and subsequently lost custody of them.

Even when women on welfare are working, their grant is inadequate for them to afford decent housing. In no state is the TANF grant even equal to the federal poverty level, which is only about $16,000 for a family of three (the average size of families on TANF is 2.6.) The average monthly grant in 2001 was $351/month.[48] Women who leave TANF earn an average of just over $7.00 per hour. Working full time, full year (which is often not the case because of personal problems, illness or employer instability) the annual earnings would only be about $14,000. Because of cuts in the federal budget, they are unlikely to receive subsidized child care after leaving TANF. The cost of housing, child care, utilities, and transportation create overwhelming economic pressures on these poor mothers and their children.

Another program under TANF in which states can choose to participate is the Domestic Violence Option. A state choosing this option must attempt to identify any applicants and recipients who have been victims of domestic violence. A number of studies have found that between 40 and 65 percent of women on welfare had experienced family violence some time in their lives—they were either abused as children, in an intimate relationship, or both. Fully 20 percent were currently experiencing abuse.[49]

## POLICY ALTERNATIVES

The Violence Against Women Act (VAWA), first passed in 1994 and reauthorized in 1995 has provided greatly needed programs and policies to benefit victims of violence. Unfortunately, although this 1995 VAWA legislation authorized new programs for court training, grants for underserved populations, a focus on mitigating the effects of domestic violence on children, interdisciplinary training, and education for health professionals, the President's budget did not request funding for any of these new programs and most of the existing programs were slightly cut.[50]

The 2006 federal Budget Reconciliation Act will have even more severe consequences and will greatly exacerbate the poverty of poor children and their families. Earlier, we discussed the dilemma faced by abused mothers who face the choice of moving to housing they can afford, often in communities with poor educational facilities for their children. As of this writing, funding for the education of the disadvantaged was reduced by 3.5 percent for 2006, a total of $520 million and special education programs serving children with disabilities and other special needs was cut by $164 million (1.4 percent.)[51] Children who have suffered abuse directly or have lived in abusive homes are more likely to have special needs. Programs for vocational education, adult education and English literacy were cut by $45 million, or 2.2 percent. What this means is that even if local TANF officials were to allow welfare recipients to pursue education instead of a work activity, the resources for such programs are less likely to be available.

This budget reconciliation package provides funding for the Child Care and Development Block Grant (CCDBG) in addition to child-care funding provided in TANF legislation for mandated work programs. The CCDBG provides child-care funding for low- and moderate-income working families. Women who have left welfare, are in danger of going on or returning to welfare, or simply earn what the average woman in America earns, are eligible for this funding. A victim of violence or a mother whose child has been abused, and who leaves the abuser could obtain funding for child care so she could try to support her family. However, in the 2006 budget, this funding, in addition to failing to address inflation-driven cost, increases has been cut by an additional 1 percent. This results in a cut of 3 percent or $65 million. The Center for Budget and Policy Priorities has estimated that under-funding of child care will mean that by 2010, "...*255,000 fewer children in low-income working families not on TANF will receive child care assistance than received such assistance in 2004*" [italics in original].[52]

We discussed earlier the need for more affordable housing, but the 2006 budget moves in the opposite direction. Section 8 Housing vouchers, which is the main rental assistance program for low-income families was also cut by 1 percent. This will result either in 65,000 fewer such households obtaining rental assistance in 2006, or each recipient will receive a smaller grant for assistance.[53]

Medicaid is the major federal health insurance program for the poor. The Congressional conference agreement on the 2006 budget made major changes in this program, reducing benefits and increasing co-payments and premiums. Under existing legislation, $3 was the maximum charge for co-payments to Medicaid recipients. This new budget agreement could mean charges of $20–$100, at states' option. A poor mother will now have to choose to delay or avoid obtaining needed health care for herself or her children—or face the possibility of going without food, not paying her utilities or losing her housing. Abused women and their children have both short and long term physical as well as mental health needs that will be even less likely to be addressed when this punitive Medicaid program is fully implemented by the states.

These cuts could have easily been avoided had Congress decided to drop two tax cuts that did not take effect until January 2006. Virtually all these tax cuts (97 %) go to households with incomes over $200,000, with over 53 percent going to households with incomes exceeding $1 million.[54] So, if we are to discuss policy alternatives for poor families with children who have been victims of abuse, the overarching recommendation is that our domestic priorities need a 180-degree about-face. Instead of reducing taxes for millionaires, these funds should be redirected for better schools, health care, child care, housing, and other services to prevent and address the effects of family violence.

### Short Term

In the short term, we need to advocate for full funding of the VAWA Reauthorization of 1995, the reversal of new tax cuts for the very wealthy and restoration of the budget cuts in the 2006 federal budget. The VAWA legislation contains provisions for providing unemployment insurance for abused women who lose their jobs because of time taken off for court appointments, health problems or other violence-related difficulties.

Some specific programs have been proposed and implemented at the local level and should be expanded nationally. In Suffolk County, New York, the Victims Information Bureau has developed a successful cross-training program for domestic violence and child protective service workers. They learn to recognize and appreciate the problems the other group faces, and domestic violence workers accompany CPS workers on home visits where partner abuse is also suspected.[55] In Maine, the Parents as Scholars program has used state "maintenance-of-effort" funds to provide welfare grants to women so they can finish their 2- or 4-year-college program without running afoul of TANF legislation.[56] Rather than expanding this nationally, new federal legislation is threatening stats' ability to use such funding creatively. TANF should be amended, instead, to define post-high school education as a viable work activity to meet the work requirements. TANF programs should provide professionally trained case managers to individualize programs for TANF recipients and to provide guidance and support for them as they negotiate their way to financial self-sufficiency within the 5-year deadline. Early identification of children with emotional difficulties in preschool and primary grades, followed by early professional intervention could go a long way to prevent the long term emotional scarring of children suffering from family violence.

### Long Term

As important as these programmatic efforts are to alleviate some of the problems faced by poor children and their families, especially those touched by violence, other more comprehensive change is needed. The United States is the only major industrialized nation that does not provide universal health care and child care as a right. We are also the only such nation not providing paid family leave for a newborn, an adoptee or a seriously ill family member. All of these government programs would improve the lives of the families we have been discussing. Economic changes should include indexing the minimum wage to the cost-of-living, similar to those annual cost of living adjustments (COLA) to Social Security recipients. A number of municipalities have recently passed "living wage" legislation, although these are usually limited to municipal employees or contractors. This requires paying wages above minimum wage. A living wag is based on estimates of the minimum a family needs to live on. For single-parent families, this legislation, if universalized for all wage earners, could make the difference between choosing to either stay with or return to an abusive partner, or to be forced to go on welfare or a homeless shelter.

Education in our nation is the ladder to economic mobility. We need to assure educational equity for children, no matter where they live. This means decoupling education budgets from property taxes and local bond issues. This current method of regressive taxation assures that children in wealthier, usually white, communities get an educational advantage over poorer white and children of color. Our continued racial segregation in housing patterns reinforces these inequalities. Moreover, in the twenty-first century, when advanced skills are a necessity, all young people capable of benefiting from college or other advanced training should be guaranteed such an education. Higher education, like health care, should be a right, not a benefit based on ability to pay.

## CONCLUSIONS

What such long-term changes imply is a basic redistribution of income addressing the built-in inequalities now experienced by women, all people of color and the poor. We must finally address the inequities in our society caused by patriarchy, racism and classism. These isms are intertwined. *Why* do women still earn less than men? *Why* do African American and Hispanic women still earn the least? To explain it by education and preparation is to beg the question. *Why* do African Americans and Hispanics, and the poor have inferior educations?

Referring back to our discussion of CPS and the courts, the question must be asked, *why* do mothers get punished for the abuse of their partners? *Why* do judges continue to ask, "Why do the women stay?" instead of asking, "Why do the men abuse?" *Why* are funds cut for health care, housing, education, and child care and *why* do we keep cutting taxes for those who already have so much?

*Why* has the proportion of white families on welfare (TANF) declined and the proportion of African American and Hispanic women increased? (From 1992 to2001 white enrollment dropped from 39 to 30 percent while African American enrollment rose from 37 to 39 percent and Hispanics from 18 to 26 percent.[57] *Why* are women on welfare, increasingly women of color, not allowed to get an education? Certainly there is no rational answer, as it is clear that if they got that education they would not only be less likely to remain on welfare, but they would also be contributing to the tax base. Could it be because our economic system benefits by maintaining a marginal, secondary labor force to keep wages low by assuring a source of cheap labor? Could it be that *we* don't want *them* competing with us for the shrinking number of well-paid jobs? Could it be that in a racist, sexist society we need to marginalize and exploit poor, abused women of color so that *we* can feel superior to someone?

We need to work for the short-term changes that can ameliorate the situation of children living lives of poverty and abuse. The long-term changes, however, cannot come about until we begin to ask the larger, more difficult questions. We must begin to make those connections between the concrete issues of child poverty and the larger constructs of racism, classism, and patriarchy, in order to move toward those changes.

## NOTES

1. Martha Davis, 1999. The economics of abuse: How violence perpetuates women's poverty. In Ruth Brandwein, ed., *Battered women, children and welfare reform: The ties that bind*, 17–30. Thousand Oaks, CA: Sage Publications.

2. *Domestic violence: Not just a family matter. Hearing before the Subcommittee on Crime and Criminal Justice of the House Committee on the Judiciary*, 103rd Cong. 2nd Sess. June 30, 1994.

3. J. Zorza, 1996. Women battering: High costs and the state of the law. *Clearinghouse Review* 28: 338–395.

4. Patricia Tjaden and Nancy Thoennes. 2000. Extent, nature and consequences of intimate partner violence. *National Institute of Justice and the Centers of Disease Control and Prevention*.

5. Diane Russell, 1990. *Rape in marriage*. Bloomington: Indiana University Press.

6. Callie Marie Rennison, February 2003. *Intimate partner violence, 1993–2001*. U.S. Department of Justice, Bureau of Justice Statistics.

7. Jody Raphael, 1999. Keeping women poor: How domestic violence prevents women from leaving welfare and entering the world of work. In Brandwein, *Battered women, children and welfare reform*, 31–43.

8. Jody Raphael and Richard Tolman, 1997. *Trapped by poverty/trapped by abuse: New evidence documenting the relationship between domestic violence and welfare*. Chicago: Taylor Institute and the University of Michigan Research Development Center on Poverty, Risk and Mental Health.

9. Davis, *Battered women, children and welfare reform*.

10. K. Waits, 1985. The criminal justice system's response to battering: Understanding the problem, forging the solutions. *Washington Law Review* 60: 267–329.

11. Ruth Brandwein, 1999. Family violence and social policy. In Brandwein, ed., *Battered women, children and welfare reform*, 147–172.

12. Sandra Butler and Luisa Deprez, 2002. Something worth fighting for: Higher education for women on welfare. *Affilia: Journal of Women and Social Work* 17: 30–54.

13. Marilyn Gittell, Jill Gross, and Jennifer Holdaway, 1993. *Building human capital: The impact of postsecondary education on AFDC recipients in five states. Report to the Ford Foundation.* New York: Howard Samuels State Management and Policy Center. City University of New York Graduate School.

14. T. Kane and C. Rouse, 1997. Labor market returns to two- and four-year college. *American Economic Review* 85: 600–614.

15. E. Sweeney, L. Schott, E. Lazere, S. Fremstad, and H. Goldberg, 2000. *Windows of opportunity: Strategies to support families receiving welfare and other low-income families in the next stage of welfare reform.* Washington, DC: Center on Budget and Policy Priorities.

16. U.S. Department of Education, 1994. *Digest of education statistics.* Washington, DC: Government Printing Office.

17. L. Bowker,, M. Arbitell, and J. Ferron, 1988. On the relationship between wife beating and child abuse. In K. Yllo and M. Bograd, eds. *Feminist perspectives on wife abuse*, 155–174. Newbury Park, CA: Sage.

18. M. McKay, 1994. The link between domestic violence and child abuse: Assessment and treatment considerations. *Child Welfare* 73: 29–34.

19. Diana Pearce, 1999. Doing the triple combination: Negotiating the domestic violence, child welfare and welfare systems. In Brandwein, ed., *Battered women, children and welfare reform*, 109–120.

20. E. Peled, 1997. The battered women's movement response to children of battered women: A critical analysis. *Violence Against Women* 3: 424–446.

21. Evan Stark and Anne Flitcraft, 1985. Women battering, child abuse and social heredity: What is the relationship? In N. Johnson, ed., *Marital Violence*, 147–171. Boston: Routledge Kegan Paul.

22. Peled, The battered women's movement response to children of battered women.

23. U.S. Bureau of Justice Statistics, 1995. *Violence against women: Estimates from the redesigned survey.* Washington, DC: Government Printing Office.

24. Demi Kurz, 1995. *For richer, for poorer: Mothers confront divorce.* New York: Routledge.

25. Angela Browne and Susan Bassuk, 1997. Intimate violence in the lives of homeless and poorly housed women: Prevalence and patterns in an ethnically diverse sample. *American Journal of Orthopsychiatry* 6: 261–278.

26. U.S. Department of Health and Human Services. February 18, 2005. Annual update of the HHS poverty guidelines. *Federal Register* 70(33): 8373–8375. Available at http://aspe.hhs.gov/poverty/05fedreg.htm (accessed March 22, 2006).

27. U.S. Department of Health and Human Services, Administration for Children and Families. *Fiscal year 2001: Characteristics and financial circumstances of TANF recipients.* Available at http://www/acf/dhhs.gov/programs/ofa/character/FY2001/characteristics.htm (accessed November 9, 2004).

28. U.S. Census Bureau. *Poverty Tables.* Available at http://www.census.gov/

29. Ibid.

30. Institute for Women's Policy Research, August 2005. *The gender-wage ratio: Women's and men's earnings, #350.* Washington, DC: Author.

31. Children's Defense Fund, 1996. *Summary of legislation affecting children in 1996.* Washington, DC: Author.

32. Daniel Pelletiere, Keith Wardry, and Sheila Crowley, 2006. *Out of Reach 2005.* Washington, DC: National Low Income Housing Coalition. Available at http://www/jlihc.org/ (accessed March 22, 2006).

33. M. Allard, M. Colten, R Albelda, and C. Cosensa, 1997. *In harm's way? Domestic violence, AFCD receipt and welfare reform in Massachusetts.* Boston: University of Massachusetts, McCormack Institute, Center for Survey Research.

34. J. Pearson and E. Griswold, Feb. 1997. *Child support policies and domestic violence.* Paper presented at the Cooperation/Good Cause Forum sponsored by the Federal Office of Child Support Enforcement. Washington, DC.

35. C. Harlow, 1991. *Female victims of violent crime.* Washington, DC: U.S. Department of Justice.

36. Ruth Brandwein, 1999. Connections between child abuse and welfare: One woman's story. In Brandwein, ed., *Battered women children and welfare reform,* 121–130.

37. Ruth Brandwein and D. Filiano, 2000. Toward real welfare reform: The voices of battered women. *Affilia: Journal of Women and Social Work* 17: 224–243.

38. Ibid.

39. Personal Responsibility and Work Opportunity Reconciliation Act of 1996 Pub.L, 104–193, 110 Stat.2105 (Aug. 22, 1996).

40. Butler and Deprez, Something worth fighting for.

41. P. Loprest, and S. Zedlewski,. 1999. *Current and former welfare recipients: How do they differ?* Washington, DC: The Urban Institute.

42. K. Harris, 1996. Life after welfare: Women, work and repeat dependency. *American Sociological Review* 61: 407–426.

43. Kane and Rouse, Labor market returns to two- and four-year college.

44. A. Gruber, 1998. Promoting long-term self-sufficiency for welfare recipients: Post-secondary education and the welfare work requirement. *Northwest University Law Review.* 93: 247–299.

45. Butler and Deprez, Something worth fighting for.

46. Pearce, *Battered women, children and welfare reform.*

47. Brandwein, *Battered women, children and welfare reform.*

48. U.S. Department of Health and Human Services, Administration for Children and Families. *Fiscal year 2001.*

49. Allard et al. *In harm's way?*

50. Women's Policy, Inc. 2006. *Summary of VAWA 2005 provisions.* http://www.womenspolicy.org/thesource/article.cfm&#x003F;ArticleID=1918 (accessed Feb. 8, 2006)

51. Arloc Sherman and Richard Kogan. January 2006 (rev.). *What do the across-the-board cuts mean for domestic appropriations?* Washington, DC: Center for Budget and Policy Priorities.

52. Sharon Parrott, Edwin Park, and Robert Greenstein. January 8, 2006 (rev). *Assessing the effects of the budget agreement on low-income families and individuals.* Washington, DC: Center for Budget and Policy Priorities.

53. Sherman and Kogan, *What do the across-the- board cuts mean for domestic appropriations?*

54. Robert Greenstein, Joel Friedman, and Aviva Aron-Dine. December 28, 2005. *Two tax cuts primarily benefiting millionaires will start taking effect January 1.* Washington, DC: Center for Budget and Policy Priorities.

55. Victims Information Services of Suffolk (VIBS).

56. Butler and Deprez, Something worth fighting for.

57. U.S. DHHS, Administration for Children and Families. *Fiscal year 2001: Exhibit II— Trends in AFDC/TANF characteristics FY 1992-FY 2001.* Avalaible at http://www.acf.dhhs.gov/programs/ofa/character/FY2001/charactistics.htm (accessed November 9, 2004)

# CHAPTER 3

# DIVERSITY IN LIVING ARRANGEMENTS AND CHILDREN'S ECONOMIC WELL-BEING IN SINGLE-MOTHER HOUSEHOLDS*

## *Pamela R. Davidson*

The sweeping reforms introduced to the federal welfare system in 1996 bolstered public scrutiny of single-mother households. The Personal Responsibility and Work Opportunity Reconciliation Act (PRWORA) was signed into law with the explicit purpose of reducing the dependence of single-parent households on public assistance and decreasing the incidence of single-parent households. These goals have led to a plethora in educational programs to reduce unwanted pregnancies, changes in welfare policies to reduce the "marriage penalty," and similar changes in the tax code. Despite these efforts, both the number and percent of children living with single mothers is on the rise (Figure 3.1)

Supporting the goals of the PRWORA has been a wealth of research on single-mother households that demonstrates their lower economic status and their negative impact on children.[1] In a nutshell, this research makes the case that children growing up in single-mother households suffer academically in school, engage in premarital sex earlier, have an increased risk of early childbearing, and suffer higher levels of depression and aggression. This research supports the policy goal of integrating single mothers into the workforce since economic standing is viewed as a correlate of poorer outcomes in children raised by single mothers. In contrast, scholarship critical of the current policy emphasis points to the difficulties that single mothers face in finding stable jobs that allow them to earn enough to provide for their families.[2] Relatedly, the need to work extended hours makes it increasingly difficult for single mothers to simultaneously provide their children with a warm and nurturing environment so essential for child development and to provide quality supervision for adolescent children.[3]

Underlying research on single-parent households and policies designed to reduce them is the notion that all single-mother households are alike.[4] In contrast to this, I

Percent Living with Single Mothers

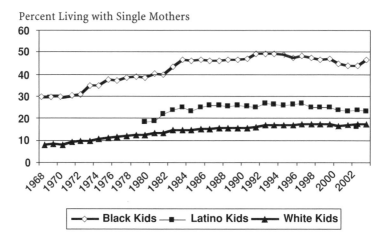

Number Living with Single Mothers

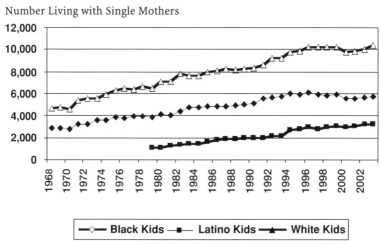

**Figure 3.1**

**Trends in Children's Living Arrangements, by Race/Ethnicity, 1968–2004.** *Source:* **U.S. Census Bureau, Annual Social and Economic Supplement: 2003 Current Population Survey, Current Population Reports, Series P20-553, "America's Families and Living Arrangements: 2003" and earlier.**

focus on the heterogeneity of children's living arrangements in single-mother households. Most studies do not consider that the category of single mother can have different meanings in different households.[5] In some households, single mothers live with boyfriends; in others with their own parents; and in still others they live with both their minor-aged and adult-aged children. This heterogeneity is not captured under the rubric of "single mother." In this chapter, I consider the impact that children's living arrangements have on their economic well-being and vulnerability.

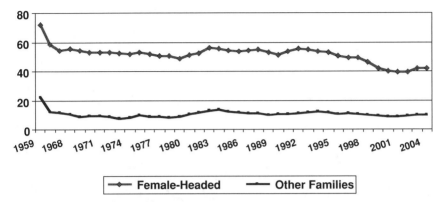

**Figure 3.2**
**Poverty Rates of Related Children in Female-Headed, Other Households, 1959–2004.**
*Source:* **Congressional Research Service, based on U.S. Bureau of the Census data. Current Population Reports, Series P-60 and CRS tabulations.**

In considering children's economic well-being, supporters of current policies point to poverty rates for both children and single mothers that have declined notably over the past decade since the start of welfare reform in 1996 (Figure 3.2). In their view, this is a positive trend and has only been possible because of the long-term incorporation of single mothers into the labor market. The argument made is that, while initially difficult, single mothers have been able to work their way up into better jobs thereby qualifying many for unemployment benefits in times of economic downturn.[6] With childhood poverty rates currently on the rise, this argument may now be put to the test. As many researchers have been quick to point out, however, the poverty rate may not have ever been an adequate measure of economic well-being.[7] The official poverty measure sets the threshold to poverty too low by failing to consider expenses that constitute a large part of every family's budgets including the cost of housing and work-related expenses such as child care and work clothes.[8] While there has been growing criticism of the official poverty measure, there is also agreement that no one measure can capture the multidimensionality of economic well-being.[9] Using different measures in addition to the official poverty rate, I hope to identify groups of children most vulnerable to shifts in social policy and most in need of attention.

## DATA AND METHODOLOGY

The data for this study come from the March Supplement of the Current Population Survey (CPS) for 2001. The 2001 CPS includes a nationally representative sample of 128,729 persons (excluding persons living in group quarters) and 49,596 households. An important advantage in using the CPS data is that its large sample size allows for a more detailed classification of household structures than smaller

All Children in CPS

All Children in Single Mother HHs

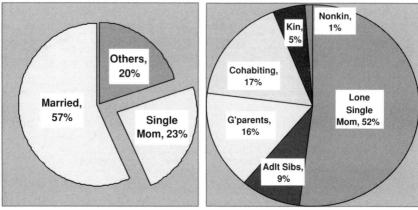

**Figure 3.3**
**Types of Households in Which Children Live.** *Source:* **2001 CPS March Supplement, author's own calculations.**

surveys. In addition, the CPS provides detailed information on income sources. The unit of analysis is the child. Children selected into the analysis include those living in single-mother households or in married parent households in which no additional adult besides the married parents live.[10] A mother is considered single if she is unmarried or married, but with no spouse present. While the CPS distinguishes between primary families and (related and unrelated) subfamilies, in this study, the presence of a single mother anywhere in the household constitutes a single-mother household. This operationalization deviates from that used to report official poverty statistics, but is more in line with the object of this study.

The dependent variables in this study measure children's economic well-being and include: mother is 125 percent above the poverty line, the household is 125 percent above the poverty line, and disposable household income covers basic household expenses. Further description of these variables is provided below. The central independent variable is household structure. The CPS consists of 34,664 children in 18,138 households. Most of these children (57.3%) live in married couple households in which no other adults are present (Figure 3.3).[11] Close to one-fourth live in single-mother households. The residual group of other children includes those living in extended married parent households, single-father households, or no-parent (e.g., grandparent-headed) households.

Households identified as single-mother households are further categorized by the type of living arrangements and fall into six categories: lone single mother, adult sibling, grandparent, kin, nonkin, and cohabiting households. Over half (52%) of children in single-mother households live with lone single mothers, that is in households in which no other adults are present besides the single mother.[12] Another 16 percent live in households where a single mother lives with her underage children and at least one of their grandparents. These multigenerational households can either be headed by the children's parents or their grandparents. Kin households consist of at least one adult who is related to the single mother and are home to approximately 5 percent of children in single-mother households. In most cases (ca. 62%), the single mother is the head of household and the adult relative is usually the mother's sibling (in 55% of the cases). Approximately 9 percent of children in single-mother households coreside with their adult siblings. Similar to kin households, adult sibling households can contain other adults besides single mothers, but at least one must be the adult child of a single mother. Only less than 2 percent of all children in single-mother households reside in nonkin households, that is in households in which all adults in the households are not related to the single mother (and are not her cohabiting boyfriend). In most cases (69%), the single mother is the head of household. The CPS contains 722 cohabiting single-mother households in which close to 17 percent of all children in single-mother households live. Because of the difficulties in using the CPS to classify cohabiting households, special steps were taken to operationalize this category.[13] Cohabiting single mothers include single mothers who indicated that they are cohabiting based on a CPS variable introduced in 1995. Because this variable is associated with a known downward bias, I additionally classified single mothers as cohabiting if they live in households with unrelated, unmarried men over the age of 15 who meet certain established age criteria to qualify them to be male partners.[14] In the event of an overlap with other household structure categories, households designated as cohabiting are retained as such and excluded from other categories.

## RESULTS

Studies that rely on simple comparisons between children in single mother and married parent households overlook the internal diversity that exists on a number of levels. A demographic profile of the sample children included in this study is given in Table 3.1. Since the focus of this study is on children's economic well-being, all results are presented using children in households as the unit of analysis. Most children (73%) in married parent households are white compared to children in single-mother households.[15] Within the population of children in single-mother households, there is great variability but with a notable pattern. Children in households with nonrelatives (nonkin and cohabiting boyfriend households) are more likely to be white than non-white. The reverse is true for the remaining categories in which relatives "double up." Particularly notable, Latino children are much more strongly represented in extended households with kin. Close to half (40.4%) of all children in kin single-mother households are Latino.

Not all children in single-mother households are being raised by single mothers. This is mostly true in extended single-mother households, but is also true in married parent households in which less than 1 percent (0.6%) is not related to either parent. In multigenerational households, over 3 percent (3.2%) of children have no parents in the home. In a nontrivial number of kin households, at least three complete

**Table 3.1**

**Characteristics of Children in Single-Mother and Married-Parent Households**

| | Households with Children Under 18 Who Are Not HH Heads | | | | | | |
| | No Other Adult but | | Extended Households: Single Mothers and... | | | | |
| Characteristics of Children | Married Parents | Lone Mother | Grand parents | Other Kin | Nonkin | Cohabiting Boyfriend | Adult Sibs |
|---|---|---|---|---|---|---|---|
| Race/ethnicity | | | | | | | |
| White (non-Hispanic) | 73.0 | 44.8 | 35.9 | 16.4 | 63.8 | 52.8 | 39.4 |
| African American | 8.0 | 37.9 | 32.7 | 34.4 | 10.2 | 21.0 | 30.2 |
| Hispanic | 13.6 | 13.6 | 26.8 | 40.4 | 20.5 | 21.7 | 26.5 |
| Other | 3.68 | 3.7 | 4.6 | 8.8 | 5.5 | 4.5 | 3.9 |
| Child's status in HH | | | | | | | |
| Has foster parent | 0.2 | 0.8 | 0.2 | 0.0 | 0.0 | 0.2 | 1.2 |
| Has no parents | 0.6 | 0.9 | 3.2 | 7.7 | 4.4 | 1.8 | 4.5 |
| Household composition | | | | | | | |
| Mean number of children | 2.4 | 2.4 | 2.6 | 3.3 | 2.4 | 2.4 | 2.2 |
| Number of persons in HH | 4.4 | 3.4 | 5.7 | 6.3 | 4.6 | 4.7 | 4.6 |
| Has employed male | 96.5 | 0.0 | 45.4 | 66.5 | 27.1 | 93.9 | 47.2 |
| Number of parent units[a] | | | | | | | |
| One | 100.0 | 100.0 | 94.7 | 51.0 | 76.8 | 80.1 | 91.0 |
| Two | 0.0 | 0.0 | 5.3 | 41.1 | 23.2 | 19.6 | 7.7 |
| Three | 0.0 | 0.0 | 0.0 | 7.9 | 0.0 | 0.4 | 1.3 |
| Characteristics of mother[b] | | | | | | | |
| Never-married mother | 0.0 | 39.2 | 64.9 | 57.1 | 37.4 | 44.8 | 19.5 |
| Has HS Diploma | 81.3 | 89.1 | 70.4 | 65.5 | 85.2 | 77.1 | 70.6 |
| In fair or poor health | 5.2 | 14.9 | 13.0 | 6.3 | 10.4 | 9.8 | 16.4 |
| Mean age | 36.2 | 34.8 | 27.9 | 30.3 | 33.1 | 31.3 | 43.2 |
| Housing characteristics | | | | | | | |
| % Homeowner property | 77.5 | 33.6 | 63.5 | 49.2 | 37.6 | 37.6 | 48.9 |
| % Rental property | 20.9 | 64.8 | 36.0 | 47.2 | 60.9 | 61.2 | 50.4 |
| % No-cash rental | 1.6 | 1.6 | 0.5 | 3.7 | 1.5 | 1.2 | 0.7 |
| Unweighted sample size | 19,743 | 4,186 | 1,267 | 413 | 113 | 1,380 | 691 |

[a] Married parents count as one unit, as does a single parent. A cohabiting couple each with their own child counts as two family units as does a grandmother with underage child and her parenting daughter.

[b] In cases in which the minor-aged child has no mother in the household, the value of the adult next of kin is used.

families live under one roof: Close to 8 percent live in households in which there are three sets of parenting units (7.9%) and the same proportion have no parents at all (7.7%).

Various other household composition characteristics set single-mother households apart from each other and from married parent households. Children in cohabiting households (94%) come closest to children in married parent households (97%) in terms of the likelihood of there being an employed male in the household. Most children with lone single mothers (61%) do not have never-married mothers. Instead, children in multigenerational and kin households are much more likely to have never-married mothers as young mothers are more likely to continue residing in their parents' homes or turn to relatives, in particular siblings, in times of need.[16] Consistent with previous research, children in married couple households have mothers who are in better health than their counterparts in single-mother households. One-sixth of children who live alone with their single mothers or only with their mothers and adult siblings have mothers who are in fair or poor health. Partly contradicting research emphasizing married mothers' higher levels of education, children living alone with their mothers or with other nonkin are only slightly less likely to have mothers with high school diplomas than children with married parents. Marital status is, however, a more foreseeable indicator of living conditions. Over three-fourths (78%) of children of married parents live in homes owned by their parents. Even children in multigenerational households do not have higher homeownership rates. Particularly notable, only over one-third (38%) of children in cohabiting households live in homes owned by one of the tenants.

## Descriptive Results for Children's Economic Well-Being

A comparison of various measures of economic well-being by household structure is presented in Tables 2a and 2b. Tables 3a and 3b present the results for a subset of these measures broken out by race and ethnicity. The results indicate that children's economic well-being varies significantly by the type of household in which they reside. As seen in Table 3.2a, children living with lone single mothers and in cohabiting households are most likely to have low-income mothers (both 52%) closely followed by children in nonkin households (45%). A mother is classified as low-income if her family income falls at or below 125 percent of the official poverty line based on the size of her family. Because the official definition of poverty excludes the income from nonfamily members (including boyfriends), the rates for low-income status may be artificially high for households in which there are household members unrelated to the single mother. Nevertheless, the family-based measure of poverty is the official measure that is most widely used to report economic well-being.

By adding in the contributions of nonrelatives and using income threshold values based on household composition instead of that for family, there is a shift in the character of children's economic well-being.[17] In cohabiting households, notably fewer children live in low-income households than with a low-income mother (17% versus 52%). This is best explained by the fact that almost all cohabiting households have an employed male (see Table 3.1). Low-income rates decrease for children in nonkin households (25% versus 45%), in kin households (28% versus 34%), and actually in every other household type considered. These differences emerge because the family definition of income ignores the incomes of unrelated adults, but also of children who may be coresiding, such as foster children and other unrelated children

**Table 3.2a**

**Children's Economic Well-Being, by Living Arrangement, Weighted Average, Percent Experiencing Hardship Using Three Different Measures**

| Child's Living Arrangement | Sample Size | % With Income Mother [a,b] | % in Low-Income Households[a,c] | % HHs: Expenses Exceed Income [d,e] |
|---|---|---|---|---|
| Married parents, no other adults | 19,743 | 11.9 | 9.3 | 10.1% |
| Lone single mother | 4,186 | 51.8 | 52.8 | 47.7 |
| Mother and | | | | |
| Grandparents | 1,267 | 30.9 | 22.7 | 26.9 |
| Other kin | 413 | 34.1 | 27.6 | 35.6 |
| Nonkin | 113 | 44.9 | 24.8 | 32.4 |
| Boyfriend | 1,380 | 51.8 | 17.3 | 28.8 |
| Grown sibs | 691 | 37.4 | 32.4 | 35.7 |

[a] Low-income refers to 125% below the poverty level.

[b] In cases in which the minor-aged child has no mother in the household, the value of the adult next of kin is used.

[c] Based on the official poverty measure applied at the household level (using the incomes of all household members).

[d] Expenses include projected costs of rent (using the fair market value formula), food (using the low budget method), transportation, and child care. Estimates take into account differences in family size and region of the country.

[e] Disposable income includes income from all cash sources plus the value of EITC, capital gains (or losses), and the family market value of food stamps, school lunch, and housing subsidy minus taxes.

who may have independent sources of income. By considering the incomes of all household members, the gulf between children with lone single mothers and those in extended single-mother households widens. Over half of children living with lone single mothers are low-income compared to about one-fourth for children in extended family living arrangements. Extended family living arrangements clearly improve the economic standing of single-mother households.

The official measure of poverty has come under fire in recent times, with one reason being that the thresholds are antiquated. Low-budget food baskets that vary by family size are used as the basis for drawing poverty thresholds despite the fact that food consumes a much smaller portion of the family budget today than 40 years ago when the poverty measure was first created. Those critical of the measure argue that the budgets used to determine poverty thresholds should take into account budget items that are more relevant to families today, including housing, transportation, and work-related expenses such as child care.[18] To address this issue, I created a measure of economic well-being that relies on the EPI Guide to Family Budgets and relies on two pieces of information: household income and household expenses.[19]

First, I estimated income. Due to the weaknesses of a family-based measure, I sum income at the household level, using the same income definition used to measure poverty. This income definition is a measure of gross cash income and ignores a number of income sources that do not take the form of cash. To address this weakness, I utilize a household level measure based on net income (e.g., I subtract out Federal Insurance and Contribution Act or FICA, state and federal taxes) that adds in the value of Earned Income Tax Credit (EITC), capital gains (or losses), the family market value of food stamps and school lunch, and housing subsidies. Second, I impute household expenses for four expenditure categories drawing on officially published estimates that take family size and region of the country into account.[20] For housing, I impute the fair market value of rent for a household of a given size by state and metropolitan statistical area (MSA).[21] For food, I rely on estimates using the low budget method.[22] Transportation cost estimates take into account not only the region of the country, but also residence within or outside metropolitan areas and the number of (potential) drivers.[23] For child-care costs, I rely on state-level estimates broken out by region (urban/nonurban), averaging the cost of age-appropriate (e.g., using three age categories) family and home-based care and imputed this value only to those families who indicated that they paid for child care.[24] Finally, I compare the imputed value of household food and total work-related expenses to the total disposable household net income to determine if basic expenses exceed income, to create my third measure of child well-being that captures the dimension of economic hardship.

Based on this measure of economic hardship, a greater proportion of all children except those in lone single-mother households face economic hardship than would be estimated using the household-based variation of the official poverty measure. Regardless of the measure of economic well-being, however, children in lone single-mother households face the greatest financial hardship. Close to half live in households in which it is not possible to make ends meet even for only the essential items. Also vulnerable are children in kin and nonkin households, and in households in which children coreside with their adult siblings. Approximately one-third of these children live in households in which disposable net household income probably will not cover basic expenses. Many children in married parent households also face serious economic constraints, with 10 percent being in households in which making ends meet appears to be impossible.

Total income is comprised of income from varying sources, some of which, from a policy perspective, have been more strongly emphasized than others. Gaining a general understanding about the sources of household income may provide more insight into the children's possible vulnerability to policy shifts and economic downturns. Throughout the welfare debate, low-income mothers have been encouraged to reduce their reliance on public assistance by becoming more integrated into the labor market. Thus, from a policy perspective income generated in the labor market through wages or even unemployment compensation is valued above the same amount of income garnered through public assistance. There has also been increased attention to the role of nonresident fathers through increased enforcement of child support and alimony rulings. Child support enforcement has been an integral component of welfare reform with income collected through the state's enforcement efforts used to offset the cost

**Table 3.2b**
**Children's Economic Well-Being, by Living Arrangement, Mean Household Income from Four Sources[a] (in Thousands), Weighted Average**

| Child's Living Arrangement | Sample Size | Labor Income | Welfare Income | Child Support Alimony | Asset Income |
|---|---|---|---|---|---|
| Married parents, no other adults | 19,743 | 72.8 | 0.2 | 0.3 | 9.0 |
| Lone single mother | 4,186 | 18.7 | 1.3 | 2.1 | 1.9 |
| Mother and | | | | | |
| Grandparents | 1,267 | 42.2 | 1.3 | 0.7 | 5.4 |
| Other Kin | 413 | 46.6 | 0.7 | 1.0 | 2.8 |
| Nonkin | 113 | 49.0 | 0.8 | 1.0 | 2.5 |
| Boyfriend | 1,380 | 44.0 | 0.8 | 1.3 | 2.9 |
| Grown sibs | 691 | 30.5 | 1.3 | 1.8 | 3.3 |

[a] Assets: Interest earned, dividends, net return on equity, capital gains, and rent income.

Labor income: Income from earnings, unemployment, workers's compensation.

Welfare: Income from public assistance (TANF), SSI, housing subsidy, family market value (FMV) of food stamps, and FMV of school lunch.

of public assistance. From a policy perspective, income from child support is valued over equivalent amounts of income from public assistance since many feel that child support payments are typically accompanied by increased involvement by the absentee father in his child's life, resulting in the provision of moral and emotional support, and often even additional financial contributions. Finally, asset income has been touted as being more valuable than its actual value in dollars.[25] Assets gained through savings, dividends, and property ownership provide a buffer in times of economic downturn, foster long-term economic security, and is sometimes thought to have a positive impact on fostering a life perspective consistent with a long-term financial planning horizon.

The results in Table 3.2b indicate that the mean amount of income from the various sources varies widely among the different living arrangement categories. Mean labor income is highest among children in married couple households ($72.8K) and lowest in lone single-mother households ($18.7K) and in single-mother households with grown siblings ($30.5K). Despite the fact that there are notably more people in extended family households, labor income in all categories thereof is almost half of the level found in married parent households. The highest average annual welfare payments ($1.3K) are available to children in lone single mother, adult sibling, and multigenerational households.

Some income portfolios render children in certain living arrangements economically more vulnerable than others. Children in lone single-mother households are not only more likely to be low-income (Table 3.2a), but the sources of income also place them into a more precarious economic status (Table 3.2b). The income profile of children in lone single-mother households reveals their significant reliance on public assistance and child support. For every $100 a lone single mother brings home in labor income, close to $13 comes in from public assistance or child support. This nontrivial portion of the household budget is a tenuous source over which the mother may have little control. Public assistance eligibility rules may be poorly understood and personal conflicts with the children's father may translate into fluctuating or even rapidly shifting amounts from one month to the next. A similar situation faces children in adult sibling households, whose household income from labor market activities is only somewhat higher than in lone single-mother households.

In grandparent households, levels of income from public assistance is comparable to those in lone single mother and adult sibling households, but not child support payments, most likely due to the youthfulness of single mothers in that population. That reduction is more than compensated by higher-income levels from labor market activities. Labor market income remains low, however, despite the fact that multi-generational households are larger, on average, than other living arrangements and at least some of its members should have greater seniority in the labor market. Their weak economic standing is evidence of the multigenerational effect of poverty in which economic hardship brings together two generations of low-income families into one household. The situation is, however, rendered somewhat less tenuous since household asset income in multigenerational households is second only to that found in married parent households. Most of this asset income is likely to be home equity, since close to two-thirds of children in multigenerational households live in privately owned (not rented) homes (Table 3.1).

The income portfolio of cohabiting households is quite similar to that found in multigenerational households with their decreased reliance on public assistance being compensated by an increased reliance on child support. Given the current living arrangements, income from child support is more likely to be even more tenuous due to potential hostility instigated by the introduction of a "substitute father" into the child's life. Adding to this are issues of resource pooling in cohabiting households. While household income from labor market activities is comparable to that found in multigenerational households, there is no guarantee that this income will be shared equally.[26] More research is needed to assess the extent to which cohabiting partners pool incomes, but it can be assumed that cohabiting boyfriends might be less inclined to share their earned incomes in an egalitarian fashion, particularly if the single mother's child is from another relationship. About one-third of labor market earnings in cohabiting households is generated by single mothers.[27] Their ability to tap into the other two-thirds can depend on many factors, making the economic situation of children therein more tenuous than in multigenerational households.

From a policy perspective, children's income portfolios in kin and nonkin extended households appear to be the strongest. Their reliance on public assistance and child support is lowest, while income from labor market activities is highest, second only to children with married parents. Nevertheless, even more so than in cohabiting households, there are certainly issues as to how income gets pooled in kin and nonkin households and these decisions have concrete implications for child economic well-being. Like in cohabiting households, about one-third of labor market earnings in kin households stems from single mothers. Single mothers in nonkin households contribute more, roughly 40 percent.[28] With less public assistance and child support in hand and lower contributions to the total household budget in a household with others who may not be immediate kin, single mothers may find themselves in a poor bargaining position which may, in turn, translate into a weaker or at least more precarious economic situation for their children. Conversely, the single mothers in these households also tend to be the household heads (close to three-fourths of children living in these households have single mothers as heads), which may increase their bargaining power. Very little research to date has been conducted on the impact of living arrangements on resources pooling making it difficult to assess children's economic well-being under these different living conditions.

### Descriptive Results by Race and Ethnicity

The results broken out by race and ethnicity reveal a relative pattern that is very similar to that found at the aggregate level. Regardless of race or ethnicity and regardless of the operational measure, children in married parent households have a higher level of well-being than their counterparts in single-mother households (Table 3.3a). What is notable, however, is the additional penalty that children pay for being African American or Latino.

White children are never as negatively impacted by alternative family structures to the same extent as African American or Latino children. Close to three-fourths (72%) of Latino children and two-thirds (63%) of African American children in lone single-mother households are low-income. The same is true for only 37 percent of white children. Even children living in socially desirable and publicly promoted married parent households are at risk of experiencing economic hardship if they are black or Latino. While 6 percent of white children with married parents live in low-income households, the same is true for 11 percent of their African American and 25 percent of their Latino counterparts. Latino children in married parent households are the most disadvantaged ethnic group and face similar economic constraints as white children in single-mother households with adult siblings and even worse economic conditions than white children in every other extended single-mother households using either household measure of economic well-being.

In comparing measures of economic well-being, the similarity in results using either operationalization (low-income rates or income gap rate) is striking. Nevertheless, there is a 10 percent or greater difference between the two measures for every racial/ethnic group for children in cohabiting households. For example, whereas 12 percent of white children in cohabiting households are in low-income households, 22 percent are in households in which disposable net income does not cover basic expenses. This suggests that children in cohabiting households face a greater financial crunch than would be suggested by considering income alone. Even measures of income that more closely reflect disposable income do not take into account life cycle or geographic residence differences that may distinguish certain family types. Cohabiting families may be more likely to live in metropolitan areas in which

**Table 3.3a**

**Children's Economic Well-Being, by Living Arrangement, Percent Living in Low-Income Households (LIHH)[a,b] or in Households with an Income Gap[c]. (Weighted Averages)**

| Child's Living Arrangement | White Children | | | African American Children | | | Latino Children | | |
|---|---|---|---|---|---|---|---|---|---|
| | Sample Size | % in LIHH | % Inc Gap | Sample Size | % in LIHH | % Inc Gap | Sample Size | % in LIHH | % Inc Gap |
| Married parents, no other adults | 13,762 | 5.9 | 6.5 | 1,147 | 10.8 | 10.9 | 3,795 | 25.3 | 27.0 |
| Lone single mother | 1,927 | 37.9 | 34.5 | 1,233 | 63.3 | 57.3 | 866 | 71.5 | 66.2 |
| Mother and | | | | | | | | | |
| Grandparents | 415 | 13.9 | 15.9 | 310 | 26.6 | 32.4 | 477 | 29.4 | 35.4 |
| Kin/Nonkin | 127 | 12.6 | 15.0 | 105 | 39.0 | 45.7 | 249 | 26.9 | 38.2 |
| Boyfriend | 708 | 11.5 | 22.4 | 205 | 21.1 | 35.6 | 384 | 26.7 | 36.8 |
| Grown sibs | 254 | 21.2 | 26.0 | 153 | 42.1 | 42.7 | 244 | 38.2 | 42.0 |

[a] Low-income refers to 125% below the poverty level.

[b] Based on the official poverty measure applied at the household level (using the incomes of all household members).

[c] The "gap" is the difference between household disposable income and basic household expenses. HH Income is disposable household net income and includes income from all cash sources plus the value of EITC, capital gains (or losses), and the family market value of food stamps, school lunch, and housing subsidy minus taxes. Basic expenses include projected costs of rent (using the fair market value formula), food (using the low budget method), transportation, and child care. Estimates take into account differences in family size and region of the country.

transportation costs are higher. Cohabiting mothers are more likely to work and to work longer hours than other single mothers (not shown), which taken together, might increase transportation costs further. Similarly, the work habits of cohabiting couples may entail a greater demand for child care while geographic location might result in higher per hour child-care costs. A similar explanation might apply for the 10 percent difference between economic well-being measures for Latino children in kin/nonkin households. Taken together, these differences provide evidence of the difficulty of capturing economic well-being with a single measure and suggest the need to draw on multiple measures.

Labor market income in white children's households is consistently higher than in the households of their black or Latino counterparts (Table 3.3b). Once again, the meaning of having married parents differs notably by race and ethnicity and it is among the married population that there are the biggest differences by race and ethnicity. Mean labor income in married parent households is almost twice as high in white children's households as in Latino children's households ($80K versus $43K) and it is approximately 40 percent higher than in African American children's households ($58K). In contrast, in all categories of single-mother households, labor income in African American and Latino children's households are remarkably similar and always between $10K and $20K less than in the households of their white counterparts. African American and Latino children's households, thus, always have less income than their white counterparts in comparable living arrangements. Not surprisingly then, income from public assistance is higher in African American and Latino children's households regardless of living arrangement. Nevertheless, the higher average income from public assistance sources in black and Latino households does not make up for the gap in labor income. For example, the highest average amount of public assistance ($1.6K) goes to Latino children in grown sibling single-mother households, but added to the average labor income for this group ($27K), it is still several thousands of dollars less than the average income in the households of their white counterparts from labor income alone ($35.6K versus $28.8K).

### Results from Logistic Regression Analyses

To follow up on the results from descriptive analyses, multivariate analyses were conducted to better assess the relationship between children's well-being and living arrangements controlling for other factors. Because the dependent variables are dichotomous, logistic regression is used. To simplify interpretation, the log odds co-efficients are presented as odds ratios. The logistic regression models rely on white standard errors which are robust to within cluster correlation by household or family.[29] Table 3.4 details the odds ratios from nested logistic regression models. This model-ing strategy is useful in confirming or eliminating reasons for differences in children's well-being between children in married parent and single-mother households. The dependent variables are coded to express a positive state of child economic well-being and include: child does not have a low-income mother, child does not live in a low-income household, and child's household can make ends meet (basic expenses do

**Table 3.3b**
**Children's Economic Well-Being, by Living Arrangement, Mean Household Income[a] from the Labor Market (Thousands) and Public Assistance (Weighted Averages)**

| Child's Living Arrangement | White Children | | | African American Children | | | Latino Children | | |
|---|---|---|---|---|---|---|---|---|---|
| | Sample Size | Income Source | | Sample Size | Income Source | | Sample Size | Income Source | |
| | | LM | PA | | LM | PA | | LM | PA |
| Married parents, no other adults | 13,762 | 80.1 | 0.1 | 1,147 | 58.2 | 0.4 | 3,795 | 42.6 | 0.3 |
| Lone Single Mother | 1,927 | 24.1 | 0.8 | 1,233 | 14.4 | 1.6 | 866 | 13.4 | 1.6 |
| Mother and | | | | | | | | | |
| Grandparents | 415 | 53.4 | 0.8 | 310 | 35.6 | 1.5 | 477 | 34.1 | 1.5 |
| Kin/Nonkin | 127 | 55.5 | 0.7 | 105 | 39.0 | 0.9 | 249 | 39.3 | 0.8 |
| Boyfriend | 708 | 48.3 | 0.5 | 205 | 38.3 | 1.2 | 384 | 40.1 | 1.0 |
| Grown sibs | 254 | 35.6 | 1.2 | 153 | 27.1 | 1.3 | 244 | 27.2 | 1.6 |

[a] Labor income: Income (in thousands) from earnings, unemployment, workers's compensation.
Public assistance: Income from TANF, SSI, housing subsidy, family market value (FMV) of food stamps, and FMV of school lunch.

**Table 3.4**
**Logistic Regression of Family Structure and Other Characteristics on Children's Economic Well-Being, Odds Ratios (Weighted Estimates)**

| | Child Has a Nonpoor Mother | | Child Not in a Low-Income HH | | Child's Household Makes Ends Meet | |
|---|---|---|---|---|---|---|
| | Simple Model | Full Model | Simple Model | Full Model | Simple Model | Full Model |
| 0 = Lone single mother | | | | | | |
| Married parents | 8.00 | 3.69 | 10.88 | 6.35 | 8.11 | 3.67 |
| SM and grandparents | 2.41 | 4.09 | 3.81 | 11.25 | 2.48 | 2.87 |
| SM and other Kin | 2.08 | 4.21 | 2.94 | 8.97 | 1.65 | 2.13 |
| SM and nonkin | 1.32 | 0.47 | 3.40 | 3.53 | 1.90 | 1.06 |
| SM and grown siblings | 1.00$^{ns}$ | 0.47 | 5.37 | 9.12 | 2.25 | 1.56 |
| SM and male partner | 1.80 | 1.19 | 2.34 | 2.17 | 1.64 | 1.03 |
| Race/ethnicity (0 = white) | | | | | | |
| African American | | 0.62 | | 0.54 | | 0.64 |
| Latino | | 0.42 | | 0.38 | | 0.46 |
| Other | | 0.53 | | 0.49 | | 0.68 |
| Youngest SM's age | | 1.03 | | 1.02 | | 1.02 |
| Mother: HS diploma | | 2.87 | | 2.56 | | 2.42 |
| Mother: Fair/poor health | | 1.00 | | 1.10 | | 1.08 |
| Number of kids in hh | | 0.60 | | 0.55† | | 0.72 |
| Metro (0 = Nonmetro) | | | | | | |
| Pop. 100k-1M | | 1.60 | | 1.92 | | 2.04 |
| Pop. 1M+ | | 2.04 | | 2.33 | | 1.56 |
| HH income sources: | | | | | | |
| Asset income | | 2.60 | | 3.07 | | 2.77 |
| Child support/alimony | | 1.96 | | 2.20 | | 1.92 |
| Welfare income | | 0.23 | | 0.26 | | 0.67 |
| Labor income ≥ $10K | | 30.74 | | 47.45 | | 15.52 |
| Pseudo $R^2$ | .1358 | .4728 | .1519 | .5313 | .1231 | .3846 |

*NOTE:* All coefficients are significant at the $P < .001$ level. The two exceptions are indicated by ns (not significant) and † ($P < .01$).

not exceed disposable income). The full models introduce controls including race, characteristics of the child's mother, number of children in the home, metropolitan residence, and dummy variables for income sources. The complete models are a good fit to the data as indicated by the pseudo-R-Squares.

The first simple model illustrates how children's economic well-being varies along the lines of living arrangement using the low-income status (above 125%-poverty level) of the child's mother as the dependent variable. I set the reference category to lone single mother in order to assess the effect on children of adding different categories of persons to their households. The first model shows the odds of improved economic well-being (e.g., of not having a low-income mother) are eight times higher for children in married parent households than for those living with lone single mothers. Children living in other types of single-mother households are also more likely than children with lone single mothers to have mothers who are nonpoor. There is no significant difference between children living alone with their single mothers and those whose extended households also include adult siblings.

The full model reveals that child and household characteristics explain part of the relationship between well-being and living arrangements since the estimates make notable shifts after adding in the control variables. The odds ratio for married parents decreases by more than one-half, indicating that a large part of the advantage that children of married parents have over children in lone single-mother households is explained by demographics and income sources. In contrast, the odds ratios for grandparent and kin households doubles in size indicating that the potential for economic advantage among these children is diminished by the demographics of their households. The odds ratios for nonkin and adult sibling households change direction indicating a greater advantage among children in lone single-mother households compared to children in nonkin or grown sibling households. As the inverse odds ratios show, children in lone single-mother households are 2.13 (1/.47) times more likely to have nonpoor mothers controlling for the demographic characteristics and income sources than children in these two household living arrangements. For a child living in nonkin extended households, lower economic standing may simply be a measurement artifact related to the use of a family and not household based measure of income. In contrast, the inverse odds ratio for adult sibling households suggest that children who return back to the "nest" or never leave, present a real economic hardship to single-mother households net of any effects related to the demographic or socioeconomic composition of these households.

Using a family-based measure of children's economic well-being may produce distortions since children are embedded in households and benefit from the income and availability of nonrelatives. In addition, children's mothers may react to the presence of other working adults in the household by, for example, working less, making it appear that children's well-being had worsened, when in fact it may have improved due to the financial resources of other household members. The second simple model illustrates how children's economic status varies along the lines of household living arrangement using household low-income status (125%-above poverty level) as the dependent variable. Not surprisingly, the odds ratios for household structure are all larger in the second simple model than in the first. After taking into account the income from all household members, there is an even greater advantage experienced by children not only in married parent households, but also in extended family living arrangements.

As seen previously, adding control variables attenuates the estimate for married parent households and increases it for grandparent and kin households. The main difference with the second full model is that the direction of the effect of nonkin and adult–sibling households does not switch. Instead, it increases suggesting an even stronger economic advantage among these children compared to children in lone single-mother households after controlling for demographic variables and income sources. This result is not surprising for nonkin households since the dependent variable in the second model counts the income of nonfamily members whereas this was not the case in the first model. The reversal for grown sibling households is more surprising and indicative of the important role of nonfamily members in potentially lifting children out of poverty. Grown sibling households are the most likely to have foster children[30] and this may be a nontrivial source of nonfamily income. They are also more likely than most household categories to have other unrelated other children who may have additional income available (e.g., social security and SSI for orphaned or disabled children). Controlling for household demographics and based on a household measure of income, three of the five extended single-mother households have larger odds ratios than for married parents. This result is consistent with the idea that much of the advantage of children in married parent households has to do with demographics and the failure to consider all income sources, instead of marriage being the ideal arrangement per se to accumulate economic resources.

Compared to children in lone single-mother households, children in any other living arrangement are more likely to live in households in which disposable household income covers basic expenses (third model in Table 3.4). Compared to previous models, the estimates remain relatively stable, with the exception of married parent households, even after adding in the control variables. Nevertheless, an odds ratio of 3.67 indicates that the odds of living in households that can "make ends meet" is still almost four times higher for children in married parent households than those in lone single-mother households. The odds ratios for nonkin and cohabiting households also decrease after controlling for household demographics, remaining statistically significant, but substantively irrelevant since an odds ratio close to unity (here 1.06 and 1.03) suggests that the odds of living in a household that makes "ends meet" is almost the same in both lone single-mother and nonkin or cohabiting households. This finding differs from that found in the previous two full models. It suggests that children living in these households fare better than children in lone single-mother households largely because their demographics are different. For example, 64 percent of children in nonkin households are white compared to 45 percent in lone single-mother households. Race and, relatedly, earnings power are likely to be important demographic factors that set these two household types apart in terms of economic well-being.

## CONCLUSION

This study examines the well-being of children in single-mother households and sheds new light on the factors that contribute to children's economic standing with a focus on different categories of single-mother households. This study demonstrates the need to consider not only marital status but also living arrangements when determining children's well-being. It also reveals the need to rethink measures of economic well-being since the poverty measure may be flawed on a number of levels.

There are notable differences not only between children in married parent and single-mother households, but also between children in different categories of living arrangements. On every measure of well-being, children in married parent households fare better than children in single-mother households. Consistent with previous research, children in married parent households are less likely to be low income (using both a family and household definition) and more likely to live in households that are able to "make ends meets." Children in lone single-mother households appear to be the most vulnerable with respect to economic well-being even after controlling for demographics and income sources. A large component of this difference is likely to be attributable to compositional differences between married family and lone single-mother households. Both the economic advantage of cohabiting households and the disadvantage of multigenerational may also be attributable to compositional differences.

## IMPLICATIONS

Beginning with welfare reform efforts in 1996, policymakers and researchers have advocated the relevance of marriage for reducing child poverty. Policies and proposals to promote marriage assume that marriage as an institution provides both direct and indirect paths to improved child well-being through such mechanisms as combined income, better parenting, and long-term orientation. Research conducted under such efforts as "Building Strong Families" (BSF) or by Child Trends recognize the challenges policymakers face in encouraging more marital unions among soon-to-be or unwed parents and recommend such measures as increasing EITC, more generous child-care subsidies, and greater assistance with educational expenses to enable poor parents to qualify for higher paying jobs.[31] While laudable, these recommendations have a blind spot in failing to recognize the relevance of demographics for the poor economic standing of single-mother families. As demonstrated here, children in single-mother families are more likely to be non-white. Within the category of single-mother households, children in cohabiting and nonkin households are more likely to be white compared to children in multigenerational, adult sibling, and kin households who are more likely to be non-white. This racial divide in living arrangements coincides closely with economic well-being. Taken together, the results suggest that policymakers need to redirect their attention back to the salience of race and ethnicity for economic well-being if they seek to reduce child poverty.

What are the factors that vary along racial lines that may be responsible for the disparities in economic well-being? In their work on the BSF project, Carlson et al. provide relevant statistics.[32] They cite as a challenge to marriage the fact that between 33 percent and 42 percent of the fathers of unwed mothers in their sample have prison records. They also state that between 74 percent and 80 percent of unwed mothers earn less than $10,000 while the median earnings of unwed fathers is between $16K and $21K. Between 79 percent and 82 percent of their sample is either African American or Latino. Given these statistics and the results of this study, it is not unreasonable to assume that racial disparities are at least as important a factor, if not a more important factor, than marriage in determining the economic well-being of children. African Americans have the highest incarceration rates which affects their future earning ability both directly and indirectly. A criminal record is looked upon negatively by employers and even explicitly disqualifies candidates from certain (e.g., federal) jobs. Some criminal records even bar incumbents from federal student loans due to the Drug Provision of the Higher Education Act federal aid provision. The income gap between whites and non-whites remains notable for these same reasons, in addition to many more that scholars of race have long studied. Nevertheless, most policy researchers make only passing reference to the relevance of race and ethnicity for children's economic well-being and instead focus on encouraging marriage. In line with this, the results of this study show that children of married parents are less likely to be poor and have higher labor market earnings regardless of race or ethnicity. The results also show, however, that low-income status is more common among non-white children regardless of marital status or living arrangement. In addition to considering the effectiveness of enlarging single-mother households with fathers, there is an urgent need to direct more attention to the barriers facing fathers—and mothers—who are predominantly minority and who continue to encounter racially linked barriers in the labor market that prevent them from earning livable wages. Ultimately, successful strategies to reduce economic disparities between children in different living arrangements may depend on reducing labor market disparities by race and ethnicity.

Finally, this study demonstrates the need to consider other measures to describe economic well-being. On the one hand, there is some confirmation of recent criticism that the poverty thresholds are too low. Results using an "income gap" measure suggest that children living 125 percent below the poverty line may be worse off than the threshold implies since officially designated near-poor households include many in which household income does not suffice to cover even basic expenses. On the other hand, the family-level unit of aggregation produces distortions not only in cohabiting and nonkin households, but also in other kinship-based extended and married parent households. This distortion arises due to omission of the income contributions of nonrelatives in the household, including unrelated children (e.g., foster children) with independent sources of income (e.g., social security). This omission takes on even more importance in light of the fact that single mothers tend not to be the main contributors to household income. As cited elsewhere,[33] the earnings of other family members are the most important factor for lifting poor women's family incomes in the post-welfare reform era. This speaks for the need for research on resource pooling to assess whether decreased disincentives for coresidency (e.g., built into the current food stamp program) and increased support for other family members (e.g., besides for 'potential' fathers) may be effective tools in increasing the economic well-being of low-income children.

## NOTES

* Part of this paper was presented at the 27th Annual Meetings of the Association for Public Policy Analysis and Management, Washington, DC, November 5, 2005. The research presented in this paper was funded, in part, by a pre-/postdoctoral research grant from the

John D. and Catherine T. MacArthur Foundation Network on the Family and the Economy and also in part from a postdoctoral fellowship grant from the NICHD.

1. Sara McLanahan and Gary Sandefur, *Growing Up with a Single Parent: What Hurts, What Helps* (Cambridge: Harvard University Press, 1994). Sara McLanahan, "Parent Absence or Poverty: Which Matters More?" In *Consequences of Growing Up Poor*, ed. Greg Duncan and Jeanne Brooks-Gunn (New York: Russel Sage Foundation, 1997); Paul Amato and Alan Booth, *A Generation at Risk: Growing Up in an Era of Family Upheaval* (Cambridge: Harvard University Press, 1997); Bernadette D. Proctor and Joseph Dalaker, "Poverty in the United States: 2001. Current Population Reports, P-60-219 (Washington, DC: US Government Printing Office, 2002); Greg Duncan and W. Rogers, "Has Children's Poverty Become More Persistent?" *American Sociological Review*, 56 (1991): 538–550.

2. Nancy K. Cauthen and Hsien-Hen Lu, *Employment Alone is Not Enough for American's Low-Income Children and Families*. National Center for Children in Poverty Research Brief No. 1, August. (Columbia University: Mailman School of Public Health, 2003).

3. Karen Randolph, Roderick Rose, Mark Fraser, and Dennis K. Orthner, "Examining the Impact of Changes in Maternal Employment on High School Completion Among High School Youth." *Journal of Family and Economic Issues*, 25 (2004): 279–299; Robin A. Douthitt, "'Time to Do the Chores?' Factoring Home-Production Needs into Measures of Poverty." *Journal of Family and Economic Issues*, 21(1) (2000): 7–22.

4. But see, Karen Fox Folk, "Single Mothers in Various Living Arrangements: Differences in Economic and Time Resources." *American Journal of Economics and Sociology*, 55 (1996): 277–292.

5. But, for research on the effect on children of cohabiting living arrangements, see: Wendy D. Manning and Kathleen Lamb, "Adolescent Wellbeing in Cohabiting, Married, and Single Parent Families." *Journal of Marriage and the Family*, 65 (2003): 876–893; Gregory Acs and Sandi Nelson, "The Kids are Alright? Children's Well-being and the Rise in Cohabitation." New Federalism Paper. National Survey of American Families, Series B, No. B-48, July (Washington, DC: The Urban Institute, 2002); Elizabeth Thomson, Sara McLanahan, and R. B. Curtain, "Family structure, gender, and parental socialization." *Journal of Marriage and the Family*, 54 (1992): 368–378; for research on the effect of multigenerational households, see: William S. Aquilino, "The Life Course of Children Born to Unmarried Mothers: Childhood Living Arrangements and Young Adult Outcomes." *Journal of Marriage and the Family*, 58(2)(1996): 293–310.; Thomas Deliere and Ariel Kalil, "Good Things Come in Threes: Single Parent Multigenerational Family Structure and Adolescent Adjustment." *Demography*, 39(2) (2002): 393–413; for research on the effect of extended households, see M. Sanford, J. Merrill Carlsmith, Steven J. Bushwall, Phillip L. Ritter, Herbert Leiderman, Albert H. Hastorf, and Ruth T. Goss. "Single Parents, Extended Households, and Control of Adolescents." *Child Development*, 56 (1985): 326–341.

6. Julia Isaacs, "Receipt of Unemployment Insurance Among Low-Income Single Mothers." ASPE Issue Brief. (Washington, DC: US Department of Health and Human Services, 2005).

7. Constance, F. Citro and Robert T. Michael, *Measuring Poverty: A New Approach*. (Washington: National Academy Press, 1995).

8. For example, child-care costs constituted only 1 percent of the total costs required to raise a child in 1960. By 2000, this percentage had increased to 10 percent. United States Department of Agriculture (USDA), *Expenditures of Children by Families*. Miscellaneous Publication 1528–2000, May (Washington, DC: U.S. Department of Agriculture, 2001).

9. Kathleen S. Short, "Material and Financial Hardship and Income-Based Poverty Measures in the USA." *Journal of Social Policy*, 34(1) (2005): 21–38.

10. The underlying logic was to use as a comparison group to single mother households a category of married parent household that best approximates the idealized "nuclear family," given data constraints (e.g., using CPS data, it is not possible to distinguish between biological and stepfathers).

11. These households can contain other children such as the parents' grandchildren to the extent that these children's parents are also not present in the home. This is true in 14 households. A somewhat larger number (83 households) contain children who are not related to the parents. Together these households make up less than 1 percent of the total number of married parent households included in this study.

12. Lone single mother households can contain other children such as the parents' grand-children to the extent that the child's parent is not coresiding in the household.

13. Lynne M. Casper, Phillip N. Cohen, and Tavia Simmons, "How Does POSSLQ Measure Up? Historical Estimates of Cohabitation." Population Division Working Paper No, 36. (Washington, DC: US Bureau of the Census, 1999).

14. Single mothers cannot be over 10 years older than the single man and the man can not be over 20 years older than the woman. Adult foster children are explicitly excluded from being considered for cohabitation. A little over half (52.4%) of all single mothers designated as cohabiting are captured through the use of the CPS variable. The remaining 47.6 percent are categorized as such using the age rules just described.

15. As discussed previously, the married parent households studied here are but a subset of the total population of married parents and are restricted to households without any other adults (including no grown children) besides the parents.

16. Larry L. Bumpass and R. Kelly Raley, "Redefining Single-Parent Families: Cohabitation and Changing Family Reality." *Demography*, 32(1) (1995): 97–109.

17. It should be noted that Bauman cautions against the use of household income based on the analysis of SIPP data from 1900 to 1992 that suggested that nonfamily members (with the exception of cohabiting boyfriends) contribute least to the family budget. See, Kurt Bauman, "Shifting Family Definitions: The Effect of Cohabitation and other Nonfamily Household Relationships on Measures of Poverty." *Demography*, 36(3) (1999): 315–325. There remains, however, little consensus in the literature. Schoeni and Blank argue that welfare reform measures have increased the relevance of resource pooling, making low-income mothers now more dependent on the earnings of other household members. See, Robert F. Schoeni and Rebecca M. Blank, "What Has Welfare Reform Accomplished? Impacts on Welfare Participation, Employment, Income, Poverty, and Family Structure. Labor and Population Program." Working Paper DRU-2268, March (Washington, DC: RAND, 2000).

18. Citro and Micheal, op. cit.

19. Economic Policy Institute (EPI). *EPI Issue Guide on Poverty and Family Budgets*, Available at http://www.epinet.org/issueguides/poverty/poverty_issueguide.pdf (Washington, DC: EPI, 2001).

20. These estimates of household expenses are closely aligned with recommendations by EPI (2001). They are conservative since other essential budget items are not considered (e.g., utilities, clothing, books) and only the low budget diet was utilized despite the fact that full-time employment makes a low budget diet increasingly difficult. See, Douthitt, op. cit.

21. Department of Housing and Urban Development, "50th Percentile and 4th Percentile Fair Market Rents, Fiscal Year 2001; Final Rule." Federal Register, 1-2-01. Available at http://www.huduser.org/Datasets/FMR/Jan50th.pdf (Washington, DC: National Archive and Records Administration, 2001). My estimates for housing allow for the tripling up of children (but not adults) in bedrooms.

22. USDA-based food cost estimates for low-cost food plans account for members' sexes and ages. See, United States Department of Agriculture (USDA), "Official USDA Food Plans: Cost of Food at Home at Four Levels, U.S. Average, March 2000." Available at http://www.usda.gov/cnpp/FoodPlans/Updates/foodmar00.pdf (Washington, DC: USDA Center for Nutrition Policy and Promotion, 2000).

23. National Household Travel Survey, "2001 NHTS Average Annual Vehicle Miles of Travel Per Driver: Mean VMT/Driver for MSA Size by Count of HH Members with Jobs." Table generated by author at http://nhts.ornl.gov/2001/index.shtml; Oak Ridge National Laboratory, *1995 NPTS Databook. Based on Data from the 1995 Nationwide Personal Transportation Survey (NPTS).* ORNL/TM-2001/248. Available at http://www-cta.ornl.gov/cta/Publications/Reports/ORNL_TM_2001_248.pdf (Oak Ridge, TN: Oak Ridge National Laboratory, 2001; accessed on January 23, 2007). Here, estimated transportation costs rely on NHTS for per driver estimates of annual vehicle miles traveled (VMT) for households with varying numbers of workers. Based on information provided in Tab 7.2 of the Oak Ridge Lab Report, VMT was multiplied by a multiple to eliminate recreational driving and to account for shared driving. The multiples include: .85 for employed heads (of households and subfamilies); .61 for nonworking heads; .36 for working nonheads; 0 for nonworking nonheads. This product was multiplied by .325, the 2000 IRS cost-per-mile rate to attain an annual cost per driver and then summed by household.

24. Karen Schulman, *The High Cost of Child Care Puts Quality Care out of Reach for Many Families*: Available at http://www.childrensdefense.org (Washington, DC: Children's Defense Fund, 2000). The CDF survey did not include some states or regions within states. These missing values were imputed based on the results of online searches of official websites (e.g., state Web sites).

25. Lingxin Lao, "Family Structure, Private Transfers, and the Economic Wellbeing of Families with Children." *Social Forces*, 75(1) (1996): 269–292.

26. Anne E. Winkler, "The Living Arrangements of Single Mothers with Dependent Children." *The American Journal of Economics and Sociology*, 52(1) (1993): 1–18; Bauman, Shifting Family Definitions.

27. A separate analysis not shown here revealed that the mean earnings of single mothers in cohabiting households is $15.7K and of others in the household is $27.4K.

28. In a separate analysis not shown here, it was found that the mean earnings of single mothers in kin households is $14.1K and of others in the household is $30.8K. The mean earnings of single mothers in nonkin households is $20.6K and of others in the household is $27.3K.

29. Robust standard errors were estimated using the cluster technique in Stata. Estimates aggregated at the family level use family and those aggregated at the household level use household as the cluster variable.

30. As shown in Table 3.1, 1.2 percent of children in these households are foster children.

31. Kristin Anderson Moore, Susan M. Jelielek, and Carol Emig, "Marriage from a Child's Perspective: How Does Family Structure Affect Children, and What Can We Do About it?" Child Trends Research Brief, June (Washington, DC: Child Trends, 2002); Marcia Carlson, Sara McLanahan, Paula England, and Barbara Devaney, "What We Know About Unmarried Parents: Implications for Building Strong Families Programs." Building Strong Families Brief, January, Number 3 (Princeton, NJ: Mathematica Policy Research, Inc., 2005).

32. Carlson et al., "What We Know About Unmarried Parents."

33. Schoeni and Blank, "What Has Welfare Reform Accomplished?"

# CHAPTER 4

# FAMILY CONTEXT, INCOME ADEQUACY, AND CHILD-CARE NEEDS: THE BOTTOM LINE FOR SAN ANTONIO'S FUTURE

## *Juanita M. Firestone*

As a result of recent demographic changes, child-care issues have become an important concern. The Southern Regional Task Force on Child Care[1] states that "child care is perhaps the most critical work-support measure in which the federal government, states, and the private sector can invest." Adequate, affordable, quality child care is necessary to maintain viable workforce, to sustain the ability of families to move off welfare, and to assure that all children are given the opportunity to participate in early childhood development programs.[2] This need for child-care services crosses all classes and race and ethnic groups, and extends across the United States. The unique demographic profile of San Antonio, with a majority of Latinos/as and high percentages of families in low socioeconomic context means that these problems are more extensive.

San Antonio MSA, is located in Bexar County in South Central Texas and includes the city of San Antonio which had a population of 1,144,646 based on the 2000 Census. The majority of the population is of Hispanic origin (approximately 58.7% based on 2000 Census; most are Mexican American). About 6.8 percent of the population is African American (2000 Census). The population is growing at about 1.4 percent, which is slightly above the 1.3 percent average for metropolitan areas nationwide.

According to the 2004 American Community Survey, approximately 17 percent of families and close to 20 percent (19.8%) of individuals live in poverty. These percentages compare to 10.1 percent of families, and 13.1 percent of individuals in the United States. As a result, a disproportionate number of families in San Antonio confront the many ancillary problems associated with living in poverty. All of these problems are more typical of women than of men, especially women in single-parent households. The high proportion of Hispanics (58.7%), as well as the young median age of residents (31.7; 32.9 for women), further contribute to these difficulties. Approximately 80 percent of residents of Bexar County reside within the city limits of San Antonio; the remaining 20 percent reside in either other wholly incorporated cities or unincorporated areas within and surrounding the San Antonio area. Like many U.S. cities, an inner city/business core, expanding suburban areas, and a slow-growing older area geographically define San Antonio.

The city is often viewed in quadrants—the west and south sides are largely Mexican American (the "West Side," especially the inner city located inside Loop 410, is the traditional Mexican and Mexican American barrio), the Eastside African American (also predominantly inside Loop 410) and the Northside (especially the suburban areas outside Loop 410) largely Anglo, with ethnic minorities with higher socioeconomic standing gravitating toward perceived better service and retail areas, better schools, and newer bedroom communities. Like many Hispanic barrios, San Antonio's "West Side" is a residential neighborhood characterized by dense housing, higher rates of crime, poverty, unemployment, and lower educational attainment and economic development compared to other areas in the city. This area, in particular, suffers from a lack of affordable, quality day care.

## CHILD CARE IN SAN ANTONIO: ISSUES OF SUPPLY

There is a clear and documented need for affordable, quality day care. Because many cannot afford quality care on their own, they rely on government subsidies. In 1998, 85,865 children received state-subsidized child care in Texas.[3] This was a substantial increase from previous years and has meant that waiting lists persist for subsidized child care. According to a report prepared by the City of San Antonio Children's Resources Division.[4] there were 1,352 child-care facilities available in Bexar County in 1999. Of those, 43 percent were child-care centers and 47 percent were registered family home-based providers. Of the private centers, 4.8 percent were accredited, while only 1.1 percent of the family-based facilities were accredited. Between 2000 and 2001 the percent of parents utilizing subsidized child-care services increased to 40.5 percent (from 32,222 to 45,275).[5] Because so few care providers opt to become accredited by national accreditation organizations such as the National Association of Education of Young Children (NAEYC) and the National Association of Family Care Centers (NAFCC), the state of Texas developed its own system similar to accreditation, although the standards are not as strict as for the national associations.[6] The Texas-based ratings are based on "stars" and range from 0 to 4 stars with 4 stars being the highest level. A minimum of two stars is necessary in order to be licensed in Texas. Of the private centers in San Antonio, only 4.3 percent were rated as four-star vendors.[7]

The majority of care providers provide only full-time care (89%), while 53 percent provide part-time care only. Most provide care only during traditional business hours 6:00 AM–6:00 PM. Only 4.7 percent of care providers offer evening or overnight care, and only 5.2 percent offer weekend care. This is an important issue tied to the types of jobs available for individuals living in poverty who typically have lower levels of education than the city average. Often available jobs are in the service sector (e.g., fast food, cleaning, sales clerks) and demand nontraditional hours at least part of the time. A related issue is finding care for children who are not feeling completely well, but are not really ill (e.g., with a minor cold). Most care facilities will not accept sick children, so one of the parents (more often than not, the mother) must stay home using his/her own "sick leave." This can have a secondary negative impact because, if parents then become ill, they often must go to work ill because they have used their sick leave to care for their children.

The average weekly price for full-time care for one child in San Antonio area day-care centers in 1999 was $82.00 for infants/toddlers, $71.00 for preschoolers, and $44.00 for school-age children. These figures compare closely to state averages for day-care centers of $83.00, $73.00 and $48.00 respectively. Home-based care was slightly lower at $72.00 for infants/toddlers, $68.00 for preschoolers and $49.00 for school-age children. State averages for home-based care were $75.00, $70.00 and $45.00. Average daily price of part-time care in day-care centers ranged from $16.00 for infants/toddlers to $10.00 for preschoolers and $9.00 for school-age children. Average daily cost for part-time care with home-based providers was $14.00 for infants/toddlers, $10.00 for preschoolers and $9.00 for school-age children. The average hourly wage for food service workers in San Antonio in 1999 was $5.99.[8] This translates into a monthly take home of about $814.00. For a single mother with an infant, employed 40 hours/week that would mean that about 40 percent of her take home would be spent on child care.[9]

Of course, additional children increase the cost of care, and according to the *1999 Texas Child Care Portfolio*, average family size in San Antonio was 3.4, and according to the 2000 Census, the average family size in San Antonio in 2000 has increased to 3.6. While additional children do not double the cost of care, the second child adds about 25 percent to the cost. Thus, an average of $82.00 for one infant would become about $103.00 with the addition of another child. In addition, child-care expenses consume a relatively large share of poor family's budgets. In 1993, estimates based on Current Population Data indicated that poor families who paid for care spent 18 percent of their income on child care compared to 7 percent for nonpoor families.[10]

A Report by the Children's Defense Fund in 2000 indicated that the shortfall between what 10 percent of their income buys and the average annual cost of child care using a child care center was $2,020 for one child and $7,376 for two children. Other analyses on national level data indicate that the cost of child care impacts the labor force participation of women with children such that increases in cost increases the likelihood that women are less likely to be employed.[11] If women have no choice in whether they must be employed, they often seek child-care assistance. Unfortunately, the demand for assistance far exceeds the supply of care providers who will accept federal or state vouchers because both limit the amount, which can be paid for care. Thus, due to insufficient funding, families eligible for assistance may not always receive help. According to information from the City of San Antonio

Children's Resource Division, there was a waiting list of 4,000 children for child-care assistance in 2001.

Focus group participants in San Antonio reinforced the lack of quality day care centers, especially those willing to accept vouchers, and the Texas Association of Child Care Resource and Referral Agencies indicate varying rates of care availability based on geography—those areas in South and Southwestern parts of the county, where there is a higher concentration of poor families, have the fewest available care facilities. Thus, even if subsidized care became available, often it requires transportation arrangements, which cannot be met. This is especially true for jobs outside the traditional 6:00 AM– 6:00 PM hours.

One important factor that impacts the availability of quality care is the low hourly wages for child-care workers. In 2006, average wages for child-care workers in the San Antonio Metropolitan Statistical Area (MSA) was $6.90/hr. These low wages are unlikely to pull many new workers into the area in spite of high levels of demand. In particular such low wages are unlikely to attract workers with educational credentials beyond a high school diploma. Clearly the developmental needs of very young children would benefit from workers with higher levels of education and a better understanding of how to instruct and educate them. The low wages associated with care workers is likely to continue to reinforce the disjuncture between the credentials of workers desired and those willing to accept the jobs.

## Child-Care Arrangements

Data from, the 1988 National Longitudinal Survey of Youth and the 1983 National Longitudinal Survey of Young Women indicated that the most common form of child care was by relatives, although use of child-care centers was more common for children between 2 and 4 than for infants.[12] Employed mothers who worked full time outside the home were less likely to use a relative and more likely to use child-care centers, those with lower educational attainment were more likely to use relatives, as were African Americans and Hispanics.[13] Ehrle and her colleagues[14] found that 30 percent of African American children and 24 percent of white children are cared for in child-care centers, while only 10 percent of Hispanic children are. They found that Hispanic families most often rely on relatives (39%, compared to 25% of white children and 27% of African American children). Interestingly, reliance on relatives does not necessarily mean no cost. Hofferth et al.[15] found that in 1990 close to 33 percent of employed mothers who relied on relatives to care for their children paid for the care.

Economic variables also had significant influence on choices related to child-care arrangements. Households in which the husband's and the wife's income are high were more likely to rely on child-care centers, although increased family size increased the likelihood that a babysitter rather than a child-care center would be used.[16]

Using data from the Current Population Reports, Casper[17] found similar results in 1993, 41 percent of respondents used relatives, while 30 percent use organized child care-facilities, and 17 percent used family day-care settings.

Demographic characteristics were associated with those choices. Children whose mothers were employed in nonday shift hours were more likely to be cared for by relatives, while women working day shifts were more likely to use commercial child-care facilities.[18] As in previous studies, African American and Hispanic mothers were more likely to use relatives than whites, as were children in one-parent households.[19] Poor families and families receiving governmental assistance (Food Stamps, WIC benefits) were also more likely to rely on relatives, although families receiving AFDC were no more likely to rely on relatives than those not receiving AFDC.[20] Single parents are more likely than two parents to rely on relatives,[21] which is likely associated with economic context. An update of that report in 2002[22] indicated that a higher percentage of fathers (36%) and grandparents (22%) were taking care of preschoolers when the mother was employed part time than were enrolled in either day-care centers (15%) or family day-care providers (9%). This may be in part due to the increasing cost of day-care centers and providers, as well as the greater flexibility of mothers employed part-time in arranging times in the workplace. For mothers employed full-time, day-care centers (26%) and family day-care providers (12%) were most used forms of care.

Not surprisingly, the cost of child care is increasing, and those increases are more of a burden for poor families. In 1993, families earning less than $1200 per month spent about 25 percent of family income on child care compared to families earning $4500 or more per month who spent 6 percent of their monthly income in child care.[23] On an average, families below poverty level spent about 18 percent of their monthly income on child care compared to 7 percent for those above the poverty level.[24] Based on data from the 1997 National Survey of America's Families, Giannarelli and Barsimantov[25] found that 27 percent of low-income families in the United States spend more than 20 percent of family earnings on child care. This proportion varies across states with a range of 19 percent in Washington to 37 percent in Mississippi.[26] In Texas, 28 percent of low-income families spend more than 20 percent of family income on child-care expenses.[27] A family living in Texas in 1998 earning minimum wages before taxes would have spent about 33 percent of their income to purchase center-based care for an infant and a 3-year-old.[28] Costs often increase for single parents whose children spend more time in day care because they do not have another adult to help transport them.

Increasing costs of child care has been documented to impact the labor force participation of women such that increasing costs decrease the labor force participation of women.[29] Lack of affordable child care has been documented as one of the major barriers to women's participation in the labor force,[30] in particular women in low-income situations.[31] This may have important consequences for poor families given the recent changes in welfare policies. These findings were supported using various simulations of the effects of changes in the federal child care tax credit.[32] Berger and Black[33] found that single mothers who received child-care subsidies were more likely to be employed,[34] and were dramatically more likely to be satisfied with their child-care arrangements than those who did not. The higher levels of satisfaction derived from increased choice in child-care options.[35] While based on data from families in Kentucky, the consistency of the impacts of cost of child care on labor force participation rates suggests that the satisfaction findings might also hold up.

Young and Miranne[36] and Sonenstein and Wolf[37] found that mothers on welfare expressed the same concerns about child care as do mothers working outside the home. Convenient hours and location, good adult supervision, low child-to-adult ratios, learning opportunities and the child's happiness were the most important factors in choosing among child-care options. Additionally, many of the women in their samples needed child-care services before 7:00 AM and after 6:00 PM, hours that are incompatible with using private child-care centers. Clearly many of the service oriented jobs available to individuals moving from welfare to work require hours outside the "normal business day" and may require informal rather than formal child-care arrangements.

While the need for child-care arrangements is high, the supply does not meet that need. Chronic shortages in regulated, quality child care exist, and those shortages are exacerbated by children with special needs, sick children, and care during nontraditional hours and holidays.[38] Shortages are particularly acute in low-income neighborhoods, which increases the likelihood that low-income families must rely on informal, unregulated arrangements.[39] The latter shortage is mirrored in the low percentages of subsidy-eligible parents receiving assistance (about 10% nationwide in 1999) and the low percentages of available subsidized slots in licensed facilities.[40] Most states in the U.S. report waiting lists for child-care subsidies.[41]

### Latinas/os and Child Care

In spite of stereotypical representations of an idealized model of motherhood reputedly common among Hispanics, which supports a patriarchal system that de-values female employment[42] recent research indicates that the labor force experience of Hispanic women is becoming more similar to other racial and ethnic groups.[43] Furthermore, demographic data show larger increases in the educational attainment of Hispanic women compared to white, non-Hispanic women, along with increasing rates of labor force participation and average number of hours in paid labor.[44]

In addition, there is some evidence that Hispanic cultural values (such as strong familism) changes with increasing contact with U.S. mainstream culture.[45] Stereotypical gender role expectations may become less restrictive toward women with respect to child-care responsibilities, as groups become more acculturated into typical U.S. value systems.[46] Increasing labor force participation is associated with less traditional gender role attitudes. Thus, as Hispanics become the largest growing minority group in the United States the need for day care for children may increase rapidly. The high levels of poverty and low levels of education among Hispanics increases the likelihood that women must rely on relatives for child care, or will remain unemployed thus remaining in poverty and in need of government assistance.[47] San Antonio, as one of the areas in the United States with a majority Mexican American population, provides an interesting arena for assessing child-care needs among different race and ethnic groups.

## Demographic Changes Shaping Child-Care Needs: The Demand Side

The percentage of women 16 years and older who are in the labor force has steadily increased since 1970. The overall percentage increased from 39.4 percent to 56.4 percent in Bexar County and from 29.5 percent to 55.3 percent in San Antonio. The largest percent increase was seen for Hispanic women whose labor force participation went from about 35 percent to about 55 percent.

Data indicate a concomitant increase in the percentage of women 16 and over living in San Antonio with children under 6 who are in the labor force. This has been one of the important trends in the female labor force nation wide and clearly San Antonio is following national trends. While the increase was largest for white, non-Hispanic women, with an increase of over 14 percent, Hispanic women followed closely with an increase of over 11 percent. The increase for African American women was less dramatic (over 7%), but a larger percentage of women with children under 6 were in the labor force in 1970 than was true for the other two groups. Finally, there has been an important increase in women in San Antonio in managerial and professional jobs between 1990 (45.6%) and 2000 (52.4%) for all race and ethnic groups. This increase is important with respect to day-care needs because these types of jobs require large time commitments and have less flexibility than many other occupational categories.

The clear increases in labor force participation of women from all race and ethnic groups, even those with young children indicate a growing need for affordable, quality day-care providers in the San Antonio area. In addition, female householder families may have even greater need for child care. If the female is the sole provider, she must maintain employment or receive public assistance. Recent changes in welfare policies limit the time individuals can receive benefits without employment, so after 2 years women must return to paid work. In addition, a higher percentage of female householder families, even those where the householder is employed full time, live below the poverty level. Individuals in this situation have even more difficulty in affording quality day care.

The proportion of African American female householder families living in Bexar County and in San Antonio has increased dramatically from about 50 percent in 1970 to close to 72 percent in 1990 and to 87.6 percent in 2000. In 2000, the percentage of Hispanic female householder families was 85.3 percent, and for white, non-Hispanic female householders was 82.3 percent. Some of the important demographic characteristics of female householder families in Bexar County and in San Antonio impact child-care needs. The proportion of these families living in poverty has been increasing over time and is about one-third for white, non-Hispanic (32.3%) families, close to 40 percent for Hispanic families, and close to 50 percent for African American (47.6%) families. Almost all of these percentages for race/ethnic groups include female householders with the presence of children under 18.

**Table 4.1**
**Median Income of Female Householder with Children in Bexar County and San Antonio, City, Texas**

| | Bexar County | | | San Antonio City | | |
|---|---|---|---|---|---|---|
| | **1980** | **1990** | **2000** | **1980** | **1990** | **2000** |
| Panel A: Median income of a female householder with own child under 18 years old | | | | | | |
| Total | $6,657 | $11,127 | $18,810 | $6,370 | $10,402 | $18,021 |
| White | $7,306 | $12,934 | $20,723 | $6,996 | $12,109 | $19,886 |
| Black | $5,794 | $9,716 | $18,569 | $5,575 | $8,103 | $17,509 |
| Hispanic | $5,066 | $7,683 | $16,022 | $4,955 | $7,371 | $15,723 |
| Panel B: Median income of a female householder with own child under 6 years old | | | | | | |
| Total | $3,894 | $7,292 | $9010.05 | $3,641 | $6,572 | $8109.45 |
| White | $4,455 | $9,607 | $9943.00 | $4,199 | $8,328 | $8948.70 |
| Black | $3,390 | $6,773 | $8754.50 | $3,291 | $6,774 | $7879.05 |
| Hispanic | $2,938 | $5338 | $7861.50 | $2,813 | $5612 | $7075.35 |

These high percentages of female headed households living in poverty is not offset much even when the householder is in the labor force, especially for members of minority race/ethnic groups. In part, because their lower levels of educational attainment, and years and type of job experience mean that they are often employed in part-time jobs, seasonal work or jobs paying less than the minimum wage. These types of jobs also often require shift work outside typical 8:00 AM–5:00 PM employment, which makes affordable, quality day care more difficult to obtain.

The median income of female householders with children under 18 was very low in 2000 and even lower for those with children under 6 years (see Table 4.1). According to the U.S. Census bureau, in 2006 the poverty threshold for a family of two, where one was a child was $9,800.00, and for a family of three, where two are children was $13,200.00 (http//census.gov). For all race and ethnic groups female householders with children under 6 earned well below those amounts. In particular, Hispanic female householders, who are more likely to have younger children in their household, fell well below the poverty levels.

## CHILD CARE AND DEVELOPMENTAL NEEDS IN SAN ANTONIO, TEXAS

Clearly, universal access to affordable, quality early education and care for children from birth to age 12 is an important community goal. The following individual-level survey data complements the census data discussed in the previous section. The issue of affordable quality child care was raised repeatedly in the focus groups, which were used to help design a telephone survey conducted in San Antonio, Texas. The following section describes the survey sample, instrumentation, and results.

## Description of Survey

### Instrumentation

The survey instrument was created using the MicroCase Analysis computer-assisted data entry system (CATI). The questionnaire began with a brief introduction of the purpose and the origin of the survey. A series of sixty-four questions related to attitudes about various services provided by the San Antonio Department of Community Initiatives, and related to community needs for which respondents believe services should be provided. In addition eight demographic questions were asked for analysis purposes and to insure that the sample adequately reflected the population of interest. Both English and Spanish language versions of the questionnaire were created. Questions appeared on the computer screen and responses were entered directly into a computer file. This allows daily monitoring to insure that completion rates within target populations are being met.

### Administration

All interviewers received a combination of telephone survey techniques training and computer data entry training prior to beginning data collection. Calls were completed Monday through Thursday evenings from 5:00 PM–9:00 PM and Saturdays and Sundays from noon until 6:00 PM. These times optimize availability of respondents, including those employed full time. In addition, the initial screen excluded anyone answering the phone who was not eighteen years or older.

### Sample

Actual telephone prefixes were paired with four random digits to produce the phone numbers. This process insures that all necessary phone prefixes are included, and that unlisted numbers are part of the sampling frame. As is typical of most telephone surveys, results for the Community Initiatives telephone survey slightly over-represent women in all race and ethnic groups compared to their demographic representation in the community. To compensate, a weight variable was created using 1990 U.S. Census data for each sex by race and ethnic category. When applied to any analysis involving race, ethnicity or sex of respondent, results will conform to the demographic distribution of men and women 18 years and older in San Antonio. The weight variable is irrelevant to any analysis where race, ethnicity or gender makes no difference. The random sampling process as well as the size of the sample combined to produce findings representative of the San Antonio adult population.

## Survey Results

Of the respondents to this survey, 19 percent (243) reported having children requiring day care. The majority of respondents had one child (20%) needing care, an additional 11 percent had two children needing child care, and smaller percentages had more than that. While the percentages reporting 3, 4, 5, or 6 children needing care are small they typically represent those with greatest need. The more children in day care, the higher the cost to the respondent.

The majority of respondents reported their children needed day care for 5 days out of the week (60%, n=99), although six respondents (4%) reported needing care for 7 days of the week. Another 17 percent (28) reported needing care for their children for 4 or fewer days. The remaining 19 percent (31) reported needing day care, but not having any currently available. Again, although the percentage is small, those needing care for 7 days have greater difficulty in finding available options and incur greater costs.

Analyses indicated that, higher proportions of individuals living inside Loop 410 report the need for child care across all weekly categories. Residents inside Loop 410 are those residing in the older, more inner city areas of San Antonio, most of them, especially on the West Side are predominantly Hispanic and of lower socioeconomic backgrounds. While individuals living outside (45.4%) Loop 410 report a greater monthly cost for day care ($153.00) than those living inside (54.6%) the Loop ($93.00) this could arise because some of the needs of individuals inside the Loop are not being met. Much of the areas inside Loop 410 are poor, inner-city neighborhoods with higher percentages of Hispanics and little access to necessary services including child care.

Twenty eight percent of respondents reported child care occurs in their home, and 72 percent reported that they take their children elsewhere for day care. Further analyses showed that of those who report that their children are cared for in their home, the majority (57%) says their primary child-care arrangements are with relatives. Of this same group (30%) hire someone to come into their home to take care of their children. Another 7 percent report leaving their children with friends, and 5 percent report their children come home after participating in after-school or sports activities. A higher proportion of individuals living inside Loop 410 reported that child care took place in their home than those living outside Loop 410. This is probably in part accounted for by the higher proportion of children in older age categories for individuals living outside the Loop.

The majority of respondents with children in need of day care report that relatives are the primary source of care (29.3%) and that use of commercial day care facilities (28.6%) was a close second. After school activities (17.2%) were third in reported utilization. When comparing respondents who live inside and outside Loop 410 we found that a larger percentage of those living outside the Loop use relatives (29.8% compared to 28.7%), a non-relative or friend paid to come to their home (10.2% compared to 6.7%), after school and sports programs (22.7% compared to 11.8%) and commercial day-care centers (29.6% compared to 27.3%). Individuals living outside Loop 410 have a larger percent utilizing friends (10.5% compared to 1.9%) and non-profit day-care facilities (12% compared to 5.1%). Additionally those living outside Loop 410 are more likely to say their children are left home alone until they return (3% compared to 0.7%). This finding again may relate to the slightly higher proportion reporting children in older age categories (18.5%) compared to respondents living inside the Loop (17.6%).

The proportions of individuals living inside and outside Loop 410 who are very satisfied or satisfied with their child-care arrangements are roughly equivalent (92.9% inside Loop; 95.4% outside Loop). Interestingly, a much larger proportion living inside Loop 410 said they were dissatisfied with their child-care arrangements (5.4% compared to 1.6%), while a larger percentage living outside Loop 410 said they were very dissatisfied with their child-care arrangements (3.0% compared to 1.7%). The latter finding could result from the larger proportion among these respondents who reported that their child stayed home alone. Also because a larger percentage reported their child(ren) engaged in sports activities this extreme level of dissatisfaction could also reflect the need to insure that the children have appropriate transportation to get to practice and to games.

While the number of cases was not large (155) overall a higher percentage of respondents reported dissatisfaction with their current child-care arrangements than reported satisfaction with them (83.8% compared to 74.4%). The largest percentage of individuals who are very dissatisfied with their child-care arrangement is of those who report their child staying with relatives as their primary care arrangement (58.6%). The next highest percentage among those very dissatisfied was of those who reported that their child(ren) stayed home with someone other than a relative or a friend (25.2%). Finally, a fairly large percent of the respondents who used commercial day care reported they were very dissatisfied with the arrangement 16.3%). Among those who reported being dissatisfied, the largest proportion left their children at home with someone other than a relative or a friend (50.9%). Those reporting their children were in after-school programs, in commercial day-care centers (18.6%), and who were left home alone (12%) also had noteworthy percentages reporting dissatisfaction. Interestingly, none of the individuals who said their children stayed home alone until they got home reported they were very dissatisfied with that arrangement.

Among those who reported satisfaction with child-care arrangements, the largest percentages used either a commercial day-care center (38.8%) or said their child(ren) were part of after school programs (25.1%). A large percentage of respondents who reported their children stayed with a relative also reported being very satisfied (34.3%). Additionally, a small but meaningful proportion of respondents using commercial day-care (24.4%) and after school programs (13.7%) reported they were very satisfied with the arrangement. While the percentage of individuals whose children were in sports programs was quite small, they all reported being very satisfied with that arrangement. This finding is likely to reflect the belief that sports activities teach a variety of important skills and values to children.

Respondents were asked about desirability of services to help them meet the developmental needs of their children, and the percent of individuals reporting specific unmet needs that they would like answered were calculated. Responses depict a high level of desired services and unmet needs in the San Antonio community. Close to 50 percent of respondents indicated they would like to see more educational programs for children, and about 20 percent reported a need for more recreational training and for more religious/moral training. Fifteen percent of respondents expressed a desire for career counseling and about 14 percent indicated a need for more group-based experiences such as Boy Scouts and Girl Scouts. Over 10 percent requested more cultural arts training, over 5 percent saw a need for personal counseling and for vocational training.

With respect to unmet needs that would support the positive development of their children, over 8 percent of respondents reported their children had behavioral problems for which they currently received no help. An additional 6 percent reported that their children needed after school programs, which were not provided, and over 5 percent reported children with learning disabilities for which they were not receiving help. Just fewer than 5 percent reported that needed recreational activities were unavailable for their children, or that their children had health care needs for which they were unable to obtain services. Finally, slightly over 1 percent of respondents reported their children experienced either mental health needs or needs created by physical disabilities that were unmet by current service provisions. The patterns displayed here were similar for individuals whether they lived inside or outside Loop 410.

Clearly members of the San Antonio community express high levels of interest in a variety of programs designed to positively influence the development of children. Additionally a smaller but significant percent of respondents reported various needs currently experienced by their children, which they are unable to meet by accessing current levels of available services. Furthermore high levels of dissatisfaction with current child-care arrangements indicate a large need in the community for various types of child-care services. While affordability is always an important issue, quality day care is needed to provide the opportunity for parents to become self sufficient as well as to provide optimal levels of development for the children of San Antonio.

### Conclusion

The growing demand for quality child care is well documented and is occurring in conjunction with critical shortages and problems on the supply side. The economic context of large demand and shortage of supply suggests increasing cost to consumers. This will undoubtedly create even more problems for city officials concerned with both boosting the Bexar County economy and providing citizens with employment opportunities that provide a living wage. Those individuals at the lower end of the socioeconomic spectrum will be most affected by a lack of quality and affordable child care. In spite of recent changes with regards to father's participation, child care remains primarily the responsibility of women. On an average, women's wages still fall below those of men, and female-headed households are far more likely than other families to be poor. Thus these issues will impact women directly to a greater extent than men. However, to label this issue a "woman's issue" is to miss the point. Children are the future of San Antonio and Bexar County. Without affordable, quality care systems many of those children will grow up in economically disadvantaged households with all of the well-documented problems associated with being poor.

It is important to keep in mind the benefits to the local economy associated with investing in adequate, quality child care. Direct benefits include the generation of jobs, and increased employment and earnings for parents. Indirect benefits include decreasing the need for government-supported services as individuals become employed. One study focused on San Antonio[48] stated that assistance to families needing child care should bring a simple annual return of about 46 percent. Thus a good child-care assistance program would not only cover its own cost, but add 46 percent in additional tax revenue for each dollar spent to the community.[49] Benefits also accrue to companies providing child-care services. Employers providing child-care benefits report higher worker morale, reduced absenteeism, increased productivity and lower turnover.[50] Despite these benefits, very few private sector companies provide benefits for child-care services, and those that do often require employees to "choose" among available benefits (e.g., health care, life insurance, child care).[51]

While this chapter has focused on care for children, there are indicators that elderly care is also becoming increasingly important. While only about 1.5 percent of the respondents to our survey indicated a need for elder care in 1999, this would have translated into about 30,000 individuals who needed this service in the MSA at that time. Given population increases and aging among some race/ethnic categories, this figures has increased substantially. All of the same issues (of demand and of supply) are likely to apply in these circumstances as well. In addition because when elderly need care they often also have health problems, the concerns addressed above may be exacerbated by the need for attendants trained in health care.

The solutions are not simple. Given the changing structure of the workforce, the increasing numbers of female-headed households and the types of jobs available in the San Antonio area (tourism, health services, educational services, retail stores), child-care systems must include school-age as well as infant/toddler programs, sick child care, transportation, and after hours care. These increasing services will be necessary, while maintaining affordable rates. Child-care assistance will produce dividends immediately and in the future. Ignoring the increasing demand will cost the community dearly, in terms of building workforce capacity, decreasing the demand for public assistance, and meeting children's developmental needs. Children are our most vulnerable group. How our children are treated reflects on all of San Antonio and Bexar County, and in the end will be the best measure of our future.

## NOTES

1. Southern Regional Task force on Child Care, 2000. "Sound investments: Financial support for child care builds workforce capacity and promotes school readiness," Columbia, SC: Southern Institute on Children and Families. Available at http://www.kidsouth.org

2. Jennifer Ehrle, Gina Adams, and Kathryn Trout, 2001. "Who's caring for our youngest children? Child-care patterns of infants and toddlers," *Occasional Paper Number* 42, Washington, DC: The Urban Institute; Southern Regional Task Force on Child Care, "Sound investments"; L. Stoney, 2000. "Child care in the southern states: Expanding access to affordable care for low-income families and fostering economic development," Columbia, SC:

The Southern Institute on Children and Families. Available at http://www.kidsouth.org/child care.html#reports

3. D. Stewart, 2000. "Protecting our future," *CPPPriority Mail* (Spring 2000). Austin, TX: Center for Public Policy Priorities.

4. City of San Antonio, Children's Resources Division. 1999. "1999 Texas child care portfolio," San Antonio, TX: City of San Antonio.

5. Texas Workforce Commission, 2005. "Evaluation of Effectiveness of Subsidized Child Care Program; Report to the 79th Texas Legislature," Austin, TX: Texas Workforce Commission

6. This information came from a telephone interview with an employee of the City of San Antonio Children's Resources Division.

7. Family home-based providers are not rated comparably.

8. Texas Association of Child Care Resource and Referral Agencies, 1999

9. Children's Defense Fund, 2000. "The High Cost of Child Care Puts Quality Care Out of Reach for Many Families," Washington, DC: Children's Defense Fund.

10. L.M. Casper, 1996. "Who's minding our preschoolers?" Current Population Reports Household Economic Studies, P70-53, Washington, DC: U.S. Bureau of the Census.

11. J. R. Veum, and P.M. Gleason 1991. "Child Care: Arrangements and costs," *Monthly Labor Review* (October): 10–17; R. Connelly, 1992. "The effect of child care costs on married women's labor force participation," *The Review of Economics and Statistics* 80: 83–90; M.C. Berger and D.A. Black, 1992. "Child care subsidies, quality of care, and the labor supply of low-income, single mothers," *The Review of Economics and Statistics* 80: 635–642.

12. Veum and Gleason, "Child Care."

13. Ehrle, Adams, and Trout, "Who's caring for our youngest children?"; B. Fuller, S. Holloway and X. Liang,1996. "Family selection of child-care centers: The influence of household support, ethnicity, and parental practices," *Child Development* 67: 320–337; U.S. Bureau of Labor Statistics, 1992.

14. Ehrle, Adams, and Trout, "Who's caring for our youngest children?"

15. S. Hofferth, A. Brayfield, S. Deich and P. Holcomb, 1991. *National child care survey, 1990* Washington, DC: The Urban Institute. Report 91–5.

16. A.M. Collins, J.I. Layzer, J.L. Kreader, A. Werner, and F.B. Glantz, 2000. "National study of child care for low-income families; state and community substudy interim report," Washington, DC: U.S. Department of Health and Human Services Administration for Children and Families; E.L. Lehrer, and S. Kawasaki, 1985. "Child care arrangements and fertility: An analysis of two-earner families," *Demography* 22(4): 499–513; D.A. Phillips, M. Voran, E. Kisker, C. Howes, and M. Whitebook 1994. "Child care for children in poverty: Opportunity or inequity?" *Child Development* 65: 472–492.

17. L.M. Casper, 1996. "Who's minding our preschoolers?" Current Population Reports Household Economic Studies, P70-53, Washington, DC: U.S. Bureau of the Census.

18. Casper, "Who's minding our preschoolers?"

19. Casper, "Who's minding our preschoolers?"

20. Casper, "Who's minding our preschoolers?"; Collins et al., "National study of child care for low-income families; state and community substudy interim report"; Ehrle, Adams, and Trout, "Who's caring for our youngest children?"

21. Ehrle, Adams, and Trout, "Who's caring for our youngest children?"; Stoney, L., "Child care in the southern states."

22. J.O. Johnson, 2002. "Who's Minding the Kids? Child Care Arrangements: Winter 2002," Current Population Reports Household Economic Studies, P70-101, Washington DC: U.S. Bureau of the Census.

23. L.M. Casper, 1995. "What does it cost to mind our preschoolers?" Current Population Reports Household Economic Studies, P70-52, Washington DC: U.S. Bureau of the Census.

24. Casper, "What does it cost to mind our preschoolers?"

25. L. Giannarelli and J. Barsimantov, 2000. "Child care expenses of America's families," Washington, DC: The Urban Institute. Occasional Paper No. 40.

26. Giannarelli and Barsimantov, "Child care expenses of America's families."

27. Giannarelli and Barsimantov, "Child care expenses of America's families."

28. G. Adams and K. Schulman 1998. "The South: Child care challenges," Washington, DC: Children's Defense Fund.

29. D. Blau and P. Robins 1989. "Fertility employment and child-care cost," *Demography* 26: 287–299; D. Blau, and P. Robins, 1992. "Child care demand and labor supply of young mothers over time," *Demography* 28(3): 333–351; R. Connelly, 1992. "The effect of child care costs on married women's labor force participation," *The Review of Economics and Statistics* 80: 83–90; Stoney, "Child care in the southern states."

30. D.E. Bloom and T.P. Steen, 1990. "The labor force implications of expanding the child care industry," Population Research and Policy Review 9: 25–44; D. Pearce 1978. "The Feminization of poverty: Women, work, and welfare," *Urban and Social Change Review* 11: 663–680.

31. Stoney, "Child care in the southern states."

32. I. Garfinkel, D. Meyer, and P. Wong, 1990. "The potential of child care tax credits to reduce poverty and welfare dependency," *Population Research and Policy Review* 9(1): 45–63; C. Michalopoulos, P.K. Robins, and I. Garfinkel, 1992. "A structural model of labor supply and child care demand," *Journal of Human Resources* 27(1): 166–203.

33. M.C. Berger and D.A. Black, 1992. "Child care subsidies, quality of care, and the labor supply of low-income, single mothers," *The Review of Economics and Statistics* 80: 635–642.

34. See also Bloom and Steen, "The labor force implications of expanding the child care industry"; Michalopoulos, Robins, and Garfinkle, "A structural model of labor supply and child care demand"; Stoney, "Child care in the southern states."

35. Berger and Black, "Child care subsidies, quality of care, and the labor supply of low-income, single mothers."

36. A.H. Young, and K.B. Miranne, 1995. "Women's need for child care: The stumbling block in the transition from welfare to work," in J.A. Garber and R.S. Turner (Eds.), *Gender in Urban Research*, 201–218, Urban Affairs Annual Review 42, Thousand Oaks, CA: Sage Publications.

37. F.L. Sonenstein and D.A. Wolf, 1991. "Satisfaction with child care: Perspectives of welfare mothers," *Journal* of Social Issues 47: 15–31.

38. Collins et al., "National study of child care for low-income families; state and community substudy interim report."

39. Collins et al., "National study of child care for low-income families; state and community substudy interim report."

40. Collins et al., "National study of child care for low-income families; state and community substudy interim report"; Southern Regional Task force on Child Care. 2000. "Sound investments: Financial support for child care builds workforce capacity and promotes school readiness," Columbia, SC: Southern Institute on Children and Families. Available on http://www.kidsouth.org

41. Collins et al., "National study of child care for low-income families; state and community substudy interim report."

42. A. Mirande and E. Enriquez, 1979. *La Chicana*. Chicago, IL: University of Chicago Press; L. Ybarra, 1988. "Separating myth from reality: Socio-economic and cultural influences

on chicanas and the world of work," in M. B. Melville (ed.), *Mexicans at Work in the United States*, pp. 12–23. Houston, TX: University of Houston, Mexican American Studies.

43. Marta Tienda and Paul Guhleman, 1985. "The occupational position of employed Hispanic women," in George J. Borjas and Marta Tienda (eds.), *Hispanics in the U.S. economy*, pp. 243–273. New York: Academic Press; M. Baca Zinn, 1982. "Mexican American women in the social sciences," *Signs* 8: 259–72; Ybarra, *Mexicans at Work in the United States*; M.P. Fernandez-Kelly, 1991. "Delicate transactions: Gender, home, and employment among hispanic women," in F. Ginsburg and A.L. Tsing (eds.) *Uncertain terms: Negotiating gender in-American culture*, 183–195. Boston, MA: Beacon Press; Norma Williams, 1990. *The Mexican American family; Tradition and change*. Dix Hills, NY: General Hall, Inc.; D.A. Segura, 1992. "Walking on eggshells: Chicanas in the labor force," in S.B. Knouse, P. Rosenfeld, and AL. Culbertson (eds.) *Hispanics in the workplace*, 173–193. Beverly Hills, CA: Sage, 1992; J.M. Firestone and R.J. Harris 1994. "Hispanic women in Texas: An increasing proportion of the underclass," *The Hispanic Journal of Behavioral Sciences*, 16(1): 176–185; Harris and Firestone, "Ethnicity, family change and labor force patterns in Texas, 1980–1990," *The Hispanic Journal of Behavioral Sciences*, 19(3): 268–280.

44. Firestone and Harris, "Hispanic women in Texas"; Harris and Firestone, "Ethnicity, family change and labor force patterns in Texas, 1980–1990."

45. F. Sabogal, G. Marín, R. Otero-Sabogal, B. VanOss Marín, and E.J. Perez-Stable (1987). "Hispanic familism and acculturation; What changes and what doesn't?" *Hispanic Journal of Behavioral Sciences*, 9: 397–412; Firestone and Harris, "Hispanic women in Texas"; R.T. Garza, and P.I. Gallegos, 1995. "Environmental influences and personal choice: A lumanistic perspective on acculturation," in A. M. Padilla (ed.), *Hispanic psychology; critical issues in theory and research*, pp. 3–14. Thousand Oaks, CA: Sage; Harris and Firestone, "Ethnicity, family change and labor force patterns in Texas, 1980–1990"; J.L. Jasinski, N.L. Asdigian,. and G. Kaufman Kantor, (1997). "Ethnic adaptations to occupational strain." *Journal of Interpersonal Violence*, 12(6): 814–831.

46. William A. Vega, 1990. "Hispanic families in the 1980s: A decade of research. *Journal of Marriage and the Family* 52: 1015–1024; A.B. Ginorio, L. Gutierrez, A.M. Cauce, and M. Acosta, 1996. "Psychological issues for Latinas," in *Bringing cultural diversity to feminist psychology: Theory, research, and practice*, 241–263. Washington, DC: American Psychological Association; Harris and Firestone, "Ethnicity, family change and labor force patterns in Texas, 1980–1990".

47. Casper, "What does it cost to mind our preschoolers?"; Casper, "Who's minding our preschoolers?"; Ehrle, Adams, and Trout, "Who's caring for our youngest children?"

48. Texas Perspectives, *Public Funding of Childcare Services*, San Antonio, TX: Texas Perspectives, Inc.

49. Texas Perspectives, *Public Funding of Childcare Services*.

50. The Southern Regional Task Force on Child Care, "Sound investments."

51. See L. Stoney and M. Greenberg, 1996. "The financing of child care: Current and emerging trends," *The future of children* 6(2): 103.

## REFERENCES

Adams Gina and Karen Schulman. 1998. "The South: Child care challenges," Washington, DC: Children's Defense Fund.

Baca Zinn, Maxine. 1982. "Mexican American women in the social sciences," *Signs* 8: 259–272.

Berger, Mark C. and Dan A. Black. 1992. "Child care subsidies, quality of care, and the labor supply of low-income, single mothers," *The Review of Economics and Statistics* 80: 635–642.

Blau, David and Phillip Robins. 1989. "Fertility, employment and child-care cost," *Demography* 26: 287–299.

———. 1992. "Child care demand and labor supply of young mothers over time," *Demography* 28(3): 333–351.

Bloom, David E., and Todd P. Steen. 1990. "The labor force implications of expanding the child care industry," *Population Research and Policy Review* 9: 25–44.

Casper, Lynne M. 1995. "What does it cost to mind our preschoolers?" Current Population Reports Household Economic Studies, P70-52, Washington DC: U.S. Bureau of the Census.

———. 1996. "Who's minding our preschoolers?" Current Population Reports Household Economic Studies, P70-53, Washington, DC: U.S. Bureau of the Census.

———. 1997. "My daddy takes care of me! Fathers as care providers," Current Population Reports Household Economic Studies, P70-59, Washington, DC: U.S. Bureau of the Census.

City of San Antonio, Children's Resources Division "1999 Texas child care portfolio."

Collins, Ann M., Jean I. Layzer, J. Lee Kreader, Alan Werner and Fred B. Glantz, 2000. "National study of child care for low-income families; state and community substudy interim report," Washington, DC: U.S. Department of Health and Human Services Administration for Children and Families.

Commission for Children and Families, 2000. Available online at http://www.ci.sat.tx.us/comminit/page46.htm

Connelly, Rachel. 1992. "The effect of child care costs on married women's labor force participation," *The Review of Economics and Statistics* 80: 83–90.

Ehrle, Jennifer, Gina Adams, and Kathryn Trout. 2001. "Who's caring for our youngest children? Child care patterns of infants and toddlers," *Occasional Paper Number* 42, Washington, DC: The Urban Institute.

Fernandez-Kelly, M. Patricia. 1991. "Delicate transactions: Gender, home, and employment among Hispanic women," in Faye Ginsburg and Anna L. Tsing (eds.) *Uncertain terms: Negotiating gender in American culture*, pp. 183–195. Boston, MA: Beacon Press.

Firestone, Juanita M. and Richard J. Harris. 1994. "Hispanic women in Texas: An increasing proportion of the underclass," *The Hispanic Journal of Behavioral Sciences*, 16(1): 176–185.

Fuller, Bruce, Susan Holloway, and Xiaoyan Liang. 1996. "Family selection of child-care centers: The influence of household support, ethnicity, and parental practices," *Child Development* 67: 320–337.

Garfinkel, Irwin, Daniel R. Meyer, and Philip K. Wong. 1990. "The potential of child care tax credits to reduce poverty and welfare dependency," *Population Research and Policy Review* 9(1): 45–63.

Garza, Raymond T. and P. I. Gallegos 1995. "Environmental influences and personal choice: A lumanistic perspective on acculturation," in Amado M. Padilla (ed.), *Hispanic psychology; critical issues in theory and research*, pp. 3–14. Thousand Oaks, CA: Sage.

Giannarelli, Linda and James Barsimantov. 2000. "Child care expenses of America's families," Washington, DC: The Urban Institute. Occasional Paper No. 40.

Ginorio, Angela B., Gutierrez, L., Ana M. Cauce, and Martha Acosta. 1996. "Psychological issues for Latinas," in *Bringing cultural diversity to feminist psychology: Theory, research, and practice*, pp. 241–263. Washington, DC: American Psychological Association.

Harris, Richard J. and Juanita M. Firestone. 1997. "Ethnicity, family change and labor force patterns in Texas, 1980–1990," *The Hispanic Journal of Behavioral Sciences*, 19(3): 268–280.

Hofferth, Sandra, April Brayfield, Sharon Deich, and Pamela Holcomb. 1991. *National child care survey, 1990.* Washington, DC: The Urban Institute. Report 91–95.

Jasinski, Jana L., Nancy L. Asdigian, and Glenda Kaufman Kantor. 1997. "Ethnic adaptations to occupational strain." *Journal of Interpersonal Violence*, 12(6): 814–831.

Lehrer, Evelyn L. and Seiichi Kawasaki. 1985. "Child care arrangements and fertillity: An analysis of two-earner families," *Demography* 22(4): 499–513.

Leibowitz, Arleen, Linda Waite, and Christina Witsberger . 1988. "Child care for preschoolers: Differences by child's age," *Demography* 25:205–220.

Michalopoulos, Charles, Philip K. Robins, and Irwin Garfinkel. 1992. "A Structural Model of Labor Supply and Child Care Demand," *Journal of Human Resources* 27(1): 166–203.

Mirande, Alfred and Evangelina Enriquez. 1979. *La Chicana.* Chicago, IL: University of Chicago Press.

National Council of Jewish Women. 1999. "Opening a new window on child care: A report on the status of child care in the nation today," New York: NCJW.

Pearce, Diane. 1978. "The feminization of poverty: Women, work, and welfare," *Urban and Social Change Review* 11:663–680.

Phillips, Deborah A., Miriam Voran, Ellen Kisker, Carolee Howes, and Marcy Whitebook. 1994. "Child care for children in poverty: Opportunity or inequity?" *Child Development* 65: 472–492.

Sabogal, Fabio, Gerardo Marín, Regina Otero-Sabogal, Barbara VanOss Marín, and Eliseao J. Perez-Stable. 1987. "Hispanic familism and acculturation: What changes and what doesn't?" *Hispanic Journal of Behavioral Sciences*, 9:397–412.

Segura, Denise A. 1992. "Walking on eggshells: Chicanas in the labor force," in Stephen B. Knouse, Paul Rosenfeld and Amy L. Culbertson (eds.), *Hispanics in the workplace*, pp. 173–193. Beverly Hills, CA: Sage.

Sonenstein, Fraya L. and Douglas A. Wolf, 1991. "Satisfaction with child care: Perspectives of welfare mothers," *Journal of Social Issues* 47:15–31.

Southern Regional Task Force on Child Care. 2000. "Sound investments: Financial support for child care builds workforce capacity and promotes school readiness," Columbia, SC: Southern Institute on Children and Families. Available online at http://www.kidsouth. &break;org

Stewart, Dianne. 2000. "Protecting our future," *CPPPriority Mail* (Spring 2000). Austin, TX: Center for Public Policy Priorities.

Stoney, Louise. 2000. "Child care in the southern states: Expanding access to affordable care for low-income families and fostering economic development," Columbia, SC: The Southern Institute on Children and Families. Available online at http://www.kidsouth.org/child care.html#reports

Stoney, Louise and Mark Greenberg. 1996. "The financing of child care: Current and Emerging Trends," *The Future of Children* 6(2): 103.

Texas Perspectives, Inc., 2000. *Public Funding of Childcare Services*, San Antonio, TX: Texas Perspectives, Inc.

Tienda, Marta and Paul Guhleman. 1985. "The occupational position of employed hispanic women," in George J. Borjas and Marta Tienda (eds.), *Hispanics in the U.S. economy*, pp. 243–273. New York: Academic Press.

U.S. Bureau of the Census, 1995. "Statistical brief: Women in the United States: A profile," SB/95-19RV, Washington, DC Bureau of the Census.

U.S. Bureau of the Census, 1998. "Data on households and families." Available online at http://www.census.gov/population/socdemo/hh-fam

U.S. Bureau of the Census, 1999. "Income and poverty thresholds." Available online at http://www.census.gov/hhes/poverty/threshld/thresh90.html

U.S. Bureau of Labor Statistics. 1992. "Work and family: Child-care arrangements of young working mothers," Report 820, Washington, DC: U.S. Department of Labor, Bureau of Labor Statistics.

Vega, William A., 1990. "Hispanic families in the 1980s: A decade of research." *Journal of Marriage and the Family* 52: 1015–1024.

Veum, Jonathan R. and Philip M. Gleason. 1991. "Child care: Arrangements and costs," *Monthly Labor Review* (October):10–17.

Waite, Linda, and Ross M. Stolzenberg. 1976. "Intended childbearing and labor force participation of young women: Insights from nonrecursive models," *American Sociological Review* 41:235–252.

Waldeman, E. 1983. "Labor Force Statistics from a Family Perspective," *Monthly Labor Review* 106:16–20.

Williams, Norma. 1990. *The Mexican American Family; Tradition and Change*. Dix Hills, NY: General Hall, Inc.

Ybarra, Lea 1988. "Separating Myth from Reality: Socio-economic and Cultural Influences on Chicanas and the World of Work," in M. B. Melville (ed.), *Mexicans at Work in the United States*, pp. 12–23. Houston, TX: University of Houston, Mexican American Studies.

Young, Alma H. and Kristine B. Miranne. 1995. "Women's Need for Child Care: The Stumbling Block in the Transition from Welfare to Work," in Judith A. Garber and Robyne S. Turner (eds.), *Gender in Urban Research*, pp. 201–218. Urban Affairs Annual Review 42, Thousand Oaks, CA: Sage Publications.

# CHAPTER 5

# CHILD CARE AND THE POTENTIAL FOR BREAKING INTERGENERATIONAL POVERTY

## *Josefina Figueira-McDonough*

Whether measured by physical and mental development, health and survival rates, educational achievement or job prospects, incomes or life expectancies, those who spend their childhood in poverty of income and expectation are at a marked and measured disadvantage.[1]

## BREAKTHROUGH EVIDENCE ABOUT THE BENEFITS OF CHILD CARE OR AT-RISK CHILDREN

The case that good child care is the most effective method for preventing intergenerational poverty of at-risk children is founded on evidence about its long-term effects that have been verified by research and experiments carried out in the United States. At the same time, examination of the shortage of public programs in the United States suggests either ignorance or indifference on the part of policy makers. Comparisons between the United States and European countries that offer universal early education programs document a stark contrast in political will and commitment to the development of children.

### Theories of the Development of Early Childhood

Interest in child care grew in tandem with the speedy rise of women in the labor market. The ranks of employed women included mothers of young children. Furthermore, attention to the quality of child care was triggered by brain research highlighting the extraordinary capacity for learning from birth to age five.[2] As a child learns, her/his experience of the world changes, and a new world emerges. Knowledge formation is a relation between children and the world around them. All of us are born with the ability to organize, classify, and impose order on our environment. In effect, children construct theories of the world. Very little of this is the result of instruction. Instead, the process involves the interaction of biological, cultural, and life experiences that shape how perceptions become organized in specific ways. As children encounter new experiences, the theory goes, existing memories in the brain are reshaped. This feedback impacts on linguistic, cognitive, social, and emotional development over time.[3] Important research on early childhood education and care (ECEC) validate this theory.

## The Impact of Child Care on the Development of Children from Birth to 5

Since the mid-1980s, research into the effects of child care on the development of infants, toddlers, and preschoolers has expanded significantly.[4] This body of work varies in terms of ages of the subjects, the sizes and characteristics of the samples, the characteristics of the services, and the outcomes measured. Nonetheless, the results are astonishingly consistent.

Studies of infants have mostly addressed the effect of child care on attachment and security. The combined results of 13 studies of infant ages 1 and 2 show that while attachment and security tend to be higher among children who stay at home with their mother than those in care, the difference narrows for those who start care before 7 months of age.[5] Research on older children (3–5) has focused more on affect, behavior, peer integration, and cognitive development, and it has paid greater attention to the characteristics of the services providing care. Parental stability and structured care result in better behavior and allow for more complex play.[6] Engaged, permanent, college-educated teachers, who engage in high interaction with the children in a setting with low children/teacher ratios, promotes greater affect, social reasoning, joint play, language, communication proficiency, and cognitive development. Nonprofit centers and those following federal interagency day-care requirements are likely to have more positive characteristics.[7]

Other studies have looked at the impact that child care has on the subsequent development of the children. These follow-up studies test the original samples up to second grade. Children who had experienced high quality child care show good outcomes on cognitive, social, and emotional outcomes through kindergarten and up to the second grade. What's more, they rate higher in competence and happiness. Such beneficial long-term outcomes are absent among children in low-quality care, more likely to exist in states with minimal child care standards.[8]

The "Cost, Quality and Outcomes Study" used more diverse samples that permitted researchers to separate out the effects of child-care quality on cognitive, emotional, and behavioral outcomes. Good care showed higher positive results, both at the time and in the follow-up studies, for children from at-risk backgrounds, compared to other children. Conversely, low-quality child care turned out to have more negative consequences for the first group than for the second.[9]

In sum, competent child care has demonstrably significant effects on cognitive, behavioral, and emotional development, and these effects carry over at least through the second grade. The ingredients of adequate child care are empirically known to include well-trained, engaged, and stable teachers as well as low child/teacher ratios (preferably 6 or 4 to 1). Standards of child care adopted by states or of child-care associations have an impact on the quality of service-providing centers. Strikingly, the benefits of competent care are heightened for at-risk children.[10]

## Experiments: Life Outcomes of Early Education

The research just outlined attests to the benefits of child care for cognitive and behavioral development. Some studies have gone even further in the assessment of the impact of early experiences during later years. The two experiments described below followed careful procedures that have earned the respect of the research community.

### The Perry School Study

High Scope, a program geared to the cognitive development of preschoolers, was designed to serve at-risk children in the largely blue-collar township of Ypsilanti in Southeast Michigan. The purpose of its founders was to improve the academic development of children living in the south part of the city, a section of rundown public housing, extensive poverty, and high crime. In the better-off schools of the city, students averaged in the 90 percentile on national achievements tests; in the area served by the Perry school, no one scored above 10 percent.

High Scope was inspired by the ideas of Jean Piaget and clearly emphasized the cognitive development of 3- and 4-year olds. These children were to spend 2 years in the program, 3 hours a day for 5 days a week. The curriculum emphasized problem solving, and the daily routine involved planning, carrying out the plan, and reviewing what had been learned. Teachers were well trained and decently paid, and the child/teacher ratio was 5 to 1. Visits to parents had the purpose of encouraging them to teach their own children and to get the parents to read to them.[11]

The experiment got underway in 1972 and involved a random sample of 127 at-risk 4-year-olds of whom half had frequented High Scope and another half who had not been part of the program. Early results were disappointing. Differences between the two groups at age 7 and 8 were not significant. Follow-up studies at ages 11, 14, 15, 19, and 27, however, came up with remarkable results.

The High Scope children were less often assigned to special classes. They had better attitudes toward school, their parents were more supportive of their schooling, and their high school grade-point average was higher. By age 19, 73 percent had finished high school as compared to 45 percent of the control group.[12] In addition, a follow-up study conducted at age 40 turned up significant differences between the two groups in education, income, crime, and family stability. Nearly twice as many of the Perry School students had earned college degrees, more had gotten jobs, and about only half as many had been arrested for crimes and sentenced to prison. Among the males, nearly twice as many of the alumni sample of High Scope raised their children on their own, as compared to the control group.[13] The economic return of the program benefits was estimated to be $17 for each dollar invested.[14]

### The Carolina Abecedarian Program

This program started in 1972 under the auspices of the Frank Porter Development Child Development Center in Chapel Hill, North Carolina. It offered quality developmental child care for high at-risk children from 4 months to 5 years of age. Care was provided 6–8 hours a week, 5 days a week, and focused on developing cognitive, social, language, and motor skills. All children were born in poverty, mostly to single mothers (75 percent) who were African American (97 percent). The caregiver to infant ratio was 3:1 and increased to 6:1 as the children got older. Activities were customized for infants and children based on readiness. As children reached three years, the preschool program was designed to be playful but targeted toward cognitive development, social and self-help skills, language and fine and gross motor skills. Children were encouraged to speak about their daily experiences. Nutritional, social work, and medical services were available to the families and children.[15]

The evaluation phase of the program included 111 children born in poverty between 1972 and 1977. Fifty-seven of the children had been in the program for 6 years, while fifty-four with the same demographic characteristics had not, although they had received the same nutritional, medical, and social work services. Follow-up data were gathered through age 21: the two groups were assessed at ages 3, 4, 5, 6.5, 8, 12, 15, and 21. At age 3, the children in the program had significantly higher IQ scores than the control group, and those who benefited most were children of mothers with low IQ scores. Through ages 8 to 21 they also had higher scores on reading and math tests, and had fewer grade retentions and special education referrals. By age 21, 35 percent of the treatment group had graduated from high school compared to 14 percent of the control group. Those in the first group were, on average, one year older at the birth of their first child. A more detailed analysis showed that those who had been in the program from 4 months old through kindergarten or until second grade showed better outcomes than those entering the program later.[16]

There is no doubt about the cumulative, consistent nature of these experiments. The results have been replicated in many countries of Europe. The key question now becomes whether care services operated by public agencies reaching vast numbers of children would produce the same outcomes.

## Early Childhood Programs Supported by Government Agencies

### Head Start

The Equal Opportunity Act of 1964 created the Office of Economic Opportunity (OEO) whose mission was to fight "the war on poverty" and to pay special attention to the needs of the young. Its mandate was to concentrate on local communities. Community Action funds were distributed in direct proportion to the number of indigent children in each state.

Head Start emerged from the implementation of these mandates. Community Action required the involvement of parents in planning the centers and their involvement as teachers' aids. An eight-week Head Start program was launched in the summer of 1965. Its policies stemmed from four premises:

- Universal opportunities for normal growth and development are a right for all children;
- disadvantaged children should be provided selected experiences to increase their level of opportunity;
- activities with sound development principles should be integrated in the home setting of families; and
- the program should eventually become available to the whole nation.

Health, nutrition, and social services were required services for the success of the program. In sum, political and professional leaders who developed Head Start called for a child-centered program that was to be locally controlled, comprehensive, and family-oriented.[17]

Head Start accorded with other programs like High Scope both with regard to the importance it attributed to early childhood education for breaking the cycle of poverty and its insistence on opening opportunities for children born in poverty. But its goals were more ambitious. The program was designed to serve as a channel for parental and community empowerment. This was the aim of Community Action. The broader objectives, the institutional diversity of the program, its size, budgetary constraints, and changes in the philosophy of the federal administration, have all made evaluation more difficult than has been the case for other, smaller programs framed from the outset as test cases for research.

For example, while some early assessments reported positive examples of parental and community empowerment, extensive documentation at later times testified to a virtual breakdown in the implementation of such goals during the decades following the War on Poverty.[17,18] And studies that showed improvement in cognitive and socioemotional development have been criticized on methodological grounds.[19] Subsequent research on academic gains indicates that progress of this sort seem to fade by the second grade, even though former students in adulthood have records of less referrals to remedial education and lower rates of dropping out.[20]

To counter findings that initial academic gains seem to disappear by the second grade, some states have tried to build continuity between preschool programs and public schools, often by having them located on the same campus. Evaluation of these transitional programs indicates that this has resulted in greater rigidity in the management and implementation of ECEC (Early Children Education and Care) as the organizational style of the public schools takes over. By contrast, physical health has been an area of great success of Head Start. Children participating in the program have received more preventive and remedial services and their immunization rates are higher than is the case among other low-income children.[21]

The failure to explore whatever long-term impacts might be associated with Head Start has to do with the lack of precise follow-ups on life outcomes of the sort captured by the samples used in High Scope and the Abecedarian programs. It is worth noting that the earlier High Scope evaluations also showed a loss of cognitive advantages among program participants by the second grade, and this happened with Head Start children as well. Positive life outcomes were discovered in later follow-ups not engaged in by Head Start. Another important difference between the Abecedarian and Head Start programs is the length of children's participation: six as compared to two years, respectively.

Finally, Joseph Califano's prediction that Head Start would become a national program for at-risk children did not come to be. In fact, while 40 percent of poor children under the age of 6 were in the program in 1990, by 2004 only about 20 percent participated. Budget cuts, population growth, and higher poverty rates took their toll.[22]

### *The Chicago Child-Parent Centers*

The Chicago Child-Parent Centers originated in the mid-70s, led by the superintendent of one of the poorer school districts of Chicago. The goal was to build academic success on early intervention and parental involvement in preschool education. Early education would follow instructional approaches, tailored to children's learning styles that developed their speaking and listening skills. This would occur in small classes that permitted individual attention. Health and nutritional services would be part of the program.

Currently there are 34 centers throughout the Chicago public schools. The centers provide preschool to disadvantaged children 3 and 4 years old. In 13 centers, the program is extended from kindergarten to third grade. Each year about 2,500 children take part in CPC. All teachers have bachelor's degrees and early childhood certificates. Each center has a parent resource room staffed by a full-time teacher. Until recently, all parents had to sign an agreement to participate for the equivalent of half a day a week. After 1996, because of TANF work requirements, this stipulation was removed. The program is funded through State of Illinois Title I.[23]

A large-scale, long-term scientific evaluation has been tracing 1,500 disadvantaged minority kids for the past 20 years. About 75 percent of the youngsters attended CPCs, and the remaining subjects came from equally impoverished neighborhoods. The study clearly shows that the program yields substantial benefits. By age 20, the CPC graduate has a 30 percent advantage in completing high school, and by age 21 nearly two-thirds achieve that goal. Furthermore, 40 percent fewer than in the comparison group were held back in school, and had one-third fewer juvenile arrests.

The researchers calculated that for every dollar invested in the preschool component of the program, $7.14 returns to society in increased earnings of participants and in reduced costs for remedial education, crime control, and rehabilitation.[24]

The findings of these two publicly supported ECEC programs demonstrate their viability and, in addition, underpin plans for future national policies. The programs have the same purpose: to equalize opportunities by means of early education for children in poverty. One program was supported by federal money, the other by state funds.

However, there are evident differences between the two. Head Start has had multiple goals, has been less focused on learning goals, and was designed for shorter periods of intervention. These differences contributed to the more favorable of CPC's impact. The conclusion, nonetheless, is that good public early education programs are viable and that they can have strong, long-term benefits for at-risk children.


## THE 1996 WELFARE REFORM AND CHILDREN CARE

### Antecedents of Temporary Assistance to Needy Families

Richard Titmuss, the English pioneer of policy analysis, argued that welfare encompassed any government economic advantage given to citizens not based on compensation for work or private exchange. Thus, tax breaks to the middle class and corporations, any type of incentive as well or compensation for farming and failing industries, as well supplements for occupational security, constitute welfare.[25]

In the United States the term "welfare" has acquired a restrictive and negative connotation inasmuch as it is applied exclusively to social assistance for the poor. This pejorative resonance has its source in the charity meanings attached to such programs. American political culture distinguishes so-called charitable beneficence from the notion of rights identified with social insurance, and this tradition has resulted in marginal entitlements.[26]

Aid to Dependent Children, one of the public assistance programs included in the Social Security Act of 1935, reflected the traditional, puritanical interpretation of poverty as self-made. The poor are poor because they are wanting in moral fiber and civic norms. Hence, they have to be treated very strictly so that they embrace the prescribed virtues. Both AFDC and subsequent programs for poor families (AFDC and TANF) perpetuate these beliefs, translated in the form of policies geared to exclude many needy families, punitive regulations applied to families that are included and marginal funding.[27]

The burgeoning of AFDC rolls by the 1960s, together with the creation of the Office of Economic Opportunity and related programs, as well as the passage of civil rights legislation, and urban riots in the wake of Martin Luther King's assassination, gave rise to a white conservative movement. AFDC was blamed for creating poverty. New theories emerged supporting the necessity of obligatory work for the poor.[28]

The eventual outcome was passage of the welfare reform act, signed by President Clinton in 1996. TANF took the place of AFDC. The new policy proclaimed its goal: promoting self-sufficiency. It did away with entitlements, and administration was delegated to the states. Federal contributions were limited and made proportional to the decrease in welfare rolls. Time limits were set on welfare recipients. Work requirements were required for benefits, while special programs encouraged marriage and chastity.[29] Contrary to the evidence, these policies were inspired by the conviction that women were on welfare because they did not want to work, that they were unmarried because of loose morals, and that they kept having children to prolong their stay on welfare.[30]

### Evidence of the Reproduction of Poverty

Gosta Esping-Andersen has argued that occasional, short-term poverty is not an indictment of the state of social justice in liberal democratic societies. However, long-term, persistent poverty *does* represent an unjust entrapment of citizens.[31] The repercussions of life-long poverty on the vulnerability of the next generation exacerbate this entrapment. This situation is incompatible with the principle of equal opportunity central to democracies.

The goal is for children to grow up to be self-sufficient and to contribute to society. The tragic irony is that the vast numbers of children living in poverty in the United States (more than 9 million in 2004, half of whom are below the age of 6) are unlikely to reach or foster that goal. They often drop out of school, have children very young, and by the age of nine have accepted a marginal future.[32]

Frequently such outcomes are blamed on single motherhood. These women form the largest group among welfare recipients. Research on intergenerational poverty has focused on poor single mothers. An analysis of five different surveys concluded that children who grow up in households with only one biological parent are worse off than those raised by both biological parents. Regardless of parental education and race, children living with a single parent are twice as likely to drop out of high school, to have a child before the age of 20, one and a half times to be idle—out of school and out of work by their late teens and early twenties.[33]

In fact, children living with single mothers are five times more likely to be poor than those in two-parent families. Forty-two percent of single mothers are poor. The assumption implicit in TANF policies is that it is single female parenthood in particular that causes poverty. However, an alternative hypothesis holds that the causal sequence is the reverse. Single mothers find themselves in poverty not because they are unmarried; rather, they are unmarried because they are poor. Various studies confirm this explanation for divorced or separated mothers, teenage mothers, and mothers on welfare and living in depressed neighborhoods where male unemployment is widespread.[34] Interestingly, the United States, as compared to western European nations, has the highest percentage of single mothers in poverty, and four times as many as in northern European nations.[35] Regardless of the beliefs that shape TANF policies, the determining reality is that children of poor families live in contexts conducive to failure and inimical to equal opportunity.

### TANF Child Care

With the implementation of TANF the obligation of adult recipients to work became inescapable. This requirement triggered a corollary need for child care. It raised, in turn, the importance of the government's role in underwriting child care. The welfare reform of 1996 combined federal programs of child-care subsidies under the Child Care Development Fund (CCDF). The devolution of welfare to the states meant that they could exercise discretion regarding eligibility and benefits. State governments could use TANF money for child care, either directly or by transferring up to 30 percent of TANF monies to CCDF, and they could add their own funds as well.[36]

Since half of the parents receiving assistance have offspring aged 6 or under, child-care subsidies grew rapidly from 1996 to 2000, and state TANF funds exceeded the primary CCD funding. The number of children receiving subsidies nearly doubled, reaching 1.9 million.[37] The subsidies are generally provided through vouchers set at 75 percent of child-care costs in the community of the recipient. The guidelines for the voucher program are parental choice, work requirement, and priority given to families leaving welfare for work. Co-payments, income eligibility, and reimbursement vary from state to state.

Despite the increase in state funding, a large proportion of low-income working families do not get subsidies. In thirteen of the sixteen states studied, 30 percent or more of eligible children do not receive subsidies. Because funds are insufficient to meet demand, states have rationed services in several ways. In nearly all (47) states, eligibility levels have been lowered. More than half (35) of the states have excluded low-income working parents who are not receiving welfare. Thirteen states require a minimum of work hours for eligibility. All states have limited outreach efforts, leaving many low-income working parents in the dark about the subsidies.[38]

A number of the usual bureaucratic obstacles have cropped up. Intakes have been frozen and waiting lists created. Priorities are set so that only excluding many applicants. Procedures to apply have become more complex, requiring lengthy paper work and office visits, forcing parents to take time from work.[39]

Other barriers stem from the inadequacy of child-care centers in areas where low-income families live. Compounding the problem is the fact that these centers charge high fees, relative to family budgets. As income declines, the proportion of child-care costs goes up. Forty-two percent of families who left welfare for low-skilled, low-wage jobs paid an average of $232 a month for child care in 1999.[40] Another hindrance is that the tight schedules that many low-income women encounter at work reduce their child-care options.

This mismatch between child-care funding and demand worsened in 2001, when many state budgets went into crisis. By then, the states served 18 percent—one in seven—of federally eligible children. The situation has deteriorated further. Thirteen states decreased their investment in child-care assistance in 2002. In one of these states, California, over 200,000 eligible children are on the waiting list.[41]

The costs of services and restrictions on these services jeopardize poor women trying to keep up their work commitments, and lack of access to quality child care aggravates the problem. Parents who get child-care subsidies in the amount calculated for services in their neighborhood are faced with hard choices. Nearly all live in poor neighborhoods, with limited choices, where child-care options may be unsuited to the mothers' work schedules. Faced with these hassles, almost 30 percent of parents with subsides have recourse to unregulated child care. This means that not even health and safety standards are monitored.[41]

Although states were instructed to devote some of their child-care money to improve ECEC services, there is no evidence that they have engaged in interventions, recommended by child-care experts, such as lower child/adult ratios and improved staff training. By 2003 about two-thirds of a million children of TANF recipients have been cut from Medicaid, SHIP, and other state health insurance programs in 36 states.

Two factors make the deficiency of child care under TANF the Achilles heel of the program. The first concerns the sheer number of children in need. According to 2001 TANF statistics, half of the parents receiving assistance have children under 6 years of age. Second, as evidenced by the research reviewed at the outset, adequate child care offers the best chance to break the intergenerational cycle of poverty.[42]

Other research shows a strong connection between the availability of child care and the participation of mothers in the work force. Child-care subsidies increase the duration of employment for welfare recipients *and* for those off welfare. Forty percent of women receiving this type of assistance are more likely to stay employed at least for two years, compared to those who go without. The impact grows to 60 percent for former welfare recipients, and the benefits show up in the quality and stability of child care.[43]

We know, then, that child care has two crucial effects. It makes it easier for low-income women to work in a sustained manner, and it helps give children a better future.

## UNIVERSAL EARLY CHILDHOOD EDUCATION AND CARE

### Barriers at Home

Some commentators point out that, at least for low-income workers, child care should not be left to the market, which by definition responds to competitive pressures and profit. But attempts to move toward universal child care have been met with failure in the United States.

By the mid-80s, when millions of children under 5 had mothers who worked, more than half attended day care, the Child and Care Federal Income Tax Credit expanded to cover 60 percent of child-care expenses. Although low-income families are eligible, they have small tax obligations to offset to begin with. At the end of the 1980s, federal expenditures for child care, which benefits mainly low income families, fell by more than 13 percent.[44] Head Start, a promising program in child care for poor children, presently covers only 20 percent of children in need. The Chicago Child-Parent Centers are a successful model but they are limited to that city. The 2006 reauthorization of TANF projects a further decline in child-care opportunities for the beneficiaries of the program. Increases for child care have been limited to 1 billion dollars over the next 5 years. Because states are required to increase the number of clients meeting the work requirement, this fixed amount will perpetuate or augment the present shortfall.

A concrete example of what will happen in California clarifies the consequences for states battling deficits. California will receive about $24 million annually for child care. But the state will also be required to increase the number of people obliged to work by 45,000. Assuming that only half these families have children under the age of 6, $320 million would be necessary to meet child-care needs. California's budget for 2006 will reduce funding for the state work program by $198,800, and 58 percent of this comes from child care. This is taking place in a state where more than 200,000 eligible children are on waiting lists.[45] For all the knowledge we have gained about how to break the cycle of poverty, the political will to equalize opportunities for children has faltered.

### Lessons from Europe

Demographic pressures in western Europe are similar to those experienced in the United States: an aging population, declining fertility, and a female labor force edging close to the participation rates of males. Similarly, the economic restructuring that accompanies globalization has produced a flight of manufacturing jobs to developing countries with low-wage labor.

These similarities notwithstanding, the response of governments has differed sharply on the two sides of the Atlantic. In the United States, top priority goes to cutting back on public expenditures on entitlements while offering market alternatives that, by definition, discriminate against low-income citizens. In most countries of Europe, the objective is to support programs that facilitate women's work and child development. These measures show ingenuity. They try to remedy the demographic imbalance by framing a new gender and family contract, one that increases the number of active workers without decreasing fertility. Most countries in northern Europe, and more and more in southern Europe, have managed to respond to growing demands for health, education, and assistance by creating jobs that are attractive to women because they offer decent pay and schedules consistent with family needs. In spite of fears of gender segregation, in a country like Sweden, women make about 77 percent of what their male counterparts earn, as compared to 52 percent in the United States. Furthermore, the poverty of single mothers in northern European countries ranges from about 10 to 20 percent as against 46 percent in the United States.[46]

An important policy tying women's work to fertility is maternity leave. Among the 12 countries surveyed in 2001 by the OECD, all the European members, including the Southern tier of countries like Italy and Portugal, have maternity leaves for 15–21 weeks with wage replacements over 80 percent.[47]

A parallel concern is with the education of children. The view that has taken hold in Europe is that in a global labor market the future of developed countries depends on creative and innovative individuals able to contribute to new technologies. Economic success and employment depend on the education of future citizens.[48]

Research on child development in Europe shows the same results as in the United States,[49] though the lead remains with United States in terms of the sheer quantity of investigative work.[50] The consequential difference lies in how governments in Europe have reacted to scientific findings through public policies. A 2001 report of the Organization for Economic Co-operation and Development (OECD) on *Early Childhood Education and Care* (ECEC) permits an evaluation of existing policies in 10 European countries.[51] In all countries, with the exception of the United Kingdom, there is a funded provision to give full time ECEC to children aged 3–6. All children can have at least 2 years of early education before beginning compulsory school. The ECEC entitlement was introduced earlier in Sweden, Norway, and Denmark. At the end of the last century, the coverage topped 90 percent in the 3- to 6-year-old group. In other countries, with the exception of United Kingdom, similar rates were expected by mid-decade.

Care for infants and toddlers below age 3 is predominantly offered in centers and family care homes, and all these places charge parental fees albeit on a sliding scale. The number of public *crèches* is growing. The simultaneous decrease of informal arrangements indicates widespread acceptance of the quality of these public, affordable systems.[52]

As in the United States, the quality of ECEC programs is defined by staff training, child/staff ratio, and pedagogical orientation. These characteristics are in turn influenced by funding, by the ministry in charge, and by national/local management. Staff training for ECEC of the 3–6 age group requires college education in all countries. In public programs for younger children, training criteria are specialized, but a university degree is not required. One of the factors influencing this difference is the fact that most of the later programs are under welfare rather than education departments.[53]

Only in Sweden have both programs been nationally planned and managed by the education ministry. Because the ECEC is integrated in the education department, staffing requirements are the same across the system, as are salary and professional status. This also facilitates the mobility of staff from ECEC to regular school programs.[54] Other countries prefer national/local joint responsibility. This arrangement gives more flexibility of implementation, allowing for adjustments to community needs, including the development of special strategies for reaching out to at-risk children. This is the case with the Capabel project in Amsterdam. It added neighborhood family groups who could use play facilities, mother–child home instruction, service referrals, and organized social and political support. Similar programs have evolved in Denmark, Belgium, and Italy.[55] In many of these cases, national regulations focus on curriculum and expected outcomes to avoid inequality in the delivery of ECEC goals.[56]

The child/staff ratios recommended by the ECEC network are somewhat larger than those favored by research teams in the United States: 1:4 for children under age 1; 1:6 for children aged 1 and 2; 1:8 for children aged 3and 4; 1:15 for children aged 5 and 6. All programs goals include cognitive, social, and value dimensions (civic and/or moral) of development.

These public programs operate with practically universal coverage of young children, and most have statutes that give priority to those with special needs or to at-risk children. Conversely, evidence from studies in United Kingdom and the United States suggests that market-driven approaches have contributed to an uneven growth in ECEC. In particular, supporting the provision of ECEC through subsidies has led to shortages in low-income areas, where private and nonprofit operators find it difficult to survive.[57] These shortfalls become even more serious once it is recognized that in the late 1990s nearly three times as many children, proportionately, were in poverty in the United States than in Denmark.[58]

According to projections based on OECD data for the same period, eliminating child poverty in the United States would represent an added cost of 0.30 percent of the GDP.[59]

While the disconnect between know-how accumulated in the United States and public policy in the implementation of ECEC has been highlighted here, it would be a mistake to infer that important groups have not attempted to improve the situation. Since the 1990s the National Council of Teachers of Mathematics, the American Association for the Advancement of Science, the National Teachers of English, the National Commission for the Social Studies, the National Association of Elementary School Principals, the National Association of State Boards of Education, the Association for Supervision and Curriculum Development have all joined forces to call for early childhood curriculum and assessment guidelines.[60] More recently, the Office of Educational Research and Improvement in the Department of Education has funded the National Center for Early Development and Learning to conduct multi-state prekindergarten programs. This includes center-based programs for 4-year-olds that are fully or partially funded by state education agencies operated in schools or under the direction of state and local education agencies.[61]

## NOTES

1. UNICEF, *A League Table of Child Poverty in Rich Countries*. (UNICEF, Florence: Innocenti Center, 2000): 3.

2. For examples of this literature, see Rebecca Shore, *Rethinking the Brain: New Insights in Early Development* (New York: Families and Work Institute, 1997); G. Lindsey, "Brain Research and Implications for Early Childhood Education," *Childhood Education* 75(2) (1998): 97–101.

3. For arguments in support of this perspective, see David Wood, *How Children Think and Learn* (Cambridge, MA: Blackwell, 1988) and C. Denise Johnson, "The Role of Child Development and Social Interaction in the Selection of Children's literature to Promote Early Literacy Acquisition," *Early Childhood and Practice* 5(2) (2003): 1–12.

4. Some further research can be found in the *Early Childhood Research Quarterly, Early childhood Research and Practice, Child development, Developmental Psychology* and in reports and publications of *The National Institute for Early Education*.

5. NICHD Early Childcare Research Network, "The Effects of Infant Childcare on Infant-Mother Attachment Security. Results of the NICHD Study of Early Care," *Child Development* 59(1) (1997): 157–167; Michael Lamb, Kathleen Sternberg and Margarita E. Prodromidis,

"Non-maternal Care and the Security of the Infant-Mother Attachment," *Infant Behavior and Development* 15(1) (1992): 71–83.

6. Loraine Dunn, " Proximal and Distal Features of Daycare Quality," *Early Childhood Research Quarterly* 8(2) (1993):167–192 .

7. Linda Hestenes, Susan Kontos, and Yvonne Bryan, "Children's Emotional Expression in Childcare Centers Varying in Quality," *Early Childhood Research Quarterly* 8(3) (1993): 295–307; Susan D. Holloway and Marina Reichartt-Erickson, "The Relationship of Day Care Quality to Children's Free Play Behavior and Social Problem-solving Skills," *Early Childhood Research Quarterly* 3(1) (1988): 39– 53; Carolee Howes and Claire Hamilton, "The Changing Experience of Child Care: Changes in Teachers and Teacher-Child Relationships and Children's Social Competence with Peers," *Early Childhood Research Quarterly* 8(1) (1993): 5–32; Carolee Howes, Deborah Phillips, Marcy Whitebook, "Thresholds of Quality: Implications for the Social Development of Children in Center-based Childcare," *Child Development* 63(2) (1992): 449–460; Carolee Howes , E.Smith, and Ellen Galinsky, *The Florida Childcare Quality Improvement Study: Interim Report* (New York: Families & Work Institute, 1995); Margatet R. Burchinal, Joanne E. Roberts, Laura Nabors, and Donnae Bryant, "Quality of Center Childcare and Infant Cognitive and Language Development," *Child Development* 67(2) (1996): 604– 620; Dunn (n. 6 above); Deborah Phillips, Kathleen McCartney, and Sandra Skar, "Childcare Quality and Children's Social Development, *Developmental Psychology* 23(4) (1987): 537–543.

8. Hestenes (n. 7 above); Howes and Hamilton (n. 7 above); Susan J. Kontos,"Childcare Quality, Family Background, and Children's Development," *Early Childhood Research Quarterly* 6(2) (1991): 249–262; Kathleen McCartney, Sandra Scarr, A. Rocheleleau, Deborah Phillips, Martha Abbot-Shim, Marlene Eisenberg, N. Keefee, S. Rosenthal, and J.Ruth, "Teacher-Child Interaction and Child care Auspices as Predictors of Social Outcomes in Infants in Infants, Toddlers and Preschoolers," *Merrill-Palmer Quarterly* 43(3) (1997): 426–450; Ellen Peisner-Feinberg and Margaret R. Burchinal, "Relations Between Pre-School Children's Childcare Experiences and Concurrent Development," *Merrill-Palmer Quarterly* 43(3) (1997): 451–447.

9. Phillips, McCartney, and Skar (n. 7 above); Peisner-Feinberg and Burchinal (n. 8 above); Ellen Peinser-Feinberg, Richard M. Clifford, Mary Culkin, Carolee Howes, and Sharon Kagan, *The Children of the Cost, Quality and Outcomes Study Go to School* (Chapel Hill, NC: Frank Porter Graham Child Development Center, 1999). Margaret Caughy, Janet DiPietro, and Donna M. Strobino, "Day-Care Participation as a Protective Factor in the Cognitive Development of Low Income Children," *Child Development* 65(2) (1994): 457–471.

10. Children are defined to be at-risk when they grow up in homes at or below the poverty level, live in dilapidated neighborhoods, with high rates of unemployment and crime. For evidence of the positive impact of good early child care on these children, see Phillips, McCartney, and Skar (n. 7 above); Dedorah Vandell and Marie Corsaniti, "Variations in Early Childcare: Do They Predict Subsequent Social, Emotional and Cognitive Differences?" *Early Childhood Research Quarterly* 23(4) (1999): 555–572.

11. For a detailed description of the characteristics of the program, see David Weikart, Linda Rogers, Carolyn Adcock, and Donna McClelland, *The Cognitively Oriented Curriculum* (Urbana: University of Illinois Press. 1971).

12. See Lawrence J. Schweinhart and David Weikart, "Success by Empowerment: The High/Scope Perry Pre-School Study through Age 27," *Young Children* 49(1) (November 1993): 54–58.

13. See Lawrence J. Schweinhart, *Life Time Effects: The High Scope Perry School Study* (Ypsilanti, MI: The High Scope Press, forthcoming)

14. See David Kirb, " Life Way After Head Start," *New York Times* (November 24, 2004).

15. For a description of the program, see Craig T. Ramey and Frances A. Campbell, "Poverty, Early Childhood Education and Competence: The Abecedarian Experment," in *Children in Poverty: Child Development and Public Policy*, ed. Aletha C. Huston (Cambridge: Cambridge University Press, 1991): 190–221.

16. For good coverage of these outcomes, see Frances A. Campbell, Elizabeth Pungelo, Shari Miller Johnson, Margaret Burchinal, and Craig T. Ramey, "The Development of Cognitive and Academic Capabilities: Growth Curves of an Early Childhood Experiment," *Development Psychology* 37(2) (2001): 231–242.

17. From Catherina J. Ross, "Effective Programs for Children Growing up in Concentrated Poverty: The Historical Roots of Head Start," in *Project Head Start: A Legacy from the War on Poverty*, ed. Edward Zigler and Jeannette Valentine (New York: Free Press, 1979).

18. See for example Linda J. Ames with Jeanne Ellsworth, *Reformed Women, Women Empowered: Poor Mothers and the Endangered Promise of Head Start* (Philadelphia: Temple University Press, 1997).

19. See Thomas J. Gamble and Edward Zigler, "The Head Start Synthesis Project: A Critique," *Journal of Applied Development Psychology* 10(2) (1989): 267–274.

20. Lisbeth B. Schorr, "Effective Programs for Children Growing Up in Concentrated Poverty," in *Children in Poverty*, ed. Aletha Huston (Kansas City: Cambridge Press, 1991).

21. See Stacey Newhart-Pritchett and Panayota Y. Mantzicopoulos, " A Bumpy Transition from Head Start to Public School," in *Critical Perspectives on Project Head Start: Revisioning the Hope and Challenges*, ed. Jeanne Ellsworth and Lynda J. Ames (New York: New York University Press, 1998): 291–319.

22. A sample of these criticisms can be found in Edward Zigler and Sally J. Syfco, "Head Start: Criticism in a Constructive Context," *American Psychologist* 49 (1994): 127–132; Joseph A. Califano, " Head Start, A Retrospective View: The Founders," in *Project Head Start, A Legacy from the War on Poverty* (n. 17 above) chap. Data for 1990 are from Patricia Hamilton, Katherine Hayes, and Henry M. Doan, "Head Start Bilingual and Multicultural Program Services," in Ellsworth and Ames (n. 21 above), p. 150. Data on the number of children under 6 in poverty are from the *2004 Census*, Table 3, Detailed Poverty Tables, Current Populations Report B60 –222. Head Start budget and enrollment is given in *Head Start Hard Facts* (Washington, DC: Administration on Youth and Families, Head Start Bureau, 2004).

23. For an historical account, see Rochelle Stanfield, *Chicago Parent-Child Centers Program Overview: The Value of Early Childhood Education in the Real World* (Baltimore, MD: The Anne E. Casey Foundation, 2006).

24. See the research report by Arthur J. Reinolds, Judy A. Temple, Dylan J. Robertson, and Emily A. Man, "Long Term Effects of an Early Childhood Intervention on Educational Achievement and Juvenile Arrests: A 15 YearFollow-up of Low Income Children in Public Schools," *Journal of the American Medical Association* 283 (May 9, 2001): 2339–2346.

25. See Richard M. Titmuss, *Social Policy: An Introduction*, ed. Bryan Adam KayTitmus (London: Allen & Unwin, 1974).

26. For an historical account of this outcome see Mimi Abramovitz, *Regulating the Lives of Women: Social Welfare Policy from Colonial Times to the Present* (Boston: South End Press, 1996).

27. For an excellent description of the evolution of public assistance, see Walter Trattner, *From Poor Law to Welfare State: a History of Social Welfare in America* (New York: Free Press, 1999). For insights into the persistence of charity ideology in welfare programs, see David

Wagner, *What's Love Got to Do with It? A Critical Look at American Charity* (New York: New Press, 2000), and Yvonne Luna and Josefina Figueira-McDonough, "Charity, Ideology and Exclusion: Continuities and Resistance in U.S. Welfare Reform," in *Women at the Margins: Neglect, Punishment and Resistance*, ed. Josefina Figueira-McDonough and Rosemary Sarri (New York: The Howard Press, 2002), pp. 321–335.

28. For an analysis of the rise of the antiwelfare movement see Alan Brinkley, *The End of Reform* (New York: Vintage, 1996). As examples of arguments supporting the new views of how to "cure" poverty see Charles Murray, *Losing Ground: American Social Policy 1950–1980* (New York: Basic Books, 1984) and Lawrence M. Mead, *Beyond Entitlement: the Social Obligations of Citizenship* (New York; Free Press, 1986).

29. A more detailed account of the 1996 reform can be found in Josefina Figueira-McDonough, *The Welfare State and Social Work: The Hesitant Pursuit of Social Justice* (Thousand Oaks, CA: Sage Publications, 2006), Chap. 8.

30. For evidence contradicting such beliefs, see Abramovitz (n. 26 above) and Kathryn Edin and Laura Lein, *Making Ends Meet: How Single Mothers Survive Welfare and Low Wage Work* (New York: Russell Sage Foundation, 1997); Gregory Duncan, *Years of Poverty and Years of Plenty* (Ann Arbor, MI: Institute for Social Research, 1985); Mary Jo Bane, "Household Composition and Poverty," in *Fighting Poverty: What Works and What Doesn't*, ed. Sheldon Danziger and Daniel Weinberg (Cambridge: Harvard University Press, 1986): 209–230; Theodora Ooms, Stacey Buchet, and Mary Parke, "Beyond Marriage Licenses: Efforts to Strengthen Marriage and Two Parents Families: A State by State Snapshot," *Center for Law and Social Policy*, April 2004; Grant Foundation, *The Declining Economic Fortunes of Young Americans* (Washington, DC: Grant Foundation, 1988); Paul Jargowsky, *Poverty and Place: Ghettos Barrios and the American City* (New York: Russell Sage Foundation, 1997); Jill D. Berrick, *Faces of Poverty* (New York: Oxford University Press, 1995).

31. Gøsta Esping-Anderson, "Towards the Good Society, Once Again?" in *Why We Need a New Welfare State*, eds. Gøsta Esping-Andersen et al. (Oxford: Oxford University Press, 2002), pp. 1–28.

32. Duncan Lindsey, *The Welfare of Children* (New York: Oxford University Press, 2004).

33. Sara McLanahan and Gary Sandfur, *Growing Up with a Single Parent* (Cambridge: Harvard University Press, 1994).

34. See Bane, Ooms, and Jagowsky (n. 30 above); W. Julius Wilson, "Public Policy Research and the Truly Disadvantaged," in the *Urban Underclass*, ed Christopher Jencks and Peter Peterson (Washington, DC: Brookings Institution, 1991), pp. 460–481.

35. Karen Christopher, " Family Friendly Europe," *American Prospect* 13 (2002): 59–61.

36. Child Care Law Center, *Child Care as Welfare Prevention* (San Francisco: Child Care Law Center, 1995): March.

37. Henry Colleen, Misha Werschkul, and Manita C. Rao, *Childcare Subsidies Promote Mothers' Employment and Children's Development* (Washington, DC: Women's Policy Research Center, 2005): #G714.

38. Gina Adams, Kathleen Snyder, and Jody Stanford, "Getting and Retaining Child Care Assistance: How Policy and Practice Influence Parents' Experience," in *Assessing New Federalism* (Washington, DC: Urban Institue, 2002): Paper #55; Rachel Schumacher, Mark Greenberg and Janellen Duffy, *The Impact of TANF Funding On Child Care Subsidy Programs* (Washington, DC: Center for Law and Social Policy, 2001).

39. Colleen et al. (n. 37 above).

40. Danielle Ewen and Katherine Hart, *State Budget Cuts Create Growing Childcare Crisis for Low Income Families* (Washington, DC: Children's Defense Fund, 2003).

41. Welfare Watcher's, *Congress Sets Up States to Fail on TANF* (Sacramento: Western Center On Law and Poverty, 2005): 12/21.

42. Leighton Ku and Sashi Ninalendran, *Losing Out: States Are Cutting 1.2 to 1.6 Million Low-income People from Medicaid, SCHIP and Other State Health Insurance Programs.* (Washington, DC: Center on Budget and Policy Priorities, 2003) POSINGS/health documents, 12–22.

43. Collen et al. (n. 37 above).

44. David M. Blau, *The Child Care Problem: An Economic Analysis* (New York: Russell Sage Foundation, 2001).

45. Welfare Watcher's (n. 41 above)

46. See Esping-Andersen (n. 31 above)

47. OECD Report, *Starting Strong: Early Childhood Education and Care* (Paris: Organization for Economic Co-operation and Development, 2001), p. 32, Table 2.2.

48. Esping-Andersen (n. 31 above) See also Robert Reich, *I Will be Short: Essentials for A Working Society* (Boston: Beacon Press, 2002).

49. For a summary of some of this research, see *Early Childhood Research and Practice* 1(2) (Fall 1999).

50. See references in the OECD report (n. 47 above), pp. 139–145.

51. European countries included in the 2001 OECD and referred to in subsequent discussion are: Belgium, Denmark, Italy, Netherlands, Norway, Portugal, Sweden, and the United Kingdom.

52. See OECD (n. 47 above), pp. 129–130.

53. Ibid., p. 98, Table 3.1.

54. Ibid., pp. 76–83.

55. Ibid., pp. 61, 119, 120.

56. Ibid., p. 46.

57. Ibid., p. 57.

58. Goodin et al., *The Real World of Welfare Capitalism* (Cambridge: Cambridge University Press, 1999), p. 287.

59. Esping-Anderson (n. 31 above).

60. Sue Bredekamp et al., *What Does Research Say About Early Education?* (North Central Regional Education Laboratory, Oak Brook, 1992).

61. North Central Regional Educational Laboratory, *Multi-stage Study of Pre-Kindergarten* (Washington, DC: Department of Education, National Center of Early Development and Learning, 2003).

# CHAPTER 6

# Under a Watchful Eye: Parents and Children Living in Shelters

## *Donna Haig Friedman*

### "BECAUSE YOU SEE ME, I EXIST"

With these six words, two mothers who had been homeless with their children opened a celebratory event in Boston.[1] Later in the program, one by one, 20 other previously homeless mothers took the microphone and each in turn addressed the audience of supporters with the words:

"Because you see me. . . . "

Each finished her statement with a uniquely personal achievement or aspiration.

"Because you see me, I am two weeks away from graduating with a Masters degree in communications."

"Because you see me, my children are doing well in school."

Not being seen is the worst hardship a human being can suffer. Consider the words of Joseph Wresinski, the founder of the international Fourth World Movement that works to break down social exclusion across the globe:

"For the very poor tell us over and over again that a human being's greatest misfortune is not to be hungry or unable to read, nor even to be out of work. The greatest misfortune is to know that you count for nothing, to the point where even your suffering is ignored. The worst blow of all is the contempt on the part of your fellow citizens. It is contempt that stands between a human being and his rights. It makes the world disdain what you are going through and prevents you from being recognized as worthy and capable of taking on responsibility. The greatest misfortune of extreme poverty is that for your entire existence you are like someone already dead."[2]

To place this perspective in context, bear in mind that:[3] "40% of the world's population does not have electricity; 33% of the world's children under five suffer from malnutrition; 47% of the world's population lives on less than two US dollars per day; while, the total wealth of the 200 richest people in the world is 1.14 trillion dollars." A little closer to home, the income gap between the wealthiest and poorest persons in the United States continues to grow,[4] and with it, homelessness of both families with children and lone individuals.

## FAMILIES IN POVERTY AND HOUSING INSTABILITY

Over the past 25 years, the U.S. government has disinvested in the production of low cost housing units and housing assistance, redirecting its resources toward urban revitalization and home ownership[5], and, in response to the subsequent growth of homelessness in the country, toward homeless assistance support services and residential programs. Likewise, radical policy shifts and budget cuts have impacted families poor enough to use or be eligible for public assistance.[6] In particular, the entitlement to welfare ended in 1996; five-year lifetime limits for welfare receipt were established; and the majority of welfare-reliant families were required to enter the paid workforce. Work as the pathway out of poverty was widely supported by both policymakers and the general public. As of 2000, only 16 percent of families in poverty in the United States were utilizing welfare; down from 46 percent in 1973.[7]

By 2006, more poor U.S. families did indeed have a head-of-household in the workforce; however, the squeeze between housing costs and incomes continues to threaten the housing stability of large numbers of working poor households. In no part of the United States can a full-time minimum wage worker pay for private market housing with just 30 percent of his/her income, a HUD standard for housing affordability.[8]

According to the U.S. Department of Housing and Urban Development, nearly 5 percent of all households in the country (5.1 million households) have worst case housing needs, that is, they pay more than 50 percent of their income for housing; they have no housing assistance, are renters, and have incomes below 50 percent of the area median income (AMI). Most of these households have extremely low incomes (below 30% of AMI) and pay an average of 76 percent of their incomes for rent; many adults heading these households work in low-wage jobs.[9] Households headed by persons of color, elders, sole women with children and, renters are more affected by the income-housing squeeze than are others.[10]

The demand for low-cost housing far outstrips the supply of housing subsidies or low-cost units. On average, an eligible U.S. household would have to wait nearly $2\frac{1}{2}$ years for a Section 8 housing voucher.[11] The wait is much longer in many communities across the country. One estimate of need, highlighted in the 2002 Millennial Housing Commission Report and cited in Bratt, Stone, and Hartman, indicates that 250,000 low-cost housing units would need to be created each year for the next 20 years to meet the demand.[12]

## MORE SHELTERS, FULL SHELTERS

Based upon the most extensive and conservative analysis to date, 23–35 million people are homeless in the United States annually, 1 percent of the United States population, 6–9 percent of those in poverty and 6–9 percent of children in poverty.[13] An estimated 3 percent of the country's population is homeless over a 5-year period.[14] Contrary to widely held assumptions that lone individuals living on the street are the most typical "face" of homelessness, children comprise 39 percent of those who are homeless in the United States each year.[15] However, many children are living apart from their parents when homelessness hits the family; homeless men and women report that 74 percent of their children are not living with them when they are using homeless assistance services.[16]

Families' use of shelter nationally has increased over the past 15–20 years. Between 1987 and 2001, emergency shelters increased in size and were more likely to be full each day and night.[17] As of 1996, emergency shelters in the United States served 239,600 persons per day on average;[18] 40,000 homeless assistance programs in 21,000 locations were providing service to homeless men, women, and children across the country's urban, suburban, and rural communities, nearly half located in central city areas.[19]

## THE COSTS OF HOMELESSNESS AND SHELTER LIVING

### The Economics

Sheltering low-income families is much more costly than providing them with rental assistance and/or other homelessness prevention resources. For example, Washington, DC, spends $7,000 on average per family household for prevention as compared to $11,500 per household for shelter. In its first 4 years, 70–80 percent of families served by its prevention program were successfully housed and had not fallen into homelessness.[20]

In Massachusetts, the state spends $43,000 to $56,000 per family each year to secure shelter space for the families the state expects to shelter.[21] In contrast, the state spent only $16,200 per family per year for a pilot transitional housing program with a history of success that allows each family to live in a private apartment and receive intensive service support.[22] The state spends an average of $3,000 or less for families served by its homelessness prevention program.[23]

For the past decade, Hennepin County, Minnesota, has been a leader in implementing a community-wide homelessness prevention network and has evidence of its success. In 2002–2003, the County spent $472 on average per family for prevention services, with a 95 percent success rate—no use of shelter for at least 12 months after intervention.[24] Using a rapid-rehousing approach for homeless families, the County significantly reduced the time families lived in shelters and have documented an 88 percent success rate; the average cost per family was $800 for this intervention. Finally, the cost of an intensive transitional housing program, an alternative to shelter, was $3,668 on average per family, resulting in a 96 percent success rate.[25]

The lion's share of resources to fight homelessness in the United States is nonetheless tied up in maintaining and expanding the country's residential emergency shelter system.[26] Housing assistance resources, on the other hand, have been inadequate for over 40 years and subject to relentless cuts, even though having a housing subsidy or access to low-cost housing clearly prevents families from falling into homelessness or returning to the shelter system.[27]

### The Human and Social Costs

Shelter as an acceptable housing option for low-income families is costly in other ways as well. The impacts of family homelessness on children and their parents are well documented. The humiliation of not being able to house one's children rips at a parent's core sense of self.[28] When a mother feels this way, her children feel the pain as well.

Children are highly vulnerable.[29] Forty percent of children in families surveyed in New York City family shelters[30], representing 75 percent of all children in shelters in the city, had asthma; half had symptoms consistent with mild to severe asthma; over half had used emergency rooms for medical care.[31] Childhood homelessness is a risk factor for homelessness as an adult.[32] Homeless mothers have reported that 39 percent of their children under 18 were not living with them and, for those children who were with their mother or father in a homeless assistance program, 46 percent of their parents reported that one or more of their children had had an alcohol, drug, or mental health problem in the past month.[33]

Relentlessly high levels of stress, frequent dislocations that result in cut off from friends, family, and familiar surroundings, discontinuity in educational experiences, and a sense of social exclusion are but a few of the realities in children's lives when they are without a home; they share these realities with their parents, whose well-being is intricately intertwined with their own.[34]

Children are also resilient.[35] Developmental, social, and emotional setbacks for children can be ameliorated if the surrounding environment provides safety and is conducive to development of their competence, curiosity, sense of empathy, and connection to at least one responsive and caring adult.[36] Parents have a greater chance of creating such an environment for their children when they themselves have a sense of economic and housing security. When families have no other alternative than shelter, the presence of a supportive, respectful, safe, and predictable environment has the potential to reverse the damage sustained by both parents and their children on their traumatizing homelessness journeys.

## UNDER A WATCHFUL EYE

Families who have secured living space in shelters in which they share kitchens, living rooms, bedrooms, and laundry facilities with others find themselves under the watchful eye of other parents and children, as well as shelter staff; the staff have the power to offer resources that lead to housing and the power to take away shelter.

Paradoxically, support for parents and children may be close at hand, however the closeness may contribute to unwanted staff intrusions into private family matters.

## Inherent Complexities of Shelter Life

### Shelter Life Is Anything but Easy for Families

"My whole family was living in one room. Granted it was the biggest room in the house, but it was barely big enough for the five beds, a crib, and one large dresser. My children previously had their (own) room, a large backyard to play in, and a screened-in porch with their own bathroom. We had to adjust to sharing the room with several different mothers who each had one small child and didn't seem to stay more than a few days . . ." [37]

The potential exists for parents living in shelters to have their *best* and *worst* moments. At times hardship brings out the best in people. However, when stress is unrelenting, it is hard to shine. In shelter settings, parents may experience their authority with their children being at odds at times with staff who have a responsibility to ensure predictability and security for all who live in the shelter. The intimacy that housed parents have with their children in the privacy of their own homes is hard to come by for families living in congregate shelters. Parental routines with children have been disrupted for extensive periods of time during families' harrowing journeys prior to entering shelters. This disruption continues in shelter settings where so many routines of daily living are alien to those of the individual families. [38] When children begin to feel safe in a shelter setting, they may need to let down; predictable clashes are likely to take place between and among children in shelters. These moments may be embarrassing for parents if support and understanding from staff is lacking. Add to this circumstance the challenge of mixing parenting and family routines, norms, and traditions with families of different ethnicities who are living together in shelters, and you have a recipe for the exacerbation, rather than amelioration, of the effects of long-standing stress on individual children and their parents.

### Working in and Managing Shelter Programs Is Also Challenging

"At times, the issues were so great for a family that they just couldn't see beyond their situation. . . . I have been cursed out, I have been called every name in the book. At times, I've wanted to throw in the towel . . . and then at that moment someone or something would happen to remind me why I was doing the work . . . I know that my life was changed and I would say that (the family's) life was changed by our interaction." [39]

Frontline staff and shelter directors also face challenges as they attempt to create environments that will ensure order, predictability, fairness, safety, and flexibility for all. For shelter staff, help-giving fatigue is not unexpected; absorbing family pain can and does take a toll. Limited time and space boundaries in shelter settings create a heightened intensity, one that is more taxing on shelter staff than is the case for help-givers who work in nonresidential human service settings. The pressure on shelter staff is considerable. At times, the chemistry among parents, children, and staff may be problematic and undoubtedly affects staff members' stress levels on the job. They are held accountable if conflicts between and among family members get out of hand or if anyone's safety is put at risk on their watch. Finally, shelter staff constantly face dilemmas related to responding flexibly to unique family circumstances and requests, while trying to apply shelter policies and rules fairly.

## MAXIMIZING SUPPORT AND MINIMIZING HARM

Being under a watchful eye and being seen are qualitatively different experiences for parents and their children in shelters. Parents speak of negative encounters as ones in which they feel as though they are under a microscope; while they view positive helping encounters, "being seen," as the triggers for transforming their lives.[40] The paradox of help-giving, simply stated, is that seeing and accepting a man, a woman, a child *as is* opens the door for growth.

### Help-Giving Approaches[41]

Professional or paraprofessional helpers, shelter staff in this case, have options regarding how they intervene in the lives of the families living in their shelters. Senge and his colleagues offer a relevant help-giving framework: helper as expert or helper as partner.[42] Determining when to use which approach and assessing the impacts of each approach is worthy of reflection.

#### The Helper As Expert: Diagnosing, Giving Advice, Taking Charge

"Parents in shelters have many outside influences pressing down on them. The anger has to go somewhere ... An asset-approach to helping parents in crisis can prove very effective, rather than using a deficit-approach or assuming that parents have negative intentions. I remember the phrase 'Keep hope alive!'. It picked me up when I felt myself sinking too low. The negative attitude of a staff person can bring down the best."[43]

An "helper as expert" model of help-giving is one in which helpers fix the problems at hand, through taking charge or giving advice aimed at changing behaviors perceived by the helper to be causing the problems. Such a "take charge" approach may be critically important for shelter staff to use during emergencies or when the safety of children and/or parents is threatened or when, after soliciting considerable input from those affected, a staff member makes a decision that simply has to be made. At its worst extreme, a "helper as expert" approach may be harmful to families; a diagnosis orientation can inadvertently become a deficit-oriented lens[44] that obscures *seeing*. Recently, a woman who directs an activist community organization in California likened her experience of being a human service client to feeling like a "turtle on its back," completely helpless and at the mercy of help-givers. She had experienced the worst impact of a help-giving framework that emphasizes pathology, dysfunction, and an obsession with compliance. These are the very barriers that lead parents to feel as though they are being treated like children or prisoners when they live in shelters.

These are the very forces that drive men, women, and youth to live on the streets, in their cars, or in their own tent cities rather than seek shelter.[45] Parents submit to oppressive shelter situations because of their children. And, when treated badly, they leave shelter with a sense of bitterness and shame.[46]

### The Helper As Teammate, Learning Partner and Facilitator

"There are many who would challenge crossing the sometimes sterile boundaries between professional and relational roles ... It is our experience that moves us to cross those boundaries. For among all of us who are first of all human beings, there is a search for meaning, a human cry for connecting, bonding ... the experience of community." [47]

An "helper as partner" model of help-giving is one in which helpers and families enter into a relationship with a vulnerability that opens the door for both to be changed in the process,[48] a "power with," rather than "power over" relationship. Using this way of building relationships with families, helpers are called to be reflective, to let go of fixed, win-lose mindsets and to work toward equality in the relationship, to actively intervene without judgment.[49] Each person has a core role to play; each holds the self and the other accountable. Both parties pay attention to active listening, teamwork, reciprocity, and the minimization of indebtedness.[50] Two-way reflection on the relationship takes place in a context of safety. Helpers invite parents to actively question their suggestions. Parents expect to actively question and to share their insights. Together helper and parent consider alternative pathways to growth grounded in a parent's dreams for herself and children. This way of working can be scary, as it requires professionals to let go of control and make a commitment to an inherently uncertain process.

This asset-oriented framework focuses more on how parents have overcome adversity and sustained their families and less on how they succumbed to hardship.[51] "Strength spotting"[52] is the detective work undertaken in assessment processes grounded in this way of seeing; professional energy is focused on recognition of parents' and children's capabilities, positive intentions, and adaptive survival strategies.[53] The result is that both helper and parent see something new; the seeing together has a "healing quality."[54] Such encounters can lead to a deep internal transformation, a radical shift in the ways in which parents see themselves and tell their life stories, from stories of self-blame and victimization to ones that acknowledge external influences on the family's circumstances and recognize parents' resiliency in the face of hardship, and efficacy and hope as they move forward into the future.[55]

### Organizational and Programmatic Approaches that Promote "Seeing"

A fundamental principle of communication is this: if we change our perceptions, we can change our feelings and ultimately our behavior ... Staff are challenged to identify themselves not exclusively by what they do—by their roles and tasks—but to go deeper and understand their primary identity, the spirit from which behaviors flow. Our roles and functions do not define who we are! We are, first of all, human beings who on life's journey have developed significant assets, capacities, and gifts, while still having multiple needs that yearn for fulfillment. This experience has a leveling effect on all of us.[56]

As reflected in the words above by the visionary leader of an agency that, among other services, operates a family shelter in Boston, an extraordinary commitment at an organizational level, from the top down, is required for reflective, respectful, and collaborative practice to become the norm as staff members interact with each other and with the families they serve. Learning to act from such a trusting and collaborative stance takes skill and time. This organizational environment is not easy to create and is always a work in progress, even for those leaders and staff who are highly committed to these values.

## *A Culture of Reflectivity*

Leaders and staff of learning organizations have to actively work toward establishing a culture of reflectivity that invites ongoing organization-wide self-examination, creativity, and imaginative thinking.[57] Across the whole organization, leaders will need to provide board, management, staff, and families with concrete and practical ways of committing themselves to building a holistic organizational environment that fosters transformational relationships and community.[58] Kofman and Senge's design principles provide a framework for building the capacities of managerial leaders to promote such an organizational environment:

> (1) The learner learns what the learner wants to learn, so focus on key managerial issues; (2) The people who need to learn are the ones who have the power to take action, so focus on key operational managers, as opposed to staff; (3) Learning often occurs best through "play," through interactions in a transitional medium where it is safe to experiment and reflect; (4) Learning often requires slowing down the action to enable reflection to tacit assumptions and counterproductive ways of interacting; or at other times, speed up time to reveal how current decisions can create unanticipated problems in the long term; (5) Learning often requires "compressing space," as well as time, so that the learner can see the effects of his or her actions in other parts of the system; (6) This transitional medium must look like the action domain of the learners; (7) The learning space must be seamlessly integrated into the work space for on ongoing cycle of reflection, experimentation and action.[59]

Concrete evidence of a dynamic learning environment, as applied to shelter settings, is the creation of leadership opportunities for staff and families, established avenues for them to have substantive decision making roles regarding the shelter's daily operations, particularly those that directly impact the quality of their lives.[60] Another example is the creation of time and space for planned, reflective conversations at staff and house meetings and using these dialogue spaces productively to reexamine organizational mission, values, purpose, and effectiveness. Success in such efforts is dependent upon effective professional development approaches that build staff competencies in teamwork, the de-escalation and mediation of conflicts, community building, and respectful, asset-oriented, and culturally competent practice.

### *Shelter Spaces*

Organizations desiring to lay the groundwork for transformational relationships and to bring out the best in parents, children, and staff will need to create shelter spaces that foster community building and convey a message of respect, safety, and warmth. The physical environment matters and deserves attention. Nearly half of the country's emergency shelters serve over 100 people at a time.[61] Barrack shelters are less common currently than they were 20 years ago; however some version of shared living is still characteristic of 69 percent of emergency shelters in the United States.[62] Only about one-third of emergency shelters have indoor or outdoor play spaces for children.[63]

To create a sense of home and to build community in shelters, while limiting tensions resulting directly from a lack of privacy and overcrowding, organizations will need to determine how many families they can maximally shelter at any given time. What are the possibilities and constraints of the physical environment? In what ways can shelter environments be designed to enable family members to remain together[64] and to ensure that they are accessible for persons with disabilities?

## RESISTANCE TO PERPETUATION OF THE SHELTER INDUSTRY: INVESTMENT IN PERMANENT SOLUTIONS

Organizations that provide shelter to homeless men, women, and children are part of an extensive industry in the United States. Originally, shelters were established as "emergency" housing; they are now woven into the fabric of most communities in the country. National, state, and local homeless assistance organizations rely for their survival on resources directed specifically for those who are homeless. Without considerable soul-searching and intentional redirection, such organizations could *inadvertently* find themselves engaged and invested in sustaining the problem, becoming dependent upon the continuation of homelessness and of ever increasing public, private, philanthropic, and other homelessness-oriented resources.

An alternative pathway for sheltering organizations is to become change agents, building up alternative futures for their organizations that are directed toward implementing and advocating for the long-term solutions, planning as if homelessness was on the decline. Such organizations, with deep knowledge of low-income households' circumstances, hopes, and capabilities, are in a strong position to contribute to the development of low-cost housing in their communities, to develop educational, income promotion and neighborhood safety net supports, and to advocate for a significant redirection of public resources toward low-cost housing, housing assistance, and homelessness prevention.

## CONCLUSION

In conclusion, it is time to invest in what are known solutions for ending family homelessness in the United States. As a country, the disinvestments and cuts in low-cost housing and housing assistance, as well as income support and education have inadvertently led to a perpetuation and institutionalization of shelter as a viable long-term family housing option; in many cases, shelter life has exacerbated family stress as well as parental depression and internalized self-blame.

Some states and local communities are mobilizing to put an end to homelessness through system-wide prevention efforts that seek to enable families to hold on to their housing before they lose it. Such efforts will fail to be successful without substantially higher federal investments in low-cost housing, housing assistance, and income supports for low-income households, as well as effective workforce development and education initiatives.[65]

Nonetheless, for now and the foreseeable future, many families without homes are left with no alternative but to live in a shelter for long or short periods of time. Real attention needs to be given to the quality of the shelter experience so that, rather than being *watched*, these families experience help-giving that effectively taps their aspirations, sets high expectations, provides high levels of support, and enables both parents and children to come out the other side full of pride, feeling whole as individuals and as a family, feeling connected, having sparkled, having been recognized, honored, and *seen*.

## NOTES

1. This event, "Mothers of Inspiration" was sponsored by the One Family, Inc., Boston, Massachusetts, May 2004.

2. J. Wresinski, *The Very Poor, Living Proof of the Indivisibility of Human Rights*. Translation of a contribution to a fundamental review of Human Rights by the National Advisory Committee on Human Rights (Paris, France: Editions Quart Monde, 1989); See also Jona M. Rosenfeld and B. Tardieu, *Artisans of Democracy: How Ordinary People, Families in Extreme Poverty, and Social Institutions Become Allies to Overcome Social Exclusion* (Lanham, NY: University of America Press, Inc., 2000).

3. Y. Arthus-Bertrand, *The Earth From Above: 365 Days* (New York: Harry N. Abrams, Inc., 2000), 1.

4. Chris Tilly, "The Economic Environment of Housing; Income Inequality and Insecurity," in *A Right to Housing*, ed. Rachel Bratt, Michael Stone, and Chester Hartman (Philadelphia, PA: Temple University Press. 2006), 25–26; Chuck Collins, "The Economic Context: Growing Disparities of Income and Wealth," *New England Journal of Public Policy* (Fall/Winter, 2004/2005): 49–56.

5. National Low Income Housing Coalition (NLIHC), "FY 07 Budget Chart for Selected Programs," http://www.nlihc.org/pubs and NLIHC, "The Crisis in America's Housing: Confronting Myths and Promoting a Balanced Housing Policy," http://www.nlihc.org/pubs. According to the NLIHC's calculations, for the entire period from 1976–2006, relative to other programs that target low income people (income security, food and nutrition, social services, and Medicaid), federal funding for housing assistance has been much lower; when federal expenditures for those other programs began to rise in the 1990s to its current levels ($150–$360 billion range), housing assistance remained low ($30–$40 billion range). Over the past 40 years, HUD's Budget Authority, resources primarily directed at low income households, decreased by 59 percent from $76.9 billion in 1976 to $31.5 billion in 2006, while federal housing-related tax expenditures, primarily benefiting investors and homeowners who have incomes high enough to file an itemized tax return, increased by 353 percent, from

$29.4 billion in 1976 to $133.2 billion in 2006. See also the Center for Budget and Policy Priorities (CBPP), "Initial Assessment President's 2007 Budget: Impacts on Housing Voucher Program and Hurricane Recovery," Barbara Sard, Douglas Rice, and Will Fischer, Revised February 17, 2006, www.cbpp.org/2-17-06hous.htm. According to the CBPP, the President's FY07 proposed budget cuts $622 million from the HUD budget (1.8%)—most cuts hit HUD programs other than homeless assistance which is proposed to increase over last year's expenditures by 15.8 percent. A slight funding increase over 2006 is proposed for HUD's housing voucher program; this increase will fund the same number of vouchers as in 2006, and will not fully make up for past cuts (65,000–100,000 federal vouchers were lost nationwide between 2004 and 2005).

6. Otherwise referred to as 'welfare' or Transitional Assistance to Needy Families [TANF].

7. Mimi Abramowitz, "Saving Capitalism from Itself: Whither the Welfare State?" *New England Journal of Public Policy* (Fall/Winter 2004/2005): 21–32.

8. National Low Income Housing Coalition, Out of Reach (Washington, DC: NLIHC, 2005).

9. U.S. Department of Housing and Urban Development, *Affordable Housing Needs: A Report to Congress on the Significant Need for Housing* (Washington, DC: December 2005).

10. Michael Stone, "Housing Affordability: One-Third of a Nation Shelter-Poor," in *A Right To Housing*, ed. Bratt et al. (Philadelphia, PA: Temple University Press, 2006).

11. Bratt et al., "Why a Right to Housing Is Needed and Makes Sense," Editors' introduction. In *A Right To Housing*, 2006.

12. Bi-Partisan Millennial Housing Commission, *Meeting our Nation's Housing Challenges*, Submitted to the House of Representative's and United States Senate's Committees on: Appropriations and subcommittee for VA, HUD and Independent Agencies and other committees, Washington, DC, May 30, 2002; Bratt et al., 2006, 12.

13. Martha Burt and L. Aron, *America's Homeless II: Populations and Services* (Washington, DC: Urban Institute, February 2000); These figures are low estimates, given that the calculations were conducted prior to August 2005 when Hurricane Katrina hit the New Orleans/Mississippi coast and an additional 2.2 million people were directly impacted by the Hurricane, according to the U.S. Census Bureau News, September 6, 2005, US Department of Commerce, Washington, DC. Available at http://www.census.gov/Press-Release/www/releases/archives/hurricanes_tropical_storms

14. B.G. Link, E. Susser, A. Stueve, J. Phelan, R.E. Moore, and E Streuning, "Lifetime and Five-Year Prevalence of Homelessness in the United States." *American Journal of Public Health* (1994): 1907–1912.

15. Burt and Aron, *America's Homeless II*.

16. Martha Burt, L.Y. Aron, T. Douglas, J. Valente, E. Lee, and B. Iwen, *Homelessness: Programs and the People They Serve. Findings of the National Survey of Homeless Assistance Providers and Clients* (NSHAPC). Prepared for the Interagency Council on the Homeless (Washington, DC: Interagency Council on the Homeless, 1999).

17. Y-L Wong, and H. Nemon, *The 2001 Survey of Homeless Service Providers: A Profile of Programs Providing Residential and Non-Residential Services for a Sample of U.S. Jurisdictions*, Report prepared under contract with Aspen Systems Corporation for the U.S. Department of Housing and Urban Development (Philadelphia, PA: University of Pennsylvania, 2001).

18. Ibid.

19. Burt et al., *Homelessness*.

20. Center for the Study of Social Policy. An Assessment of the District of Columbia's Community Care Grant Program (Washington, DC: June 2003).

21. One Family, Inc. *An Unprecedented Opportunity*. Presentation by Susanne Beaton at the Massachusetts State House (Boston, MA: Author, February 7, 2006).

22. John McGah and Amy Carlin, *Massachusetts Department of Transitional Assistance Homeless Prevention Pilots*, A report prepared for The Boston Foundation (Boston, MA: The Boston Foundation, June 2005).

23. Outcome data are not yet available.

24. Donna Haig Friedman, John McGah, Julia Tripp, Michelle Kahan, Nicole Witherbee, and Amy Carlin, *Partners in Prevention: Community-Wide Homelessness Prevention in Massachusetts and the United States*. A report prepared for The Boston Foundation (Boston, MA: The Boston Foundation, June 2005).

25. Martha Burt and Carol Pearson, *Strategies for Preventing Homelessness*. Prepared for the Office of Policy Development and Research, U.S. Department of Housing and Urban Development (Washington, DC, U.S. Dept of Housing and Urban Development: May 2005); Friedman et al., *Partners in Prevention*.

26. Center for Budget and Public Priorities, 2006.

27. Cushing N. Dolbeare, *Changing Priorities: The Federal Budget and Housing Assistance, 1976–2006*, NILHC, May 2001 at www.nlihc.org/pubs; Dennis Culhane, *Family Homelessness: Where to from Here?* Presentation to Associated Grant Makers foundations (Boston, MA, May 23, 2005); Marybeth Shinn and Jim Baumohl, "Rethinking the Prevention of Homelessness," *Proceedings of Practical lessons: The 1998 National Symposium on Homelessness Research,* cosponsored by the U.S. Department of Housing and Urban Development and the U.S. Department of Health and Human Services (Washington, DC, 1998); Marybeth Shinn, Beth C. Weitzman, Daniela Stojanovic, James R. Knickman, Lucila Jimenez, Lisa Duchon, Susan James and David H. Krantz, Predictors of Homelessness Among Families in New York City: From Shelter Request to Housing Stability, *American Journal of Public Health* (1998): 1651–1657; Debra Rog, C.S. Holupka, K.L McCombs-Thornton, Implementation of the Homeless Families Program: 1. Service Models and Outcomes. *American Journal of Orthopsychiatry* (1995): 502–513.

28. C.G. Coll, J.L. Surrey, K. Weingarten, *Mothering Against the Odds: Diverse Voices of Contemporary Mothers* (New York: Guilford Press, 1998), see Chapter 3: Homeless: Mothering at Rock Bottom, Koch, Lewis, and Quinones.

29. National Research Council and Institute of Medicine, *From Neurons to Neighborhoods: The Science of Early Childhood Development*. Committee on integrating the science of early childhood development, ed. Jack P. Shonkoff and Deborah A. Phillips, Board on Children, Youth and Families, Commission on Behavioral and Social Sciences and Education (Washington, DC: National Academy Press, 2000).

30. Representing 75 percent of all children in NYC family shelters; D.E McLean, S. Bowen, K. Drezuer, et al., "Asthma among Homeless Children: Undercounting and Under-treating the Underserved," *Archives of Pediatric Adolescent Medicine* (2004): 244–249.

31. Ibid.

32. Burt, *Homelessness*.

33. Ibid.

34. National Research Council and Institute of Medicine, *From Neurons to Neighborhoods*.

35. Ibid.

36. Ibid.

37. Deborah Gray, Mother, from Donna Haig Friedman, *Parenting in Public: Family Shelter and Public Assistance* (New York: Columbia University Press, 2000), 73.

38. Although standardization of daily routines is hard on families, guidelines for meal times, chores, curfews, supervision of children, and many other daily routines are necessary to ensure smooth operations and predictability for all who live and work in shelter settings.

39. Rosa (Clark) Almanzar, Mother and Shelter Director, Project Hope, in Friedman, *Parenting in Public*, 151–152.

40. Friedman, *Parenting in Public*.

41. Peter Senge, C.O. Scharmer, J. Jaworski, and B.S. Flowers, *Presence: An Exploration of Profound Change in People, Organizations and Society* (New York: Doubleday Press, 2000); Carl J. Dunst, Carol M. Trivette, and Angela G. Deal, *Enabling and Empowering Families: Principles and Guidelines for Practice* (Cambridge: Brookline Books, 1988).

42. Ibid.

43. Deborah Gray, *Parenting in Public*, 114.

44. Steven Friedman and Margot T. Fanger, *Expanding therapeutic possibilities: Getting results in brief psychology*. (Lexington, KY: Lexington Books, 1991), 167.

45. Friedman, *Parenting in Public*; Ian Urbina, Keeping it Secret as the Family Car becomes a Home, New York Times, April 2, 2006. Available at www.nytimes.com/2006/04/02/us/02cars.html

46. Friedman, *Parenting in Public*.

47. Margaret Leonard, Executive Director of Project Hope, in Friedman, *Parenting in Public*, 153.

48. Senge et al., *Presence*.

49. Donald A. Schon, *The Reflective Practitioner: How Professionals Think in Action* (New York: Basic Books, Inc, 1983).

50. Dunst et al., *Enabling and Empowering Families*.

51. Sally Brecher and Steven Friedman, "In Pursuit of a Better Life: A Mother's Triumph," in *New Language of Change*, ed. Steven Friedman (New York: Guilford Press, 1993); and Steven Friedman, *Creating a Balanced Life: Transformative Possibilities*. Presented at the Commonwealth Educational Seminars (Danvers, MA: September 15, 2006).

52. Friedman, *Creating a Balanced Life*.

53. Brecher and Friedman, *New Language of Change*.

54. Senge et al., *Presence*, 107.

55. Michael White, "Deconstruction and Therapy," in *Experience, Contradiction, Narrative And Imagination: Selected Papers Of David Epston And Michael White, 1989–1991*, ed. David Epston and Michael White (South Australia: Dulwich Centre Publications, 1992); Brecher and Friedman, *New Language of Change*; Friedman and Fanger, *Expanding therapeutic possibilities*.

56. Leonard in Friedman, *Parenting in Public*, 216.

57. F. Kofman and P. Senge, "Communities of Commitment; The Heart of Learning Organizations," *Organizational Dynamics* (1993): 5–23.

58. Ibid.

59. Kofman and Senge, "Communities of Commitment; The Heart of Learning Organizations," 18–19.

60. Wong and Nemon, *The 2001 Survey of Homeless Service Providers*. Only 36 percent of shelters in the cities surveyed have resident or consumer councils.

61. Burt, *Homelessness*, 1999.

62. Wong and Nemon, *The 2001 Survey of Homeless Service Providers*.

63. Ibid.

64. By disallowing adolescents and fathers, many shelters in the United States contribute at times to harmful family separations.

65. Roberta L. Rubin and Donna Haig Friedman (manuscript under review). Welfare Reform and Federal Housing Policy: Impacts on Educational Opportunities and Economic Security for Low-Income Families.

# CHAPTER 7

# THE WORK OF COORDINATING CHILD CARE FOR RURAL LOW-INCOME MOTHERS[*]

## *E. Brooke Kelly*

Transformations in the nature of employment and the demographics of families have prompted increasing attentiveness to the interface of work and family life. Declines in manufacturing jobs have contributed to increasing unemployment rates and an overall decline in men's earnings. At the same time, service jobs are on the rise, with a large share of jobs that are deskilled, nonunion, poorly paid, with little autonomy and job security. These jobs are typically filled by teenagers, women, and people of color.[1] As industrial jobs that previously afforded men a wage that could support a family become scarcer and women's earnings become more crucial to families, women have been increasingly pulled into the labor force.[2] Such changes in the sort of jobs that are available have not only affected two-parent families, however. Men's decreased earning power has also contributed to higher numbers of female-headed households due to a decline in the number of men who are viewed as suitable marriage partners.[3] These single-mothers often struggle to support their families on low-wage service jobs, contributing to the feminization of poverty,[4] an increase in the number of women and children living in poverty.

Rural areas have experienced a similar, yet slower decline in industry and increase in service jobs. These changes have been accompanied by a decline in agricultural jobs as farms become larger due to increased mechanization.[5] The distribution of jobs by sectors, however, varies greatly from one rural area to the next. Jobs in rural areas are more dispersed, with fewer employers in the local labor market and less variety of jobs than in urban areas.[6] The share of workers in jobs that are low-skilled and at the low end of the pay scale is well above the nation's in rural America.[7] An increasing number of African Americans, Latinos, and Asian Americans are being pulled into rural communities to fill low-wage jobs. Accordingly, farm workers have one of the lowest median weekly earnings by occupation with the largest percentage of workers who belong to a minority group, most of whom are Hispanic.[8]

Services are now the source of slightly more than half of all rural jobs, compared to about two-thirds of urban jobs, providing 73 percent of rural women's total employment Within rural service sectors, women are relatively concentrated in retail trade, which has the lowest average pay of any major industry.[9] In their research on rural economies and families, Albrecht et al. found that when the proportion of the labor force working in the service sector increased, men were less likely to be employed, and, in turn, female-headed households were most prevalent. Although the rural poor are more likely to be married than those in central cities, the number of female-headed families is growing. Albrecht et al. argue that such changes are related to higher levels of rural poverty.[10]

Such transformations demonstrate the dynamic interchange between the realms of work and family. Accordingly, a growing body of scholarship[11] has developed to investigate the ways these two realms of life intersect and overlap at both macro levels, as in the economic transformations and trends addressed above, and micro levels, as individuals attempt to juggle, balance, and, more recently, weave[12] the competing and often contradictory demands of work and family life. Central to the study of work and family and the demystification of work and family as separate spheres[13] of life is the issue of child care. For working parents, managing child care around the demands of paid work can be a challenging endeavor. However, until recently much of the literature on work and family has focused on middle-class dual-earner families (with two employed parents), assessing changes in the division of labor in child care and housework as increasing numbers of women take on "second shifts"[14] at home after coming home from their first shift of paid work.[15]

In anticipation of and following welfare reform in 1996, research on low-income families has increased, largely in an effort to assess the impact of such policy changes on the well-being of children and families. Much of this and previous research on low-income families has focused on survival strategies, such as Edin and Lein's work on how low-income single-mothers "made ends meet" on low-wage work and/or welfare prior to welfare reform. Within this literature, child care is one of many needs that must be met through a number of creative strategies, along with transportation, food, shelter, and health care, to ensure family survival.[16] Survival strategy has been an important focus because it reveals and centers the material conditions and needs of families, while demonstrating the agency of parents in their attempts to deal with those conditions. Affordable quality child-care options are central needs, and low-income parents undertake many strategies to manage limited child-care options.[17]

Most research on low-income families has focused on urban contexts, leaving a dearth of knowledge about the particular effects of rural contexts.[18] Important questions requiring further investigation include: Do rural contexts necessitate a different array of material circumstances, and therefore, survival strategies? Do rural contexts necessitate different strategies for managing child care? Key to differentiating rural contexts from urban are the greater dispersion and limited availability of jobs, lack of public transportation, and greater dispersion and limitations of health care and social services. Because of the limited resources in rural areas, parents are more likely to rely on informal child-care options through family and friends.[19]

By focusing on two groups of mothers in two different rural county contexts, this chapter builds on the work of others in promoting a better understanding of how rural contexts affect the lives of low-income families. Rather than add to the on-going list of survival strategies used by these mothers to meet their child-care needs, I take a different approach by focusing on the conditions of low-wage work, demonstrating how such conditions are pivotal in structuring the child-care options to which mothers have access and the amount of energies or labor mothers must expend to manage inconsistent child-care options with inflexible and inconsistent working conditions. I argue that the conditions of low-wage work to which these mothers have access actually create constant work for them in configuring and reconfiguring child-care arrangements. Such energies expended by mothers clearly have implications for child well-being and child poverty.

## METHODS

To analyze mothers' efforts at coordinating low-wage jobs and managing child care, in-depth open-ended interviews were conducted in 2000 and 2001 with 33 Latina mothers, many of whom migrate to perform agricultural work in Harvest County, and in 2002 with 12 white mothers primarily employed in service sector jobs in Delta County. Both Harvest and Delta Counties are rural counties in Michigan.[20] This chapter draws from a larger research project focused on the invisible and taken for granted work necessary for these two groups of mothers to attain and sustain low-wage employment.[21]

In Harvest County, Latinas involved in agricultural labor with at least one child under 12 and incomes 200 percent of the poverty level or lower were targeted. Interviewers developed a sample by visiting labor camps, through their connections in their own community work and personal interactions, through the referrals of other community/human service workers, friends, friends of friends, and eventually through friends and acquaintances of other mothers interviewed. Thirty-three Latina mothers were interviewed in 2000 and again in 2001.[22]

The Delta County sample began with the informant list from a previous research project in the studied county,[23] contacts made through a community worker in the county, flyers posted at local businesses, and eventually through friends and acquaintances of other mothers interviewed. Twelve mothers with at least one child and incomes 200 percent of the poverty line or lower were interviewed in 2002.

Mothers interviewed in Harvest County all identified as Latina or Hispanic. Twenty-three mothers (70%) regularly migrated to work in Harvest County. Most considered Texas their home. The majority of women and their partners were employed in agricultural labor in Michigan, and a third of the women were laid off between crops, while 12 percent were unemployed at the time of the first interview. Over three-fourths of the women reported an education of high school or less and over half reported an eighth grade education or less. The women were not asked about their English language skills, but over half chose to conduct the interview in Spanish. Of the 33 women from Harvest County only one reported no partner or husband. Seventy-nine percent of mothers had more than one child and 20 women had at least one child aged 5 or under in the household.

Delta County women self identified as white. Although all of the women reported previous work experience, half were not employed at the time of the interview. Seventy-five percent reported completing high school. Nine were living with or married to a partner. Three-fourths of the women had more than one child, and over half had at least one child aged 5 or under.

## WORKING CONDITIONS AND CHILD-CARE OPTIONS

Although the women's circumstances differed in significant ways, the working conditions with which they contend and their struggles to manage child care illustrate some important parallels. The job contexts that both groups of mothers described mirror national trends for rural areas addressed previously: low-skill, low-pay, unfriendly-to-family jobs.[24] Such job contexts shape the working conditions to which mothers have access and, therefore, the amount of effort necessary for mothers to coordinate and manage child care.

### Low Pay and the Costs of Child Care

The jobs to which mothers in both counties had access generated little income for them to support their families and secure child care for their children. Gail, who worked as a cashier at a local branch of a discount chain, compared her salary with those of other employees working at other branches of the chain across the country and found that "the lowest hourly wage, let's say in . . . South Carolina was $7.50 an hour . . . I was making five and a half an hour up here."[25]

Agricultural labor is characterized by particularly low pay. An oversupply of agricultural labor, shaped by immigration laws, helps explain why the low pay and poor working conditions make these workers one of the most disadvantaged groups in the United States.[26] Mothers interviewed in Harvest County were no exception.

Such low pay severely restricts child-care options, particularly formal child-care arrangements. Mothers in both counties struggled to manage the costs of paid child care on their low-wage jobs, as addressed by Liz, a Delta County mother, below:

> The money I shelled out on day care was ridiculous because you drop them off at 8 o'clock in the morning and you didn't pick em up until 7 o'clock at night because that's when proofs got done. Granted, the bank closed at 5 o'clock, but we still had two hours of checks to be processed and balanced to get out of there.

Extended workdays necessitated additional hours of child care, increasing the cost of that care. Such economic dilemmas about the costs of care were not limited to single mothers, however. Ellie, a Delta County mother of three, expressed similar concerns about the cost of child care, given the income she derived from her employment:

> Two dollars an hour per kid. And it wasn't bad when [one child] was there, but if they had breaks for the schooling, the Christmas break, or anything like that where the kids were off, Suzy would be there, so it would be four dollars an hour and then with him [youngest son], it would be six, so I'd only be making, you know, fifty cents an hour and that wouldn't even pay for gas back and forth.

Ellie was not alone in noticing that the pay of low-wage work often did not cover the costs of care. Several mothers from both counties made similar comments, some noting times when they were unable to work because of the costs of care or because of other complications finding adequate child care. Celina, a Harvest County mother, explained below:

> Well, last year we paid two thousand dollars in one month to take care of the four children. . . . If I get a good job I don't qualify for the childcare [assistance] and there are four [children]; it already happened to me . . . the job didn't work out [because of the cost of] the baby sitter. Two thousand dollars in one month is a lot, and that's just part-time for the children.

Thus, formal (paid) child-care arrangements were cost prohibitive for many families and some were unable to work at times due to a deficit of care.

To deal with the exorbitant costs of child care, mothers from both counties turned to informal child-care arrangements with family members and friends and worked separate shifts from their partners.[27] Others relied on Head Start programs and other subsidized child-care arrangements through the state. Nevertheless, mothers (and their partners) often encountered problems qualifying for assistance for one or all their children. For example, Flavia reported that:

> For two children I have to pay because they don't qualify for the government to pay; for two of them they pay and for two they don't. . . . I had to pay a lot if I worked Saturday and Sunday, [yet] I had to work Saturday and Sunday to be able to pay [for child care].

Thus, Flavia and other parents found themselves in a Catch-22.

Though child-care subsidies helped offset the high costs of child care for some mothers, problems with waiting lists and regulations remained. A Delta County mother explained the dearth of child-care options common in rural areas, "I know that the state has programs for low-income [families], but then you have to have a licensed babysitter, and that's not easy [to find] around here either." Thus, negotiating quality care around the requirements and restrictions needed to subsidize costly child care presented mothers with difficult child-care dilemmas, as illustrated by Clara, a Delta County mother's, circumstances:

The day care that I had for [my children] last year would not accept FIA payments, . . . but it was the best day care we could get. . . . And we just couldn't afford ninety dollars a kid each week. She didn't accept FIA [Family Independence Agency] because she said it's just too much time to wait for them because sometimes they don't send their checks out on time.

One Harvest County couple explained it well: "When the two of us work, how nice. . . . When there is someone to take care of [the children], both of us work." Their comment illustrates the additional hardships for families who migrate to Harvest County: the lack of support networks in finding and securing formal child-care arrangements.

## Inconsistencies in Hours and Scheduling of Work

Not only was pay an issue for the mothers, but in some cases the work that Delta County mothers found was only part-time, temporary, and/or fewer hours than promised when they were hired. For example, one young, single mother, Brandy, needed more hours than she was getting at her gas station job. She said, "I was hired in, supposed to be full time and I was about 32 if I got lucky."

On the other hand, several Delta County mothers reported periods in which they were working 60–80 hour weeks, either at one job or at multiple jobs they took on for economic reasons. According to Erin, "I worked seventy-two hours in one week and never got paid over-time, never got anything. I was supposed to be a part-timer."

Women in Delta County also encountered temporary or seasonal jobs. For example, Liz, a school bus driver has to manage her finances carefully with her seasonal work: "When school's in, I work. So, basically I work on an average, maybe six months out of the year." Nancy, a young mother says her job is mostly "a summer kind of thing . . . so I only work Friday, Saturday, and Sunday."

Though seasonal work encountered by Delta County mothers offered some predictability in annual schedules, Harvest County mothers found less regularity in the scheduling of agricultural labor. Mothers and their partners contend with—and in some cases travel significant distances to contend with—unstable and inconsistent working conditions:

You could say there were good times and bad times [during the year]. They stop us, they give us one or two weeks and then they come two or three days and now there isn't any [work] and that it how it is. (Yesenia, non-migrant agricultural laborer)

Women who live in Harvest County year round (approximately 30%), like Yesenia quoted above, are often employed as seasonal agricultural laborers. The work lasts only as long as a given crop. Moreover, agricultural workers did not work consistently throughout any given season. Temporary layoffs were common. Gitana reported: "Well, right now we're not working at all. . . . Sometimes we work forty hours per week; sometimes . . . up to eighty hours per week . . . sometimes . . . twelve hours a day; sometimes ten . . . hours." The work available and the length of a season varied from year to year. Mothers (and their partners) could not predict the next year from the prior year. As Francisca explained: "Well, . . . last year we worked seven months. I do not know about this year."

The availability of work is also conditioned by the weather, including freezes or lack of rain as well as the whims of employers. Needless to say agricultural labor in Harvest County is characterized by feast or famine and the unstable work schedule makes formal child-care arrangements extremely challenging to negotiate.

## Inconsistencies and Complications in Child-Care Arrangements

Not only did the accounts of mothers in both counties suggest that many encounter inconsistencies in scheduling and hours of work, but those conditions complicate child-care arrangements for some, particularly for those who rely on formal child care. When asked if anything made it more difficult for her to work, Tomasa, a Harvest County mother, responded:

Most of it was day care, and that you have to leave too early [in the mornings and evenings] and the day care was still closed at those time[s]. . . . [At] 6:30[a.m.] I would drop [my daughter off], and . . . the day care close[d] also by 6:30[p.m.]. So, I would . . . be there just barely on time to get her. And then I would still have to take her for a couple of minutes more to the field until I finished [harvesting crops].

Low pay of such work affected the child care to which mothers had access, but so too did fluctuations in hours and scheduling. It meant a never-ending cycle. Thus, turnover in child-care arrangements was not uncommon, nor was instability in many mothers' employment circumstances. For example, Jenna, a single mother in Delta County, recounted a string of child-care arrangements that patched together formal and informal arrangements, such as a reliable friend who was unlicensed but trustworthy and a teenage daughter who watched her youngest on weekends. Arrangements seemed to fluctuate with her changes in employment and other circumstances.

Although the flexibility of informal care from family and friends often offset the inflexibility and inconsistencies of work schedules, this sort of care was not isolated from fluctuations and change. Jenna also spoke of using her older daughter as a babysitter until her daughter went to college. Similarly, changes in informal child-care arrangements among migrant workers in Harvest County were not unusual from one season to the next. Afra explained that her niece who had cared for her children during the previous season was no longer her child-care provider "because she wanted to work in the fields." Even though social services in the state of Michigan provides subsidies for informal child care by family or friends, the amount of the subsidy, less than a living wage, does not insure consistency of care providers. In addition, one might expect that others in the social networks of mothers in both counties would live in similarly tenuous economic circumstances, subject to frequent life fluctuations.[28]

Scheduling of formal child-care arrangements may also change,[29] particularly since even formal arrangements are often provided by mothers who care for their own and others' children from their homes. Brandy's account below illustrates the complications that fluctuations in day-care provider schedules can present:

> The day care provider told me that she does twenty-four hour care, but about a week later she told me that they wanted their family time after five o'clock so I had to switch my hours [at work], which was really hard because they didn't want to work with me on it.

Brandy's account reveals the feedback between fluctuating work and child-care schedules that leads to constant work for mothers to try to manage.

### Inflexibility

Not only was inconsistency in hours and scheduling a problem for families, but mothers in both counties also encountered inflexible employers and/or working conditions. For example, Brandy, the single Delta County mother of two addressed above, found her job as a gas station attendant to be inflexible:

> There were a couple of days where I had to call in because the kids were sick or transportation didn't work out and they didn't like that at all. They didn't want to work with me . . . even though hiring in they knew that I was a single mother and had quite a few problems with stability because of transportation. . . .

Family emergencies created issues for many parents. For example, Candida, a Harvest County mother, noted that her workplace instituted a policy that says if an employee leaves early they cannot return to work the next day. Antonia said that:

> They told us that we could leave only if it is an emergency. And I said like if my daughter has the flu, I said I'd go to see how she is and take her to the hospital or the clinic. And they told me, "You can't ask for permission, only in the case of an emergency." And I said to them, "What is an emergency only if someone dies?" . . . I said, "No. An emergency is if someone gets sick"

Flavia reported that her boss did not tell her that her babysitter called to tell her that her daughter was sick. Engracia's husband was not even told about a death in his family until his shift was through. Such incidents illustrate the brittle and unyielding nature of their work conditions—truly a contested terrain for families.

## THE "WORK" OF COORDINATING CHILD CARE AND LOW-WAGE WORK

As illustrated above, low pay and inconsistencies in employment structure the often fluctuating child-care options to which mothers have access. Such circumstances create constant work for mothers (and their partners), as they attempt to piece together and reconfigure fluctuations in employment and child care. Managing affordable child care of acceptable quality around the schedules of low-wage and often inflexible employment involves stress and expending energy, a precious commodity. Mothers must manage getting children to child-care providers, often at unusual times, negotiate with formal and/or informal (friends and family) child-care providers, coordinate with the schedules of partners/fathers, manage the care of older children, and constantly worry that the house of cards does not collapse.

### The Work of Getting Children to Day Care

Making sure children get to and from child-care providers also involved additional preparation and planning such as packing a bag ahead of time and getting children ready. Gail and Ellie, Delta County mothers who had to be at work at seven and six a.m. respectively, prepared a bag the night before to send with their children to the child-care provider with clothing and other things they would need:

> [I'd] usually come home and get [the bag] right then. Take the dirty stuff out and put it right by the door. . . . I had to be out of here at six because I had to start at seven. So, I was up, nine out of ten times the bag was packed. . . . [My daughter] went in her jammies, wrapped in a blanket, and then I had to talk . . . the day care provider into getting up early to take her, because she didn't start till seven, and I had to be at work at seven. (Gail)

With the odd hours required of low-wage service and agricultural labor, several mothers discussed having to wake their children at very early hours to transport them to formal or informal care arrangements. Celina, a Harvest County mother, explained the difficulties of transporting her children at the early hours necessitated by harvesting, "sometimes it is hard to wake up my children at five o'clock in the morning, and they do not sleep well." Celina's account provides a glimpse into the world of stress for children's lives as well as parents.

### Negotiating with Child-Care Providers

Whether mothers relied on formal or informal child-care arrangements, Brandy's previous example and that of Gail above both demonstrate the need for them to negotiate with child-care providers (and employers) in order to try to accommodate the often inflexible and fluctuating hours of low-wage work. For example, so that a friend who she trusted but was not licensed could provide care for her children, Jenna, a Delta County mother negotiated an arrangement that would work for both parties. "She would watch [my children] after school. She would watch them when I worked nights at the bar. . . . And the pay off was, I helped take food down there. And I didn't' put her on my taxes or claim her at the end of the year or anything like that." Because of the dispersion of child-care options in rural areas, mothers are more likely to rely on informal care arrangements,[30] leaving more room for such negotiations. Accordingly, as others have confirmed, child-care arrangements of low-income families often change.[31] Because work schedules and child-care arrangements are in a state of flux, such negotiations must happen again and again.

## Bringing Children to Work

Because of cost prohibitions or other difficulties finding care, for a few mothers bringing children to work was at least part of the child-care arrangements they pieced together, as Ellie, a Delta County mother, explained:

> We didn't know anybody really around that area. My sister-in-law lived like fifteen miles away, and the paper route was going the opposite direction, you know. At eleven o'clock at night, it was hard to take them out there. . . . So, nine times out of ten, I just took them with me or had one of the neighbors come over and just sleep overnight and watch them there.

On such occasions, the children slept in the car while Ellie delivered papers.

Similarly, Tomasa, a Harvest County mother, talked about bringing her six-month-old child to the fields with her due to a deficit of care at later hours. "There was no day care for her. There was nobody I knew that [sic] could take care of her so I would take her to the fields." Such an arrangement required coordination and planning on her part:

> I would . . . fix it up for her and I'd put her there [in the fields] to sleep and sometimes my aunt would lend me her daughter. She was . . . eight years old and she would keep an eye on her. . . . We'd find a place that looked safe, you know, for them to stay there and we would take her, you know, formula and everything.

Tomasa reflects on her child-care strategy with great sadness, wondering if the time her daughter spent in the fields is related to the serious health problems she developed later in life: "I didn't want her in the fields 'cause I knew how hot it was and, you know, they would spray stuff and I didn't want to have her there in the fields." Nevertheless, faced with no other viable alternative, Tomasa negotiated this arrangement.

## Coordinating with Partners' Schedules

Some mothers with partners managed child care through an arrangement in which both parents worked different shifts. Though such an arrangement allowed one parent to be present at all times, this strategy required a lot of coordination, as illustrated by Francisca, an agricultural worker who lives in Harvest County with her husband and three children year-round:

> I get up at four thirty in the morning, I make lunch for my husband, because he works at night and arrives at five in the morning or five thirty. . . . At six I get the children up and

when he comes I have lunch, tortillas and everything. [In the evening, I get the children ready for school], and then in the morning I just get them up so that they stay awake and I go to my job. . . . [My husband] arrives, eats lunch, gets the children up and takes them to the bus and in the afternoon he picks them up and when I arrive, the children already ate dinner and they are just waiting for me to arrive to bathe them and everything.

Although Francisa points out that her children are never alone, such a strategy requires a lot of effort and coordination on her and her husband's part.

## Managing Care with Older Children

To fill in deficits of care on weekends and at odd hours, some mothers relied on older children. Such an arrangement, however, requires monitoring and preparation of children for such responsibility. For example, when asked how she combines her work and family responsibilities, Columba, a Harvest County mother, explained: "I started, you know, with my kids teaching them a little bit of responsibility like throwing out trash, picking up their stuff. So they get the feel of responsibility and help me out."

Although older children were often assets in filling gaps in care, sometimes planning for the care of and coordinating the supervision of older children required as much effort, and, perhaps, more emotional work than coordinating care for younger children.[32] Mothers worried about their children's abilities to care for themselves and their siblings and to stay out of trouble. When Gail, a Delta County mother, was at work, for example, her children would "terrorize my house. . . . Yeah. The older they get, there's always more worries."

One common concern of mothers was ensuring that children got on the bus to school. This was a particular problem for mothers, like Laurel, who had to leave for work before their children's school bus arrived:

I'd have to be at work at sometimes five, six o'clock in the morning. Well, then there was nobody here for my kids when they got on the bus, so. And teenagers you kind of like to pay attention to what they're wearing to school, . . . and make sure they're getting on that bus. Several times I was getting phone calls [at work]. . . . "Mom I missed the bus." Well, mom can't run all the way home now to get you. . . . They would miss school. Yeah, so that got frustrating.

To deal with this situation, Laurel and her husband, Jeff, would make plans:

Well, you call home and make sure the kids are up. I'll call home right around bus time to make sure they're ready for the bus . . . But then there was times, you know, where you're at work, and you just can't take that time. You're busy at the time, and you can't get to the phone to check. And by the time you did get to the phone, they were all gone. And then you kind of sit there and wonder how their day started out.

Although mothers often planned ahead to the time when they could simplify their child-care needs as children became school age and/or able to take care of themselves and/or their siblings, their accounts illuminate often overlooked labors involved in managing the care of older children around the schedules of work.

### The Insatiable Need for Coordinating Child Care

These mother's circumstances and challenges might resonate with any parent. Indeed, many working parents recognize the taken for granted and often invisible backstage labors[33] they go through to coordinate child care around the schedules of their employment: the labors of worrying, checking in, coordinating with partners' schedules, and many other efforts they make. Increasingly, parents can make use of a growing body of literature (in the research community as well as within popular culture) that legitimizes these previously invisible efforts and struggles. Then what sets apart these two groups of mothers from every other parent? One of the key differences is the material with which parents have to work. The conditions of low-wage work necessitate constant coordination, as Brandy's circumstance from above illustrates:

> The day care provider told me that she does twenty-four hour care, but about a week later she told me that they wanted their family time after five o'clock so I had to switch my hours [at work], which was really hard because they didn't want to work with me on it.... But I ended up getting, I got off at like seven, which [the day care provider] worked with me on.... She decided that was okay. And then [my employer] gave me pretty much the hours that I needed for day care, but they put me on weekends, and I didn't have day care on weekends, so that was a hard spot.

Brandy's account reveals how the fluctuations and inconsistencies of low-wage work and child-care arrangements necessitate such coordination and reconfiguring happens over and over again. The schedules of low-wage work along with the child-care arrangements they afford both appear to be in a state of flux that requires constant reconfigurations for mothers. Garey has offered the metaphor of weaving to illustrate mothers' attempts to mesh their family and working lives.[34] However, these two groups of mothers appear to be working with constantly unraveling threads, attempting to piece together an improvisational patchwork of care.[35]

## CONCLUSIONS AND IMPLICATIONS FOR CHILD POVERTY AND WELL-BEING

Based on these mothers' accounts, their common conditions of work (low pay and inconsistencies) are pivotal in creating the constant labors necessary to manage child-care arrangements. Such findings have important implications for child poverty and child well-being.

This chapter has focused on two important groups within a changing rural landscape.[36] Such a focus on the particular issues facing parents and children in rural areas is crucial since child poverty rates are higher in rural areas than in urban areas, and the gap between rural and urban poverty grew significantly during the later

1990s. Poverty is highly concentrated in rural counties. Of the 50 counties with the highest child poverty rates, 48 are located in rural areas. The employment conditions of parents seem to be crucial to child poverty rates. Many full-time jobs in rural areas cannot support a family. For example, 27 percent of children live in low-income work-ing families in rural America versus 21 percent in metro areas. A growing number of female-headed households live in poverty (43% in rural areas vs. 34% in urban areas), contributing to a phenomenon known as the feminization of poverty.[37] Rural workers are more likely to be underemployed and less likely than their urban counterparts to receive cash public assistance to supplement or substitute for low wages. In addition, because of the low quality of jobs in rural areas and the likelihood of employment at smaller companies, rural children are more heavily dependant on health insurance from public sources versus benefits through their parents' employment. Such health care options are often of lower quality.[38]

The implications of parents' employment options on child poverty and well-being are clear. The amount of pay and benefits to which parents have access determine the material circumstances with which they live and whether a family falls above or below the poverty line. In addition to this more obvious connection, the mothers' accounts discussed in this chapter also suggest that the conditions of employment determine the array of child-care options available to mothers and, in turn, the amount of efforts and energies needed to manage the child-care options available to them. Not only does the quality of child-care options available have implications for child well-being, but the labors and reconfigurations in managing child care on the part of parents potentially sap them of time and energy they could be investing in their children. Therefore, if the goal is to address child well-being and child poverty, then one way to foster more consistent care for the children of low-wage parents is to improve the conditions of employment. For example, increasing the minimum wage could make formal child care more accessible to low-wage working parents. Since an increasing percentage of the poor consists of women and their children, addressing the gender wage gap that persists (women's average full-time earnings are still 76% of men's earnings) could have a significant impact on child poverty by affording single-mothers and dual-earner families alike greater earning power.

Improving the child-care options available to parents and children is another way to affect child well-being. Supplementing the cost of and creating more quality care could have significant positive impacts on children.[39] Parents also desperately need care that is flexible and available during unconventional hours (early mornings, evenings, and weekends). However, in reality, those with lower incomes appear to be saddled with the least flexible work and child-care options.[40] These mothers' accounts also suggest a need for care and/or supports of older children. Finally, special attention to the particular child-care needs and obstacles of rural parents is necessary. Because of the dispersion and deficit of formal child-care options in rural areas, supporting informal care from family and friends may be the best routes to improving child-care conditions.[41] More research focused on rural child-care issues is needed.

All these potential measures (improving working conditions and child-care op-tions) could serve to lessen the amount of work that mothers need to undertake to manage child-care arrangements. Although attention to the particular contexts and circumstances of low-income parents in rural areas is necessary, policies aimed at lessening the labors necessary to manage work and family could benefit all working parents and their children. All working parents labor to manage care for their children. Policies that make work more flexible for parents (such as paid family leave and flexibility in scheduling and hours) could benefit all parents and children. Thus, to tackle child poverty and the well-being of all children, we cannot overlook the work that parents do, both inside and outside the home.

## NOTES

* The research reported was supported in part by the Rural Poverty Research Center (www.rprconline.org) of the Rural Policy Research Institute (RUPRI) through a dissertation fellowship funded by the Office of the Assistant Secretary for Planning and Evaluation, the U.S. Department of Health and Human Services, and the Annie E. Casey Foundation. The research conducted in Harvest County was supported in part by USDA/CSREES/NRICGP Grants - 2001-35401-10215, 2002-35401-11591, 2004-35401-14938. Data were collected in conjunction with the cooperative multistate research project NC-223/NC-1011 Rural Low-income Families: Tracking Their Well-Being and Functioning in the Context of Welfare Reform. Cooperating states are California, Colorado, Indiana, Kentucky, Louisiana, Massachusetts, Maryland, Michigan, Minnesota, Nebraska, New Hampshire, New York, Ohio, Oregon, and Wyoming, though this chapter draws from data gathered in Michigan only. The author would like to thank the editors of this volume for their editorial suggestions and Dr. Barbara Wells for her assistance and support during the interviewing process in Delta County.

1. Maxine Baca Zinn and D. Stanley Eitzen, *Diversity in Families*, 7th ed, (Boston: Allyn & Bacon, 2005); Maxine Baca Zinn and D. Stanley Eitzen, "Economic Restructuring and Systems of Inequality," in *Race, Class, and Gender*, ed. Margaret L. Andersen and Patricia Hill Collins (Belmont, CA: Wadsworth Publishing Company, 1998); Bennett Harrison and Barry Bluestone, *The Great U-Turn: Corporate Restructuring and the Polarizing of America* (New York: Basic Books, Inc., 1998).

2. Zinn and Eitzen, *Diversity in Families*.

3. William Julius Wilson, *When Work Disappears: The World of the New Urban Poor* (New York: Vintage Books: A Division of Random House, Inc., 1996); also see Kathryn Edin and Maria Kefalas, *Promises I Can Keep: Why Poor Women Put Motherhood Before Marriage* (Berkeley: University of California Press, 2005).

4. Diana Pearce, "The Feminization of Poverty: Women, Work and Welfare," *The-Urban-and-Social-Change-Review* 11 (1978): 28–36.

5. Domer 1983 and Paarlber 1980, as cited in Don E. Albrecht, Carol Mulford Albrecht, and Stan L. Albrecht, "Poverty in Nonmetropolitan America: Impacts of Industrial, Employment, and Family Structure Variables," *Rural Sociology* 65 (2000): 87–103; Robert M. Gibbs, "Rural Labor Markets in an Era of Welfare Reform," in *Rural Dimensions of Welfare Reform*, ed. Bruce A. Weber, Greg J. Duncan, and Leslie A. Whitener (Kalamazooo. MI: W.E. Upjohn Institute for Employment Research, 2002); Saskia Sassen, *Globalization and Its Discontents: Essay on the New Mobility of People and Money* (New York: New Press, 1998).

6. Gibbs, *Rural Dimensions of Welfare Reform*.

7. Gibbs and Parker, as cited in Robert M. Gibbs, *Rural Dimensions of Welfare Reform*.

8. Jack L. Runyan, "The Number of Hired Farmworkers Increased in 2000 and Most Now Come from Minority Groups," *Rural America* 16 (2001): 44–50.

9. Robert M. Gibbs, *Rural Dimensions of Welfare Reform*.

10. Don E. Albrecht, Carol Mulford Albrecht, and Stan L. Albrecht, "Poverty in Non-metropolitan America: Impacts of Industrial, Employment, and Family Structure Variables," *Rural Sociology* 65 (2000): 87–103; "Rural Sociological Task Force on Persistent Poverty," *Persistent Poverty in Rural America* (Boulder, CO: Westview Press, 1993).

11. For examples see Stephanie Coontz, "Complicating the Contested Terrain of Work/Family Intersections: A Review Essay," *Signs: Journal of Women in Culture and Society* 22 (1997): 440–452; Arlie Hochschild, *The Time Bind: When Work Becomes Home and Home Becomes Work* (New York: Metropolitan Books, 1997); Arlie Hochschild, *The Second Shift: Working Parents and the Revolution at Home* (New York: Viking Press, 1989); Rosabeth Moss Kanter, "Jobs and Families: Impact of Working Roles on Family Life," in *Work and Family*, ed. Patricia Voydanoff (Palo Alto, CA: Mayfield, 1985); Elizabeth Menaghan, "Work Experiences and Family Interaction Processes: The Long Reach of the Job?" *Annual Review of Sociology* 17 (1991): 419–444; Judith Stacey, *Brave New Families: Stories of Domestic Upheaval in Late Twentieth Century America* (New York: Basic Books, 1990).

12. Anita Ilta Garey, *Weaving Work and Motherhood* (Philadelphia, PA: Temple University Press, 1999).

13. Rosabeth Moss Kanter, "Jobs and Families: Impact of Working Roles on Family Life," in *Work and Family*, ed. Patricia Voydanoff (Palo Alto, CA: Mayfield, 1985).

14. Arlie Hochschild, *The Second Shift: Working Parents and the Revolution at Home* (New York: Vcking Press, 1989).

15. For examples, in addition to endnote 9 above, see Scott Coltrane, *Family Man* (New York: Oxford University Press, 1996); Kathleen Gerson, *No Man's Land: Men's Changing Commitments to Family and Work* (New York: Basic Books, 1993); Beth Anne Shelton, "The Division of Household Labor," *Annual Review of Sociology* 22 (1996): 299–322.

16. For examples see Kathryn Edin and Laura Lein, *Making Ends Meet: How Single Mothers Survive Welfare and Low-Wage Work* (New York: Russell Sage Foundation, 1997); Bonnie Thornton Dill, "A Better Life for Me and My Children: Low-Income Single Mothers' Struggle for Self-Sufficiency in the Rural South," *Journal of Comparative Family Studies* 29 (1998): 419–428; Margaret K. Nelson and Joan Smith, *Working Hard and Making Do: Surviving in Small Town America* (Berkeley: University of California Press, 1999); Roberta Spalter-Roth, Bererly Burr, and Heidi Hartmann, *Welfare That Works: The Working Lives of AFDC Recipients* (Washington, DC: Institute for Women's Policy Research, 1995); Jarrett, Robin L. "Living Poor: Family Life Among Single Parent, African-American Women," *Social Problems* 41 (1994): 30–49.

17. See Ajay Chaudry, *Putting Children First: How Low-Wage Working Mothers Manage Child Care* (New York: Russell Sage Foundation, 2004).

18. For exceptions see www.ruralfamilies.umn.edu; Barbara D. Ames, Whitney A. Brosi, and Karla M. Damiano-Teixeira, "I'm Just Glad My Three Jobs Could Be During the Day: Women and Work in a Rural Community," *Family Relations* 55 (January 2006): 119–131; Janet L. Bokemeier et al., "Lost Kids in Rural Poverty: Viewpoints of Community Professionals and Low Income Mothers," Paper from Rural Sociological Society Annual Meetings, Washington, DC, August 19, 1995; Bruce A. Weber, Greg J. Duncan, and Leslie A. Whitener, *Rural Dimensions of Welfare Reform* (Kalamazoo, MI: W.E. Upjohn Institute for Employment Research, 2002).

19. O'Hare, William P., and Kenneth M. Johnson. "Child Poverty in Rural America," *Population Reference Bureau* 4 (March 2004); Susan Walker and Kathy Reschke, "Child-Care

Issues Facing Contemporary Rural Families," in *Family Focus*, National Council on Family Relations, March 2003.

20. County names are pseudonyms, as are all names of subjects. According to the 2003 Rural-urban Continuum Classification Coding system, "a classification scheme that distinguishes metropolitan counties by size and nonmetropolitan counties by degree of urbanization and proximity to metro areas . . . resulting in a 9-part county codification," Delta County is a nonmetro county with an urban population of 2,500–19,999, adjacent to a metro area. The same coding system designates Harvest County as a non–metro county completely rural or less than 2,500 urban population, adjacent to a metro area, U.S. Department of Agriculture (USDA), Economic Research Service (ERS), "Rural-urban Continuum Codes," www.ers.usda.gov/data/ruralurbancontinuumcodes, accessed on September 3, 2003; for a history of the coding system also see Margaret A. Butler, *Rural-Urban Continuum Codes for Metro and Non-metro Counties* (Washington, DC: U.S. Dept. of Agriculture, Economic Research Service, Agriculture and Rural Economy Division, 1990).

21. E. Brooke Kelly, Working for Work in Rural Michigan: A Study of How Low-Income Mothers Negotiate Paid Work, Ph.D. diss., Michigan State University, 2004.

22. These mothers were initially interviewed as part of a larger longitudinal study, formally identified as NC-1101 "Rural Low-Income Families: Tracking Their Well-Being and Functioning in the Context of Welfare Reform," (www.ruralfamilies.umn.edu). Though the larger project draws on data collected in several states, this chapter relies on interviews conducted in Harvest County, Michigan only. For additional information about data collection, samples, and/or analysis, see E. Brooke Kelly, *Working for Work in Rural Michigan*, or contact the author directly.

23. David R. Imig et al., "The Context of Rural Economic Stress in Families with Children," *Michigan Family Review* 2 (1997): 69–82; Barbara Wells, *Family Continuity and Change in a Restructured Economy: A Case Study from Rural Michigan*, Ph.D. diss., 1999, Michigan State University.

24. Gibbs and Parker, as cited in Robert M. Gibbs, *Rural Dimensions of Welfare Reform*.

25. The conditions of work in this section are further addressed for Delta County mothers in E. Brooke Kelly, "Leaving and Losing Jobs: Resistance of Rural Low-Income Mothers," *Journal of Poverty*, 9 (2005): 83–103.

26. René R. Rosenbaum, "Migrant and Seasonal Farmworkers in Michigan: From Dialogue to Action," *JSRI Working Paper* #39, The Julian Samora Research Institute, Michigan State University, East Lansing, Michigan, 2002.

27. For a discussion of child care strategies, see Kelly, *Working for Work in Rural Michigan*.

28. Stacey J. Oliker, "Work Commitment and Constraint Among Mothers on Workfare," *Journal of Contemporary Ethnography* 24 (1995): 165–194.

29. Other research has confirmed that low-income families use multiple child care arrangements and that changes in child care arrangements are common, Holloway et al., as cited in Ellen K. Scott, Andrew S. London, and Allison Hurst, "Instabilities in Patchworks of Child Care When Moving from Welfare to Work," *Journal of Marriage and Family* 67 (May 2005): 370–386.

30. Walker and Reschke, "Child-Care Issues Facing Contemporary Rural Families."

31. Holloway et al., "Instabilities in Patchworks of Child Care When Moving from Welfare to Work."

32. see Demie Kurz, "Caring for Teenage Children," *Journal of Family Issues* 23 (2002): 748–767.

33. Irving Goffman, *The Presentation of Self in Everyday Life*. New York: Doubleday, 1959; Kelly, *Working for Work in Rural Michigan*.

34. Garey, *Weaving Work and Motherhood.*

35. Scott, London, and Hurst, "Instabilities in Patchworks of Child Care When Moving from Welfare to Work."

36. However, rural America is diverse and the experiences of these two particular groups of mothers discussed in this paper should not be generalized to represent all rural mothers or even all white or all Latina rural mothers. Additional research is needed to gather more information about other groups, contexts, and circumstances in rural areas.

37. Diana Pearce, "The Feminization of Poverty: Women, Work and Welfare."

38. O'Hare, William P., and Kenneth M. Johnson. "Child Poverty in Rural America."

39. Loeb, Fuller, Kagan, and Carrol 2004; National Institute of Child and Health Development (NICHD] Early Child Care Research Nework, 2000; Votruba-Drzal, Coley, and Chase-Lansdale, 2004, as cited in Scott, London, and Hurst, "Instabilities in Patchworks of Child Care When Moving from Welfare to Work"; Ajay Chaudry, *Putting Children First.*

40. Randy Albelda, "What's Wrong with Welfare-to-Work," in *Work, Welfare, and Politics: Confronting Poverty in the Wake of Welfare Reform*, ed. Frances F. Piven et al. (Eugene: University of Oregon Press, 2002); Sonya Michel, "The Politics of Child Care in America's Public/Private Welfare State," in *Families in the U.S.: Kinship and Domestic Politics*, ed. Karen. V. Hansen and Anita I. Garey (Philadelphia: Temple University Press, 1998); Scott, London, and Hurst, "Instabilities in Patchworks of Child Care When Moving from Welfare to Work."

41. Walker and Reschke, "Child-Care Issues Facing Contemporary Rural Families."

# REFERENCES

Albelda, Randy. "What's Wrong with Welfare-to-Work." In *Work, Welfare, and Politics: Confronting Poverty in the Wake of Welfare Reform*, edited by Frances F. Piven, Joan Acker, Margaret Hallock, and Sandra Morgen, Eugene: University of Oregon Press, 2002.

Albrecht, Don E., Carol Mulford Albrecht, and Stan L. Albrecht. "Poverty in Nonmetropolitan America: Impacts of Industrial, Employment, and Family Structure Variables." *Rural Sociology* 65 (2000): 87–103.

Ames, Barbara D., Whitney A. Brosi, and Karla M. Damiano-Teixeira. "I'm Just Glad My Three Jobs Could Be During the Day: Women and Work in a Rural Community." *Family Relations* 55 (January 2006): 119–131.

Baca Zinn, Maxine, and D. Stanley Eitzen. "Economic Restructuring and Systems of Inequality" In *Race, Class, and Gender*, edited by Margaret L. Andersen, and Patricia Hill Collins. Belmont: Wadsworth Publishing Company, 1998.

———. *Diversity in Families.* 7th ed. Boston: Allyn & Bacon, 2005.

Bokemeier, Janet L., Barbara Wells, Patricia Gross, David Imig, and Dennis Keefe. "Lost Kids in Rural Poverty: Viewpoints of Community Professionals and Low Income Mothers." Paper from Rural Sociological Society Annual Meetings, Washington, DC, August 19, 1995.

Butler, Margaret A. *Rural-Urban Continuum Codes for Metro and Non-metro Counties.* Washington, D.C.: U.S. Dept. of Agriculture, Economic Research Service, Agriculture and Rural Economy Divison, 1990.

Chaudry, Ajay. *Putting Children First: How Low-Wage Working Mothers Manage Child Care.* New York: Russell Sage Foundation, 2004.

Coltrane, Scott. *Family Man.* New York: Oxford University Press, 1996.

Coontz, Stephanie. "Complicating the Contested Terrain of Work/Family Intersections: A Review Essay." *Signs: Journal of Women in Culture and Society* 22 (1997): 440–452.

Dill, Bonnie Thornton. "A Better Life for Me and My Children: Low-Income Single Mothers' Struggle for Self-Sufficiency in the Rural South." *Journal of Comparative Family Studies* 29 (1998): 419–428.

Edin, Kathryn, and Maria Kefalas. *Promises I Can Keep: Why Poor Women Put Motherhood Before Marriage.* Berkeley: University of California Press, 2005.

Edin, Kathryn and Laura Lein. *Making Ends Meet: How Single Mothers Survive Welfare and Low-Wage Work.* New York: Russell Sage Foundation, 1997.

Garey, Anita Ilta. *Weaving Work and Motherhood.* Philadelphia: Temple University Press, 1999.

Gerson, Kathleen. *No Man's Land: Men's Changing Commitments to Family and Work.* New York: Basic Books, 1993.

Gibbs, Robert M. "Rural Labor Markets in an Era of Welfare Reform." In *Rural Dimensions of Welfare Reform,* edited by Bruce A. Weber, Greg J. Duncan, and Leslie A. Whitener. Kalamazooo, MI: W.E. Upjohn Institute for Employment Research, 2002.

Goffman, Irving. *The Presentation of Self in Everyday Life.* New York: Doubleday, 1959.

Harrison, Bennett, and Barry Bluestone. *The Second Shift: Working Parents and the Revolution at Home.* New York: Viking Press, 1989.

———. *The Great U-Turn: Corporate Restructuring and the Polarizing of America.* New York: Basic Books, Inc., 1998.

Hochschild, Arlie. *The Time Bind: When Work Becomes Home and Home Becomes Work.* New York: Metropolitan Books, 1997.

Imig, David R., Janet K. Bokemeier, Dennis Keefe, Cynthia Struthers, and Gail L. Imig. "The Context of Rural Economic Stress in Families with Children." *Michigan Family Review* 2 (1997): 69–82 .

Jarrett, Robin L. "Living Poor: Family Life Among Single Parent, African-American Women." *Social Problems* 41 (1994): 30–49.

Kanter, Rosabeth Moss. "Jobs and Families: Impact of Working Roles on Family Life." In *Work and Family,* edited by Patricia Voydanoff. Palo Alto: Mayfield, 1985.

———. *Working for Work in Rural Michigan: A Study of How Low-Income Mothers Negotiate Paid Work.* Ph.D. diss., Michigan State University, 2004.

Kelly, E. Brooke. "Leaving and Losing Jobs: Resistance of Rural Low-Income Mothers," *Journal of Poverty: Innovations on Social, Political, and Economic Inequalities* 9 (2005): 83–103.

Kurz, Demie. "Caring for Teenage Children." *Journal of Family Issues* 23 (2002): 748–767.

Menaghan, Elizabeth. "Work Experiences and Family Interaction Processes: The Long Reach of the Job?" *Annual Review of Sociology* 17 (1991): 419–444.

Michel, Sonya. "The Politics of Child Care in America's Public/Private Welfare State." In *Families in the U.S.: Kinship and Domestic Politics,* edited by Karen. V. Hansen and Anita I. Garey. Philadelphia: Temple University Press, 1998.

Nelson, Margaret K., and Joan Smith. *Working Hard and Making Do: Surviving in Small Town America.* Berkeley: University of California Press, 1999.

O'Hare, William P., and Kenneth M. Johnson. "Child Poverty in Rural America." *Population Reference Bureau* 4 (March 2004).

Oliker, Stacey J. "Work Commitment and Constraint Among Mothers on Workfare." *Journal of Contemporary Ethnography* 24 (1995): 165–194.

Pearce, Diane. "The Feminization of Poverty: Women, Work and Welfare." *The-Urban-and-Social-Change-Review* 11 (1978): 28–36.

Rosenbaum, René R. "Migrant and Seasonal Farmworkers in Michigan: From Dialogue to Action." *JSRI Working Paper* #39, The Julian Samora Research Institute, Michigan State University, East Lansing, Michigan, 2002.

Runyan, Jack L. "The Number of Hired Farmworkers Increased in 2000 and Most Now Come from Minority Groups." *Rural America* 16 (2001): 44–50.

Rural Sociological Task Force on Persistent Poverty. *Persistent Poverty in Rural America.* Boulder, CO: Westview Press, 1993.

Sassen, Saskia. *Globalization and Its Discontents: Essay on the New Mobility of People and Money.* New York: New Press, 1998.

Scott, Ellen K., Andrew S. London, and Allison Hurst. "Instabilities in Patchworks of Child Care When Moving from Welfare to Work." *Journal of Marriage and Family.* 67 (May 2005): 370–386.

Shelton, Beth Anne. "The Division of Household Labor" *Annual Review of Sociology* 22 (1996): 299–322.

Spalter-Roth, Roberta, Bererly Burr, and Heidi Hartmann with the assistance of Jill Braunstein and Robin Dennis. *Welfare That Works: The Working Lives of AFDC Recipients.* Washington, DC: Institute for Women's Policy Research, 1995.

Stacey, Judith. *Brave New Families: Stories of Domestic Upheaval in Late Twentieth Century America.* New York: Basic Books, 1990.

Walker, Susan, and Kathy Reschke. "Child-Care Issues Facing Contemporary Rural Families." In *Family Focus.* National Council on Family Relations, March 2003.

Weber, Bruce A., Greg J. Duncan, and Leslie A. Whitener. *Rural Dimensions of Welfare Reform.* Kalamazoo, MI: W.E. Upjohn Institute for Employment Research, 2002.

Wells, Barbara. *Family Continuity and Change in a Restructured Economy: A Case Study from Rural Michigan,* Michigan State University, Ph.D. Dissertation, Volumes 1 & 2, 1999.

Wilson, William Julius. *When Work Disappears: The World of the New Urban Poor.* New York: Vintage Books: A Division of Random House, Inc., 1996.

# CHAPTER 8

# CONFLICTS BETWEEN WAGE WORK AND CARE WORK: HOW SINGLE-PARENT FAMILIES OF CHILDREN WITH DISABILITIES MANAGE TO JUGGLE COMPETING DEMANDS

## *Ellen K. Scott*

In a system of privatized care such as the United States, the family, regardless of the number of adults present or the resources available, is fully responsible for all dependents—be they elderly, young, sick, or disabled. In the context of a capitalist economy, jobs are structured such that employees are expected to be able to negotiate the demands of wage work as if there were no competing demands of care work. To the extent that there are services and work supports available to enable families to manage care work and wage work, they are aimed at making more feasible this privatized system of care and more efficient the unencumbered worker. That there is a conflict between wage work and care work is not a new idea, nor is it news that single parents, particularly parents caring for children with special needs, face unique demands as they juggle the competing terrain of employment and care work. As indicated in the review below, the existing literature tells us something about patterns of care work and employment in families of children with disabilities, but we know less about the nuanced processes of decision making, the experiences of employment and care and how they do or do not conflict, and parents' emotional experiences as they negotiate these competing demands. In this paper, I look at a subset of parents, single parents, who are most likely to face conflicts between employment and care work in this system of privatized care and a capitalist economy.

For both single- and two-parent families, that balance between wage work and care work is shaped by a number of factors, including the financial resources available; structure of the employment, and the benefits such as health insurance, sick leave and vacation benefits; presence of an involved network of family and friends; severity of the child's condition; availability of alternative care; availability of other services, which can be beneficial to the child and thus potentially reduce disability-related disruptions to employment, but can also can require transportation and presence of parents during work hours; and the parent's beliefs about, and approach to, wage work and care work. In families with more intense obligations of care, for example, in the case I examine here, single parents and disabled children, caregivers are forced to juggle competing obligations that often greatly exceed those in the families of typically developing children. In the context of a reigning ideology of individualism, a privatized and market-based system for the provision of care, and the absence of public means for aiding families in the provision of care for chronically ill or disabled members, parents find themselves largely on their own. If they have the economic means to purchase extra support, or if they have family members who are willing to help out, the provision of care may be spread to more than one person. But most often the care work for disabled children has been the responsibility of the parent, with occasional respite help from other family or network members, if they are lucky.

## BACKGROUND

Estimates of the rate, and the number, of Americans under the age of 18 who experience limiting conditions due to illness and disability vary with definitions of disability, but indicate that between 6.5 and 15 percent of all children in the United State have a chronic condition.[1] However, rates of children with disabilities and chronic illnesses are disproportionately high in low-income families.[2] Researchers have found that those living below the poverty line are twice as likely to report that they have children with limitations or a disability as those living above the poverty line.[3] Children with limiting conditions also disproportionately live in single-parent families.[4]

Given the relationship between poverty, family structure, and rates of disability, it is not surprising to find the rate of disability is high among welfare-reliant families.[5] Loprest and Acs (1996) found that nationally 11–16 percent of families on AFDC had at least one child with some functional limitation, and Meyers, Lukemeyer, and Smeeding (1996; 1998) found that one-fifth of welfare-reliant families in four California counties reported having at least one child with chronic health problems or disability. Post-welfare reform data indicate that 20 percent or more families receiving welfare have a child with a health problem.[6] Further, researchers find that having a child with a disability is often an obstacle to leaving welfare.[7]

Families caring for children with disabilities face substantial challenges. Such children often require more frequent medical, psychological, or social service appointments; early intervention and special education programs; time-consuming and demanding routines for dressing, feeding, and minding, especially for those with mild to severe physical or emotional difficulties; more frequent school appointments; sometimes hospital trips and stays for urgent care; and time-consuming arrangement and management of alternative care when parents are employed and not able to provide the care themselves. Care for children with disabilities is more time consuming and more costly than caring for typically developing children.[8] Hence, parents often face difficult tradeoffs between providing this care informally within the family or working outside the home and coordinating formal care for their children.

The decision to reduce or stop work in order to provide necessary care is contingent on a host of factors, including: the severity of the child's disability or illness; the child's age and the presence of other children in the family; the presence of more than one child with special health care needs; the presence of another potential income-earner in the household; access to alternative sources of care; and the family's financial resources.[9] Cultural norms dictate that in both single- and two-parent families, the primary caretakers are the mothers in the vast majority of the cases. Therefore, the consequences for employment of care work for children with disabilities have been born primarily by mothers.[10] Compared to mothers of children without disabling conditions, mothers of children with disabling conditions have lower labor force participation rates.[11]

Effects of a child with special health care needs on employment vary by race/ethnicity, income/poverty status, and family structure.[12] Mothers in white, two-parent families with a disabled child have a significantly lower probability of work compared to similar families without a disabled child, but income is a crucial variable in this story. In high-income families, parents have more resources with which to purchase alternative care and the rates of maternal employment are similar to those families without disabled children. Work reduction is significantly greater in low-income families than it is in middle- and upper-income families. In two-parent families with a stable worker earning at least a moderate income, the costs of alternative care discourage maternal labor force participation and encourage maternal caregiving for the disabled child. However, in white single-parent families and all non-white families, the reduction in maternal work is *not* significant compared to similar families without a disabled child, perhaps because in very low-income and/or single-parent families, parents have less freedom to reduce work hours or leave the labor force altogether.[13]

Historically, some very low-income single-parent families have relied on cash welfare to support their care for disabled children.[14] However, extended reliance on cash welfare to provide this care is no longer possible. In 1996, the federal Personal Responsibility and Work Opportunity Reconciliation Act, or PRWORA, replaced Aid to Families with Dependent Children with Temporary Assistance to Needy Families. Among other changes, states were required to implement mandatory work requirements and establish time limits to cash benefit programs for poor families with children. These changes prevent low-income families of disabled children from relying on cash assistance and providing direct care until their child turns 18 years of age. Therefore, those families not included in state exemptions from these regulations have had to find a way to provide the care and do the wage work necessary to support their families financially.

Employment rates are affected by the challenge of finding reliable child care, which can be quite difficult.[15] Nonetheless, some mothers do manage to work when their children are in school, and others are able to arrange alternate center-based and relative care. While some studies find that mothers who have children with special health care needs are employed at the same rate as mothers in the general population, mothers of children with special health care needs often work part-time rather than full-time.[16] Such part-time work may be the result of work reductions to provide care.

The existing literature tells us something about patterns of care work and employment in families of children with disabilities. Much of it focuses on two-parent families. We know little about the processes of decision-making, the experiences of employment and how they conflict (or not) with care work, and the emotions single parents experience as they negotiate these competing demands. In a longer paper entitled "In this Labor of Love We Are Up Against the World," I drew on open-ended interviews with 20 families to examine how single- and two-parent families navigated the conflicts between wage work and care work when also caring for children with disabilities. Here I present the data from the interviews with 11 single parents, who were the most impoverished members of my sample and who faced the biggest challenges in juggling work and care and providing for their families. Their stories reveal the difficulties of privatized care in a nation committed to resisting any notion of communal responsibility for our young, our elderly, and our disabled or chronically ill. In these stories, the contradictions inherent in a philosophy of individualism as the grounding ideology in a society could not be more apparent. I look at how parents' attempts to juggle employment and care work reveal the untenable nature of our system of privatized care.

## METHODS AND SAMPLE

During spring and summer of 2005 I conducted 20 pilot interviews with families recruited primarily through two service organizations in Eugene, Oregon, and with a few families I knew personally or had met in the course of doing this project. As this was intended to be a pilot project in which I began to explore the issues families caring for children with disabilities face, I did not restrict the sample in any manner. That is, I did not define the sample by disability type, age of child, family structure, family income, or any other potential criteria. My intention was to use the opportunity to interview diverse families in order to deepen my sense of the issues they face, the strategies they use to negotiate the competing demands in their lives, and the potential differences between social/emotional/behavioral disorders and motor or other kinds of physical disabilities, or differences across income and family structure.

The majority of the families (14/20) in the study had children with social/emotional/behavioral disorders (including the autism spectrum, ADHD, bipolar disorder, and developmental delays) and some had more than one child with a disability. The disabilities in the group of 6 families I label "other medical" include Usher syndrome (involving hearing and sight impairment), Down's syndrome, cerebral palsy, and congenital diaphragmatic hernia. There were more single-parent families (11) than two-parent families (9). Nine of the single-parent families and 5 two-parent families had children with emotional/behavioral disorders. Two single-parent families and 4 two-parent families had children with other medical problems. Eleven families in my sample were low-income (9 of these single-parent families).

My current sample doesn't allow me to investigate some of the other issues which I plan to consider in the future when I expand my sample, for example, the different issues that rural families face when they are far from services and especially if they lack transportation, and the issues that immigrant and sometimes non-English speaking families and Native American families face in negotiating the demands of caring for children with disabilities, particularly given the cultural and linguistic barriers to the services available to them.

## THE JUGGLE OF CARE WORK AND WAGE WORK
## FOR SINGLE PARENTS

Most of the single parents in my sample had children with emotional/behavioral disorders (9 of 11); two single-parent families had children with other medical problems, in both instances cerebral palsy. All of these families were headed by women. Five single parents did not work outside the home and six did. All five women who were not employed had children with emotional/behavioral disorders. Two of these five women were also disabled themselves, and one had serious health problems. Of the women who were employed, two had health problems.

### Single Unemployed Parents

For three of the single unemployed parents with whom I spoke, the demands of the care work for their disabled children constituted merely one of a myriad of problems which prevented them from sustaining employment. They described their struggles with serious mental and/or physical health problems, histories of involvement with men who were substance abusers and violent, and other serious challenges besides their children's disabilities. They relied (intermittently) on cash benefits from TANF and sometimes SSI to support their families, often in combination with food stamps and the Oregon Health Plan (the state Medicaid program). Linda's story illustrates:

Linda had three boys, the youngest diagnosed with autism. She was severely disabled from a back injury sustained about 15 years ago. She left her husband, the father of her three children, many years ago due to his drug use. She worried that perhaps his drug use had something to do with her youngest child's autism and her oldest child's defiant conduct disorder. The chronic pain she suffered required almost heroic efforts on her part to continue the daily tasks of raising three boys, regardless of their disabilities. Despite her pain and immobility, she spent enormous time and energy managing her children's problems, advocating for them, arranging appropriate services through the schools, struggling to find summer programs that would take them, and often searching for appropriate school settings for each of her two troubled boys. In reflecting on what it has taken to manage her own pain and her children's needs, she said: "I was beginning to wonder if I could be a mom anymore, that they were going to have to go somewhere else. That the pain was getting me down so much I can't always keep the house clean, I just don't feel like I can do the things a mom needs to do [crying] and I love them so much."

The other two single unemployed parents do not face additional severe obstacles to employment. In one instance, the sole reason she is not currently employed is the care work demanded because of her son's autism. I include her story below in the discussion of employment and care work.

## Single Parents' Struggles to Sustain Employment and Care for their Kids

The single parents with whom I spoke all told stories of the extraordinary difficulties they had managing their paid work and their care work. Their stories included tales of jobs lost due to the conflicts between the job and the work of managing their child's illness. Those who were currently employed told stories of unusual employers who were willing to create as much job flexibility as they needed to manage their paid work and care work without conflict. Their stories make clear: their children always come first. Parents' accounts reveal that they see themselves as the experts in managing their child's illness ("no one knows my child the way that I do"), and in their opinion, there is no one else who can do the job as well as they can.

Their care work involved a range of activities from arranging for services provided by others to learning how to provide necessary therapeutic interventions at home to advocating on the child's behalf in the school system. There was little or no respite care available to them, either for the occasional break parents needed to preserve their mental health, or on an ongoing basis, for example, after school. Thus, the obstacles to their employment were many, including the hours needed to manage and provide the care their child needs, the appointments that often disrupted a work day, the lack of alternative care necessary to free the parents to work a full day, and finally the sheer exhaustion from doing not just a typical second shift but care work that far exceeds the demands of a typically developing child.

## Losing Jobs

A number of parents lost jobs due to the difficulties of managing their children with social/emotional/behavioral disorders. Vivian, who was not employed when I interviewed her, talked about the steady decline in her employment situation culminating in her unemployment and reliance on SSI and child support in order to get by while she was managing her child's treatment for autism.

Vivian had been employed as a paramedic for years. She left this job when her husband became abusive and ultimately she could not trust him at home with the children, nor did she trust him with her children's caretaker. She quit her job in order to care for her family. Initially, she tried to run a day care out of her home, but she said:

> The abuse was horrible. The women's shelter came and rescued us and the police removed him. Because the police were involved, I lost my child care license. Ever since then, it's been down hill.

After leaving the shelter, getting situated in a new home, she found employment in a large national chain retail store. Around the time her son turned 3, she, the Head Start teachers, and doctors began to suspect he had some problems and when he was in first grade he was diagnosed with autism. Vivian felt that there "were no resources for him [in that town]," hence the difficulty finding the diagnosis.

During those years, Vivian had a very difficult time juggling paid work and care work. She said:

> [My son's] needs became more and more, him needing me. He failed in child care, failed in school, the school called me: "Come get him, he's out of control, he's hurting himself, or he's not being safe, or he's running [away]." [My employer] finally said, "We have to put you on FMLA (Family Medical Leave Act) . . . ." The problem was that there were no physicians, no counselors, no one who was trained in [autism], that had any clue what to do for [my son], what meds he should be on. . . . So we were just getting no where. We were just spinning our wheels, and I was losing my job because I couldn't go to work. Every single day the school was calling me, and I couldn't find child care because the providers were quitting on me.

After her employer suggested she take family medical leave for a while, she "begged" for a transfer to the Eugene store because Eugene had "rave reviews for autism resources." Desperate for help, Vivian chose to uproot her entire family from their home and move them to a new place. Her employer agreed to the transfer: "They made a slot for me because I had done so well. I mean I really was a valuable employee, a good worker; I was head of their marketing department, despite everything that was going on. So they went ahead and transferred me."

She managed to find a school she liked for her autistic son and the child care she needed for the additional hours when she was at work, but she soon found herself unable to work. Her abusive ex-husband found them and seeing him caused her son to regress severely. Once again, Vivian found herself overwhelmed by his needs. The child care provider quit because he was throwing tantrums and was unmanageable; the school began calling her every day again. She again used family medical leave to try to sort out the problems, but with only a few weeks left of FMLA, she was ultimately terminated from her job. She continued to be involved daily with his care—at school, staying home so that she was available when he was kicked out of school, developing an IEP, finding a new school for him, getting the therapy he needed, etc. She briefly tried to work for a construction company, but again could not find the after school care she needed. Furthermore, she needed to keep her income low so that she still qualified to have his medical care covered by SSI. "His pills alone cost $3000 per month. That's just his meds. That doesn't include the weekly doctor's visits, counselors, etc." When we spoke, Vivian felt stuck. Her 9-year-old son's care needs were too demanding and she needed to keep her earnings down in order remain eligible for the health insurance she needed desperately.

As Vivien told this story, she did not describe a sense of despair, but rather was fairly matter-of-fact about the situation. Her son had been doing better of late and that gave her optimism that they might be turning a corner. Not so the story of Karen, who expressed considerable distress over the ways in which she found her life unmanageable due to her son's emotional-behavioral problems. Karen's 8-year-old son was diagnosed with a number of problems: oppositional defiant disorder, obsessive-compulsive disorder, ADHD, and possible Asperger's. Karen had recently lost a job as a medical transcriptionist at a hospital as a result of her inability to juggle her son's needs and her work. She said:

> The reason I lost my job is that I couldn't get there on time [because of the struggles in the morning with my son]. The interesting thing about that is that I'm such a responsible person. In my life, I've been very responsible and on time and worked for powerful people, and there has never been a problem about being late. In the last few years, with the stress of [my son] and the divorce, I could not get there on time . . . and I pretty much lost my job because I couldn't get there on time.

Karen's days were consumed with advocacy for her son at school, working with teachers to develop systems that would achieve results with her son. She had found that positive reinforcement was the key with her son; some teachers were willing to participate and others were not. She was considering home schooling for him after two very frustrating years trying to establish a program that worked for him in the public schools. As I discuss below, Karen was arranging her employment to accommodate the demands of caring for her son, but she also felt enormously frustrated by the limitations in her own life as a consequence of caring for him.

Other single parents with children with emotional/behavioral disorders also reported that they had lost jobs when the demands of care work conflicted with their employment obligations. The most typical scenario was that they needed to be available to go into school at a moment's notice because their children were having a bad day. Without a job that could or would allow for such flexibility, they were either fired or had to quit because they needed to leave work on repeated occasions to be with their children. Such unpredictable care work obligations were not issues the parents of children with other medical problems talked about. Emotional/behavioral disorders were particularly demanding in this regard.

### Jobs that Work, Employers Who Care

Most crucial in the employment of the single parents caring for children with disabilities is job flexibility: the ability to leave when called to care for their child, work different times to make up hours, take days off when necessary for doctor and therapeutic appointments, and in some instances the ability to work part-time or split shifts. Among the women with whom I spoke, this was available in the context of small companies in which employers or supervisors explicitly understood and supported parents' obligations to care. Sometimes mothers worked in organizations that provided services to families with children or adults with disabilities and there they found tremendous empathy for their plight. In each instance, the women had jobs that worked, and employers who cared.

Karen, whose story is introduced above, had tried to get a graduate degree in counseling but caring for her son had prevented her finishing her degree. After her divorce, she had resorted to medical transcription, a skill she'd acquired in the military, although she hated the work. She did it for the flexibility if afforded her. This was the job from which she was fired the year before I interviewed her. It was to this work that she was just returning when we spoke:

> [After being fired and taking a break from work], I had to find a job. I've been really kind of looking at my options. I said I would never transcribe again. So I'm compromising now going back to transcription only because it gives me the flexibility that is required for [my son]. I can't have, I can't do the 9–5, it's just not possible. Unless we had an assistant, unless we hired someone to come and be here. And there goes my whole income, and my ex just refuses [to pay for care].

Despite loathing the work, Karen found a company that would hire her to do transcription, but allow her to work at home doing a split shift, 4 hours in the morning and 4 hours in the evening. With this schedule, Karen thought that she could manage the dual demands of her care work and her wage work.

Sarah, the mother of two boys aged 7 and 4, had an associate's degree in accounting and worked full time for a company that manages data. Her older son had multiple diagnoses: ADHD, pervasive developmental disorder, and potentially bipolar disorder. She said it was possible for her to be employed full time at this small company because her employer understood her situation and is willing to accommodate her needs. When she was arriving late for work after driving both her children to school because the older child had missed the bus, her employer offered her a flexible schedule. He said, "Why don't you just work 8:30 to 5:30 instead, or if you make it in by 8:15 then work until 5:15. It's okay." Further, she said,

> I can take a full day off if I have to, or a half-day off, and it's not a problem. I don't have to make up the work on the weekend or anything. School calls and says, "Hey, your kid can't ride the bus because he's not being safe, he won't put his seat belt on," and my boss will say, "Okay, go get your kid. I got it. It's okay." . . . He himself has told me family's first. "Take care of your kids."

Having lost at least one job because she was being called into school frequently, Sarah was amazed by and deeply appreciative of her boss's attitude. However, this flexibility was a product of his generosity, and Sarah could not rely on it. She had only been in the job for 6 months when I spoke with her. Hopefully, her employer's patience did not wear thin.

Diane, the mother of an 8-year-old son with autism, said that job flexibility was the most critical asset for her. Receiving $650/month child support, Diane made do in a job paying $12/hour with no benefits (her son was covered by the Oregon Health Plan, but she had no health insurance). She said, "I have no benefits. I just have the flexibility and that in itself is a benefit and their support. I could not ask for a better place to work." She worked 20 hours/week and was able to take time off when she or her son got sick, or during the summer when her son was out of school and she could find no alternative care. Recounting a time when she missed work for weeks, she remarked: "Where I work, they are very supportive and understanding. I was worried, am I going to lose my job, but they like me so they are very flexible."

The company, where she worked as a research assistant, created educational materials for people who have developmental disabilities. Therefore, perhaps they had greater understanding of her situation than other workplaces might have. For Diane, it was also very important that she work part-time so that she could be present for the demands of her son's care work: "The reason I work part-time is that I fit my schedule into [my son's] needs so that I can be present with him after he's out of school. I can do his homework with him, like if he had OT or any other needs, I'm there. . . . Keeping the routine, keeping [my son] on task, making sure his health is okay, all those things that come up with kids with autism—the cycling, the behaviors, all those issues." His schedule was crucial, she explained: "You have to be on it every day. You cannot let up."

It was financially feasible for Diane to manage because she had some child support income and she lived in low-income housing. Her priority was the care work for her son. For her, the job was perfect, and greater income from full-time work could not compensate for the time she would lose with her son. Further, she like most of the parents I interviewed, could not find regular alternative care that would allow her to work full-time or during the summers if she wanted to. But Diane's story was another story of a small company with a compassionate employer. It is hard to imagine how she would be able to provide the care she does for her son in more typical, less flexible work situations.

Other parents found similarly flexible employment situations and/or worked part-time, but not everyone was so lucky. Anna, for example, worked for a large timber company, and had a 14-year-old son with ADHD, depression, and a possible bipolar diagnosis. She could not leave work if she was called in to his school. Therefore, she worried a lot about whether she would be sanctioned for missing work, or whether she would ever risk losing her job. After years of cycling from welfare to low-wage work, this stable job with decent pay and benefits was well worth holding on to, so Anna did everything she could to be the reliable employee she knew her company expected. Although things were better by the time I interviewed her, Anna had gone through periods of having to contend with her son's disruptions at school. During those periods, she relied on the one friend she could call for help. "I'm being called once a week at least [before when he was in middle school]. . . . Sometimes he'd get suspended for 3 days at a time. And it was frequent enough that work was telling me that, you know, you have to try to make a plan because this can't happen all the time." Sometimes, if she couldn't leave work and her friend was unavailable, Anna would let him walk home when he was kicked out. Other times she would bring him home and go back to work and stay late. Her employer had not yet actually threatened to fire her, but she worried about it a lot.

## CONCLUSION

These single-parent families reflected the national population of single parent families in a number of respects: compared to the two-parent families in my sample, they were more likely to have incomes below 200 percent of poverty, the parent was more likely to also endure a chronic illness or disability, and they were more likely to have more than one child with a disability. With only one adult in the household, their struggles to manage the competing demands of caring for a child with a disability and sustaining employment were extreme.

Those, like Vivian, who could not find work that was sufficiently flexible and that had the additional work and health care benefits necessary to enable them to meet their child's predictable and unpredictable needs, eventually opted out of the workforce, at least for a period of time. Others suffered from their own disabilities and could not manage to work and provide care for their children.

These single unemployed parents relied on combinations of multiple sources of financial and material support—TANF, SSI, child support, Food Stamps, and housing assistance, if available. But these sources were often unreliable. Families receive child support when fathers have an income and they are willing to provide it or the child support division is capable of enforcing their parental obligations. Receipt of Supplemental Security Income is contingent on children fitting into ever-narrowing definitions of qualified disabilities. The process of applying for SSI is long and cumbersome and many parents do not pursue it, because they assume that their child will not be eligible for benefits. Waiting lists for housing assistance are long, and it is often difficult to find landlords who accept subsidies. In order to rely on TANF to provide care, parents of children with disabilities must be exempt from work requirements (something that varies with case workers and state policy). In most states, they eventually face time limits which prevent them from relying on this source of income for an extended period. In Oregon, until summer of 2005 the state was given a federal waiver from the implementation of time limits. As long as a recipient participated in employment activities, there was no 5-year time limit imposed. As of summer 2005, the state was no longer exempt from time limits and DHS was required to begin cutting anyone who received cash benefits for 36 months continuously between summer 2003 and 2006.

Public sources of income available to support a family caring for a child with a disability are inadequate and/or short-term. Without private resources to rely on, single parents find it virtually impossible to care for their children without working. Those parents who are not employed often sacrifice the family's financial well-being in order to provide care. Those who do work, struggle to find inadequate, expensive alternative care, which is often unavailable at all, and they are often forced to compromise the care their children receive

The single parents in this sample who were employed told stories of losing jobs, having to rely on the kindness of employers for the kind of flexibility they needed, and working part-time in order to have adequate time to care for their children. They had difficulty finding alternative care either to allow them to work more, or to provide them with the occasional respite they desperately needed. Typically, work schedules were entirely organized around their children's care needs. In the one case in which the parent (Anna) worked full time in a relatively inflexible job, her child was a young teen and she had to rely occasionally on him to care for himself. She was not comfortable with this solution, but she saw no other option. After years of relying on welfare to support herself and her child, she was determined not to lose this relatively good job.

These stories reveal the conundrum of the privatized provision of care and jobs structured by a liberal, free-market economy. They reveal the extraordinary struggle of single-parent families to manage the needs of their children and the demands of their jobs, in the absence of other sources of financial support or alternative care for their kids. Families are isolated. There are few public resources to assist with care needs. The labor market is organized such that employers are entitled to ignore completely the care demands of an employee; they have no social or economic obligation to accommodate the conflicts between the wage labor and the caring labor. Single parents manage to provide financially for their families and provide the care work that is needed through creative and often lucky solutions, given this unforgiving and seemingly untenable context. They manage on little money; they rarely take a break from work or care; they find employers who provide the flexibility they need; they are resilient when they lose jobs and must begin again.

In the context of a society which presumes parents, usually mothers, can and ought to be fully responsible for the care of their children with few public resources to assist them, parents demonstrate an extraordinary capacity to accommodate this double bind structured by work and care. They do more than simply manage their circumstances: they face the demands with dedication, resilience, and often the creativity necessary to make it all work. Despite the constraints on their lives and the lack of public resources to assist them, most parents expressed a sense of optimism about, and commitment to, their child's well-being, born of the deep and enduring love they felt for their child. Their resilience was staggering, especially in the single-parent households. This was reflected in children who were doing relatively well, considering the scarcity of resources. Mixed with this, however, was a sense of fear and despair as parents looked to the future, with no end to their care work in sight and no apparent resources available to help ease the load.

As the parents endure by paying an enormous personal and economic cost to give their kids the best life they can manage, perhaps we should ask how much better off parents and children might be if we considered this labor a social good, a community service, as is now being debated among TANF reformers? As community service, we might provide this work the public support it deserves? The Americans with Disabilities Act demands that as a society we commit to creating the conditions under which people with disabilities have equal opportunities to thrive. This begins in childhood and it begins in the home. Providing parents with the financial resources necessary for them to care for their special needs children directly or to purchase care, and investing in training and building the public infrastructure of services necessary to adequately care for children with disabilities, are first necessary steps toward this goal of equality of opportunity.

## NOTES

1. Barbara Leondard,  Janny Dwyer Brust, and James J. Sapienza, 1992. "Financial and Time Costs to Parents of Severely Disabled Children." *Public Health Reports* 107(3): 302–312;

Paul W. Newacheck and Neal Halfon, 1998. "Prevalence and Impact of Disabling Chronic Conditions in Childhood." *American Journal of Public Health* 88: 610–617.

2. Glenn T. Fujiura, Kiyoshi Yamaki, and Susan Czechowicz, 1998. "Disability Among Ethnic and Racial Minorities in the United States." *Journal of Disability Policy Studies* 9(2): 111–130; Glenn T. Fujiura and Kiyoshi Yamaki, 2000. "Trends in Demography of Childhood Poverty and Disability." *Exceptional Children* 66: 187–199; Dennis P. Hogan and Michael E. Msall, 2002. "Family Structure and Resources and the Parenting of Children With Disabilities and Functional Limitations." In *Parenting and Child's World: Influences on Academic, Intellectual, and Social-Emotional Development*. Mahwah, NJ: Lawrence Erlbaum Associates; Jane E. Miller, 2000. "The Effects of Race/Ethnicity and Income on Early Childhood Asthma Prevalence and Health Care Use." *American Journal of Public Health* 90: 428–430; Paul W. Newacheck, 1994. "Poverty and Childhood Chronic Illness." *Archive of Pediatric Adolescent Medicine* 148: 1143–1149; Newacheck and Halfon, "Prevalence and Impact of Disabling Chronic Conditions in Childhood," for example.

3. Fujiura and Yamaki, 2000. "Trends in Demography of Childhood Poverty and Disability." ; Paul W. Newacheck, W. J. Jameson, and Neal Halfon, 1994. "Health Status and Income: The Impact of Poverty on Child Health." *Journal of School Health* 64: 229–233.

4. Fujiura, Yamaki, and Czechowicz, "Disability Among Ethnic and Racial Minorities In the United States"; Dennis P. Hogan and Michael E. Msall, *Parenting and Child's World: Influences on Academic, Intellectual, and Social-Emotional Development.*; Newacheck and Halfon, "Prevalence and Impact of Disabling Chronic Conditions in Childhood."

5. Peter D. Brandon and Dennis P. Hogan, 2004. "Impediments to Mothers Leaving Welfare: The Role of Maternal and Child Disability." *Population Research and Policy Review* 23(4): 419–436; Pamela Loprest and Gregory Acs, 1996. *Profile of Disability Among Families on AFDC*. Washington, DC: The Urban Institute; Marcia K. Meyers, Anna Lukemeyer, and Timothy Smeeding, 1998. "The Cost of Caring: Childhood Disability and Poor Families." *Social Service Review* June: 209–233; Denise F. Polit, Andrew S. London, and John M. Martinez, 2001. *The Health of Urban Poor Women. Findings from the Project on Devolution and Urban Change*. New York: Manpower Demonstration Research Corporation.

6. Sandra Danziger, Mary Corcoran, Sheldon Danziger, Colleen Heflin, Ariel Kalil, Judith Levine, Daniel Rosen, Kristin Seefeldt, Kristine Siefert, and Richard Tolman, 2000. "Barriers to the Employment of Welfare Recipients." In Robert Cherry and William M. Rodgers III (eds.), *Prosperity for All? The Economic Boom and African Americans*, pp. 245–287. New York: Russell Sage Foundation Press; Polit, London, and Martinez, *The Health of Urban Poor Women. Findings from the Project on Devolution and Urban Change*.

7. Brandon and Hogan, 2004. "Impediments to Mothers Leaving Welfare: The Role of Maternal And Child Disability" ; Pamela Loprest and Gregory Acs, 1996. *Profile of Disability Among Families on AFDC*. Washington, DC: The Urban Institute; Debra Skinner, William Lachicotte, and Linda Burton, 2007. "The Difference Disability Makes: Managing Childhood Disability, Poverty, and Work." In Jane Henrici (ed.), *Doing Without: Women and Work After Welfare Reform*. Tucson, AZ: University of Arizona Press.

8. Frank J. Floyd and Erin M. Gallagher, 1997. "Parental Stress, Care Demands, and Use of Support Services for School-Age Children with Disabilities and Behavior Problems." *Family Relations* 46: 359–371; P. Jacobs and S. McDermott, 1989. "Family Caregiver Costs of Chronically Ill and Handicapped Children: Method and Literature Review," *Public Health Reports* 104: 158–163; Andrew S. London, Ellen K. Scott, and Vicki Hunter, 2002. "Health-related Carework for Children in the Context of Welfare Reform." In Francesca Cancian, Demie Kurz, Andrew London, Rebecca Reviere, and Mary Tuominen (eds.), *Child Care and*

*Inequality: Re-thinking Carework for Children and Youth*. New York: Routledge Press; Michelle Rogers and Dennis Hogan, 2003. Family Life with Children with Disabilities: the key role of rehabilitation. *Journal of Marriage and the Family* 65(4): 818–833; Sloper, Patricia and Stephen Turner, 1992. "Service Needs of Families of Children With Severe Physical Disability." *Child: Care, Health and Development* 18: 259–282.

9. C. L. Booth, , and J. F. Kelly, 1999. "Child Care and Employment in Relation to Infants' Disabilities and Risk Factors." *American Journal on Mental Retardation* 104: 117–130; Peter D. Brandon, 2000. "Child Care Utilization Among Working Mothers Raising Children With Disabilities." *Journal of Family and Economic Issues* 21(4): 343–364; Michelle Rogers and Dennis Hogan, 2003. Family Life with Children with Disabilities: The key role of rehabilitation. *Journal of Marriage and the Family* 65(4): 818–833; D.S. Salkever, 1985. "Parental Opportunity Costs and Other Economic Costs of Children's Disabling Conditions." In N. Hobbs and J. M. Perrin (eds.), *Issues in the Care of Children with a Chronic Illness*, pp. 864–879. San Francisco: Jossey-Bass.

10. Brandon, "Child Care Utilization Among Working Mothers Raising Children With Disabilities"; N. Breslau, D. Salkever, and K.S. Staruch, 1982. "Women's Labor Force Activity and Responsibilities for Disabled Dependents: A Study of Families With Disabled Children." *Journal of Health and Social Behavior* 23: 169–183; S. L. Ettner, 1995. "The Impact of "Parent Care" on Female Labor Supply Decisions." *Demography* 32: 63–80; Dennis P. Hogan and Michael E. Msall, 2002. "Family Structure and Resources and the Parenting of Children With Disabilities and Functional Limitations." In *Parenting and Child's World: Influences on Academic, Intellectual, and Social-Emotional Development*. Mahwah, NJ: Lawrence Erlbaum Associates; Rogers and Hogan "Family Life with Children with Disabilities: The Key Role of Rehabilitation."

11. Brandon, "Child Care Utilization Among Working Mothers Raising Children With Disabilities" ; Breslau, Salkever, and Staruch,1982. "Women's Labor Force Activity and Responsibilities for Disabled Dependents: A Study of Families With Disabled Children." ; Marji E. Erickson and C.C. Upshur, 1989. "Caretaking burden and social support: Comparison of mothers of infants with and without disabilities." *American Journal on Mental Retardation* 94: 250–258.

12. Breslau, Salkever, and Staruch, 1982. "Women's Labor Force Activity and Responsibilities for Disabled Dependents: A Study of Families With Disabled Children."; Hogan and Msall, *Parenting and Child's World: Influences on Academic, Intellectual, and Social-Emotional Development*. Mahwah, NJ: Lawrence Erlbaum Associates; Meyers, Lukemeyer, and Smeeding, "The Cost of Caring: Childhood Disability and Poor Families"; Salkever, *Issues in the Care of Children with a Chronic Illness*.

13. Breslau, Salkever, and Staruch, 1982. "Women's Labor Force Activity and Responsibilities for Disabled Dependents: A Study of Families With Disabled Children"; Salkever, *Issues in the Care of Children with a Chronic Illness*. San Francisco: Jossey-Bass.

14. Brandon and Hogan, "Impediments to Mothers Leaving Welfare: The Role of Maternal and Child Disability"; London, Scott, and Hunter, *Child Care and Inequality: Re-thinking Carework for Children and Youth*; Pamela Loprest and Gregory Acs, 1996. *Profile of Disability Among Families on AFDC*. Washington, DC: The Urban Institute; Marcia K. Meyers, Anna Lukemeyer, and Timothy M. Smeeding, 1996. *Work, Welfare, and the Burden of Disability: Caring for Special Needs of Children in Poor Families*. Syracuse, NY: Syracuse University Maxwell School of Citizenship and Public Affairs, Center for Policy Research.

15. Katherine Beh Neas and Jennifer Meazey, 2003. *Addressing Child Care Challenges for Children with Disabilities: Proposals for CCDBG and IDEA Reauthorization*. Washington, DC:

Center for Law and Social Policy; Brandon, "Child Care Utilization Among Working Mothers Raising Children with Disabilities"; Breslau, Salkever, and Staruch, 1982. "Women's Labor Force Activity and Responsibilities for Disabled Dependents: A Study of Families With Disabled Children"; Marji Erickson Warfield and Penny Hauser-Cram, 1996. "Child Care Needs, Arrangements, and Satisfaction of Mothers of Children with Developmental Disabilities." *Mental Retardation* 34(5):294–302.

16. L. Landis, 1992, "Marital Employment and Child Care Status of Mothers with Infants and Toddlers with Disabilities." *Topics in Early Childhood Special Education* 12: 496–507.

## REFERENCES

Beh Neas, Katherine, and Jennifer Meazey. 2003. *Addressing Child Care Challenges for Children with Disabilities: Proposals for CCDBG and IDEA Reauthorization.* Washington, DC: Center for Law and Social Policy.

Booth, C. L., and J.F. Kelly. 1999. "Child care and employment in relation to infants' disabilities and risk factors." *American Journal on Mental Retardation* 104: 117–130.

Brandon, Peter D. 2000. "Child care utilization among working mothers raising children with disabilities." *Journal of Family and Economic Issues* 21(4): 343–364.

Brandon, Peter D. and Dennis P. Hogan. 2004. "Impediments to mothers leaving welfare: The role of maternal and child disability." *Population Research and Policy Review* 23(4): 419–436.

Breslau, N., D. Salkever, and K.S. Staruch. 1982. "Women's labor force activity and responsibilities for disabled dependents: A study of families with disabled children." *Journal of Health and Social Behavior* 23: 169–183.

Danziger, Sandra, Mary Corcoran, Sheldon Danziger, Colleen Heflin, Ariel Kalil, Judith Levine, Daniel Rosen, Kristin Seefeldt, Kristine Siefert, and Richard Tolman. 2000. "Barriers to the employment of welfare recipients." In Robert Cherry and William M. Rodgers III (eds.), *Prosperity for All? The Economic Boom and African Americans*, pp. 245–287. New York: Russell Sage Foundation Press.

Erickson, Marji E. and C.C. Upshur. 1989. "Caretaking burden and social support: Comparison of mothers of infants with and without disabilities." *American Journal on Mental Retardation* 94: 250–258.

Ettner, S. L. 1995. "The impact of 'parent care' on female labor supply decisions." *Demography* 32: 63–80.

Floyd, Frank J. and Erin M. Gallagher. 1997. "Parental Stress, Care Demands, and Use of Support Services for School-Age Children with Disabilities and Behavior Problems." *Family Relations* 46: 359–371.

Fujiura, Glenn T., and Kiyoshi Yamaki. 2000. "Trends in demography of childhood poverty and disability." *Exceptional Children* 66: 187–199.

Fujiura, Glenn T., Kiyoshi Yamaki, and Susan Czechowicz. 1998. "Disability among ethnic and racial minorities in the United States." *Journal of Disability Policy Studies* 9(2): 111–130.

Hogan, Dennis P. and Michael E. Msall. 2002. "Family structure and resources and the parenting of children with disabilities and functional limitations." In *Parenting and Child's World: Influences on Academic, Intellectual, and Social-Emotional Development*. Mahwah, NJ: Lawrence Erlbaum Associates.

Jacobs, P. and S. McDermott. 1989. "Family caregiver costs of chronically ill and handicapped children: Method and literature review." *Public Health Reports* 104: 158–163.

Landis, L. 1992. "Marital employment and child care status of mothers with infants and toddlers with disabilities." *Topics in Early Childhood Special Education* 12: 496–507.

Leondard, Barbara, Janny Dwyer Brust, and James J. Sapienza. 1992. "Financial and time costs to parents of severely disabled children." *Public Health Reports* 107(3): 302–312.

London, Andrew S., Ellen K. Scott, and Vicki Hunter. 2002. "Health-related carework for children in the context of welfare reform." In Francesca Cancian, Demie Kurz, Andrew London, Rebecca Reviere, and Mary Tuominen (eds.), *Child Care and Inequality: Re-thinking Carework for Children and Youth*. New York: Routledge Press.

Loprest, Pamela and Gregory Acs. 1996. *Profile of Disability Among Families on AFDC.* Washington, DC: The Urban Institute.

Meyers, Marcia K., Anna Lukemeyer, and Timothy Smeeding. 1996. *Work, Welfare, and the Burden of Disability: Caring for Special Needs of Children in Poor Families.* Syracuse, NY: Syracuse University Maxwell School of Citizenship and Public Affairs, Center for Policy Research.

Meyers, Marcia K., Anna Lukemeyer, and Timothy M. Smeeding. 1998. "The cost of caring: Childhood disability and poor families." *Social Service Review* June: 209–233.

Miller, Jane E. 2000. "The effects of race/ethnicity and income on early childhood asthma prevalence and health care use." *American Journal of Public Health* 90: 428–430.

Newacheck, Paul W. 1994. "Poverty and childhood chronic illness." *Archive of Pediatric Adolescent Medicine* 148: 1143–1149.

Newacheck, Paul W. and Neal Halfon. 1998. "Prevalence and impact of disabling chronic conditions in childhood." *American Journal of Public Health* 88: 610–617.

Newacheck, Paul. W., W. J. Jameson, and Neal Halfon. 1994. "Health status and income: The impact of poverty on child health." *Journal of School Health* 64: 229–233.

Polit, Denise F., Andrew S. London, and John M. Martinez. 2001. *The Health of Urban Poor Women. Findings from the Project on Devolution and Urban Change.* New York: Manpower Demonstration Research Corporation.

Rogers, Michelle and Dennis Hogan. 2003. "Family life with children with disabilities: The key role of rehabilitation." *Journal of Marriage and the Family* 65(4): 818–833.

Salkever, D. S. 1985. "Parental opportunity costs and other economic costs of children's disabling conditions." In N. Hobbs and J. M. Perrin (eds.), *Issues in the Care of Children with a Chronic Illness*, pp. 864–879. San Francisco: Jossey-Bass.

Skinner, Debra, William Lachicotte, and Linda Burton. Forthcoming. "The difference disability makes: Managing childhood disability, poverty, and work." In J. Henrici (ed.), *Doing Without: Women and work after welfare reform*. Tucson, Arizona: University of Arizona Press.

Sloper, Patricia and Stephen Turner. 1992. "Service needs of families of children with severe physical disability." *Child: Care, Health and Development* 18: 259–282.

Warfield, Marji Erickson and Penny Hauser-Cram. 1996. "Child care needs, arrangements, and satisfaction of mothers of children with developmental disabilities." *Mental Retardation* 34(5): 294–302.

CHAPTER 9

# CHILDREN'S EXPOSURE TO NEIGHBORHOOD POVERTY AND AFFLUENCE IN THE UNITED STATES, 1990–2000*

## *Jeffrey M. Timberlake and Joseph Michael*

American social scientists have long been interested in the effects of poverty on children's physical, psychological, and social development. This scholarly focus issues from at least two sources: first, the United States exhibits the highest child poverty rates in the Western industrialized world.[1] In the year 2000, the U.S. child poverty rate stood at 22 percent, compared to 15 percent in Canada, Australia, and the United Kingdom, 10 percent in Austria, Germany, and the Netherlands, and less than 5 percent in Denmark, Finland, Norway, and Sweden.[2] Of the 30 member nations in the Organization for Economic Cooperation and Development, only Mexico suffers a higher child poverty rate than the United States (27% in 2000).[3]

Second, research has demonstrated that family poverty is strongly associated with indicators of child well-being.[4] According to national-level estimates from the late 1980s and early 1990s, children aged 5 to 7 from poor families (incomes in the lowest quintile) score an average of one-half to four-fifths of a standard deviation lower on standardized reading and math tests and two-fifths of a standard deviation higher on an index of behavioral problems, compared to children reared in affluent families (incomes in the upper quintile). By the teen years, girls from poor families are over eight times more likely to become a teen mother than girls from affluent families, and the high school dropout rate is more than five times higher for poor children relative to children from affluent families.[5]

Thus, the combination of high rates and strong associations with measures of child well-being has led scholars to focus on family poverty in understanding outcomes for American children. And, given that family poverty rates have historically been at least two to three times higher for blacks and Hispanics than for whites and Asians,[6] much scholarly attention has been paid to understanding the influence of exposure to family poverty on racial and ethnic inequality in children's well-being.

Complementing this well deserved focus on family poverty, scholars have increasingly added a focus on *neighborhood* poverty in attempting to understand variation in outcomes for children, particularly variation by race/ethnicity and social class. Although sociological inquiry into the effects of neighborhood characteristics on the behavior and life chances of individuals spans nearly the entire history of the discipline, William Julius Wilson is frequently credited with rekindling sociologists' concern with "neighborhood effects" on children.[7] In *The Truly Disadvantaged*, Wilson argues that a combination of urban deindustrialization and the migration of middle-class blacks out of inner city neighborhoods in the 1970s resulted in sharp increases in the concentration of poverty in urban black neighborhoods. According to Wilson, these trends have had catastrophic effects on the capacity of inner city parents to socialize children successfully.[8] Wilson's work triggered an avalanche of inquiry into the effects of neighborhood context on child well-being.[9] Scholars have tended to focus on childhood because there are sound theoretical reasons to suspect that neighborhoods have powerful influences on children's life chances. Early childhood and adolescence are crucial periods in which life trajectories are shaped via the influences of peer relationships, schooling, and initial labor market experiences, and children are overwhelmingly exposed to these influences in their local neighborhood.

Among the many outcomes that have been studied recently are school achievement,[10] teenage sexual behavior,[11] and delinquency.[12] Taken as a whole, the findings of this research have been mixed;[13] however, the bulk of the evidence indicates that neighborhoods exert small to moderate independent effects on children. Prior research has also shown that black and Hispanic families are much more likely than statistically equivalent white families to live in poor neighborhoods,[14] and that the concentration of neighborhood poverty soared in the 1970s and 1980s, and then declined somewhat in the 1990s.[15] However, with rare exceptions,[16] prior studies have not explicitly focused on children's exposure to neighborhood poverty, and virtually no research examines children's exposure to neighborhood affluence.

The purpose of this chapter, therefore, is to provide a detailed picture of the context of poverty and affluence in which children live in the contemporary United States, and an assessment of what has changed for better and for worse in the decade between the last two decennial censuses. Specifically, we present data on children's exposure to neighborhood poverty and affluence (1) across racial/ethnic and poverty status groupings; (2) by region and urban area type (i.e., nonmetropolitan and metropolitan areas, comprising central cities and suburban rings); and (3) over time, by examining changes in the distributions in (1) and (2) from 1990 to 2000. We believe this exercise is useful for at least two reasons. First, if the notion of "neighborhood effects" on children is to be taken seriously, then it is important to get a basic sense of the conditions under which American children have been living over the past several decades. Perhaps surprisingly, we are aware of no other research that presents the data shown in this chapter in as comprehensive and easily interpretable a format. Due in part to this dearth of such descriptive research, we also suspect that many scholars, policy makers, and interested lay persons are unaware of the massive levels of inequality in children's neighborhood contexts demonstrated in the following pages. We hope that this chapter will spur these audiences to pay more attention to the effects of neighborhood poverty and affluence on children's lives. To this end, we conclude the chapter by briefly discussing some implications of our findings for public policy efforts aimed at improving the lives of America's children.

## DATA AND MEASURES

### Data

Our data come from the 1990 and 2000 U.S. Decennial Censuses, concatenated in the Neighborhood Change Database (NCDB). The NCDB was developed by the Urban Institute in conjunction with GeoLytics, Inc.[17] The units of analysis are census tracts, which serve as a proxy for the neighborhoods in which children live.[18] A unique feature of the NCDB is that all tracts are matched to consistent 2000 boundaries. This means that comparisons of geographic units over time are not hampered by systematically changing boundaries of those units. We analyze metropolitan area, central city, and suburban census tracts separately, and include a residual "nonmetropolitan area" category to capture children's exposure to neighborhood poverty and affluence in small towns and rural areas.[19]

### Measures

#### Dependent Variable

We measured neighborhood poverty and affluence by adapting a typology widely used in urban sociological and demographic research. Paul Jargowsky and Mary Jo Bane developed a categorical measure of neighborhood poverty by defining neighborhoods with poverty rates of less than 20 percent as "nonpoor," 20 percent to 40 percent as "poor," and greater than 40 percent as "extremely poor." The authors and local census officials confirmed the validity of these categories by visiting neighborhoods in several cities, finding that neighborhoods in poorer categories appeared more distressed on several subjective indicators.[20]

We follow Jargowsky and Bane by defining "high poverty" neighborhoods as those with between 20 percent and 40 percent of their residents in poverty, and "extreme poverty" neighborhoods as those with poverty rates in excess of 40 percent. We also extend their typology by disaggregating the "nonpoor" neighborhood type into three components: "affluent" neighborhoods have 3 percent or less of their residents in poverty,[21] "low poverty" neighborhoods are those with poverty rates of between 3 percent and 10 percent, and "moderate poverty" neighborhoods are defined as having poverty rates of 10 percent to 20 percent. This extension obviously yields more detailed information on inequality in children's exposure to neighborhood poverty and affluence; however, we find that our extended typology also reveals substantively important findings. This is because there are much higher levels of inequality at the upper end of the distribution than in the middle, inequality that an aggregated "less than 20 percent" category would obscure.

### Independent Variables

Our geographic independent variables are census region (Northeast, Midwest, South, and West) and urban area type, including nonmetropolitan and metropolitan areas, the latter comprising central cities and suburban rings. At the child and family level, we assess the effects of race/ethnicity on exposure to neighborhood poverty and affluence by defining five mutually exclusive (though not exhaustive) racial/ethnic groups: non-Hispanic white, Asian, black, and American Indian, and Hispanic of all census racial categories. We also compute distributions for poor and nonpoor children, based on the Census Bureau's family poverty designation. Finally, because the NCDB does not provide child poverty status by race or ethnicity, we use a proxy measure—poor and nonpoor families with children.[22]

Table 9.1 presents the 2000 distributions of children and families with children by race/ethnicity and poverty status, by region and urban area type. We present these data for two reasons: first, they give an overall picture of the racial/ethnic and poverty status demography of America's children, plus an initial glimpse of variation in their distribution by geographic and urban area type. Table 9.1 also enables interested readers to calculate the absolute and relative magnitudes of the percentages presented in Figures 9.2 through 9.13. For example, Figure 9.10 shows that in 2000 about 16 percent of black children in central cities lived in extremely poor neighborhoods. Combining this figure with data from Table 9.1 yields the percentage (8.6%) and absolute number (about 927,000) of black children living in poor central city neighborhoods in 2000.[23]

## FINDINGS

### Neighborhood Poverty and Neighborhood Context

In the first stage of our analysis we demonstrate why, on average, neighborhood poverty is likely to be harmful for children and why neighborhood affluence is likely to be beneficial. To do this, we present tract-level averages from 2000 census data of six frequently analyzed indicators of neighborhood socioeconomic status (SES) across our five neighborhood types. This analysis also validates our use of neighborhood poverty rates as a single indicator of neighborhood SES.

Figure 9.1 below presents averages across the neighborhood types of median family income (in 1999 thousands of dollars). At the neighborhood level, family income is, among other things, an indicator of purchasing power in a neighborhood,[24] which has effects on the ability of a neighborhood to support a thriving commercial sector. In addition to their instrumental and symbolic functions, local businesses are an important source of adolescents' early labor market experiences. Second, we examine the percentage of neighborhood residents with a college degree or more, an indicator of the human capital available to a neighborhood. This indicator likely

**Table 9.1**

**2000 Distributions of Children and Families with Children by Race/Ethnicity and Poverty Status, by Region and Urban Area Type**

| | Total[a] | | Region (%) | | | | Urban Area Type (%) | | Metropolitan Areas | |
| | n (000) | % | Northeast | Midwest | South | West | Nonmetro Areas | Total | Central Cities | Suburbs |
|---|---|---|---|---|---|---|---|---|---|---|
| **Children** | | | | | | | | | | |
| *By race/ethnicity* | | | | | | | | | | |
| White | 49,547 | 68.7 | 18.9 | 26.3 | 33.9 | 21.0 | 23.1 | 76.9 | 21.3 | 55.6 |
| Asian | 2,554 | 3.5 | 20.2 | 12.6 | 18.5 | 48.7 | 4.9 | 95.1 | 41.0 | 54.1 |
| Black | 10,750 | 14.9 | 17.0 | 19.5 | 55.0 | 8.5 | 13.8 | 86.2 | 53.1 | 33.0 |
| Hispanic | 12,264 | 17.0 | 13.7 | 9.3 | 30.8 | 46.1 | 9.8 | 90.2 | 45.8 | 44.4 |
| American Indian | 814 | 1.1 | 5.9 | 17.4 | 27.3 | 49.4 | 49.1 | 50.9 | 22.4 | 28.5 |
| *By poverty status* | | | | | | | | | | |
| Poor | 11,747 | 16.6 | 16.6 | 18.5 | 40.2 | 24.7 | 23.1 | 76.9 | 43.4 | 33.5 |
| Nonpoor | 59,178 | 83.4 | 18.3 | 23.9 | 34.5 | 23.2 | 19.2 | 80.8 | 26.7 | 54.1 |
| **Families with children** | | | | | | | | | | |
| *By race/ethnicity and poverty status* | | | | | | | | | | |
| White | 25,788 | 73.2 | 18.9 | 26.1 | 34.5 | 20.4 | 22.8 | 77.2 | 21.5 | 55.7 |
| Poor | 2,574 | 10.0 | 16.6 | 21.1 | 39.8 | 22.4 | 31.4 | 68.6 | 29.1 | 39.6 |
| Nonpoor | 23,214 | 90.0 | 19.2 | 26.7 | 33.9 | 20.2 | 21.9 | 78.1 | 20.7 | 57.5 |
| Asian | 1,343 | 3.8 | 20.8 | 11.7 | 19.6 | 47.8 | 4.3 | 95.7 | 39.7 | 55.9 |
| Poor | 169 | 12.6 | 23.8 | 10.3 | 17.0 | 48.9 | 5.4 | 94.6 | 56.9 | 37.8 |
| Nonpoor | 1,174 | 87.4 | 20.4 | 11.9 | 20.0 | 47.7 | 4.2 | 95.8 | 37.3 | 58.5 |
| Black | 4,668 | 13.2 | 16.8 | 18.7 | 55.7 | 8.8 | 13.2 | 86.8 | 51.9 | 34.9 |
| Poor | 1,494 | 32.0 | 16.2 | 19.6 | 56.9 | 7.3 | 17.8 | 82.2 | 59.6 | 22.6 |
| Nonpoor | 3,174 | 68.0 | 17.0 | 18.2 | 55.1 | 9.6 | 11.1 | 88.9 | 48.2 | 40.7 |
| Hispanic | 4,905 | 13.9 | 15.0 | 8.8 | 32.9 | 43.3 | 9.3 | 90.7 | 46.3 | 44.4 |
| Poor | 1,296 | 26.4 | 18.5 | 6.6 | 32.9 | 42.0 | 10.8 | 89.2 | 54.5 | 34.7 |
| Nonpoor | 3,609 | 73.6 | 13.8 | 9.6 | 32.9 | 43.8 | 8.7 | 91.3 | 43.3 | 47.9 |
| American Indian | 333 | 0.9 | 6.4 | 17.4 | 29.9 | 46.3 | 44.2 | 55.8 | 24.7 | 31.1 |
| Poor | 103 | 30.8 | 6.3 | 18.0 | 24.5 | 51.2 | 53.6 | 46.4 | 24.0 | 22.4 |
| Nonpoor | 230 | 69.2 | 6.5 | 17.1 | 32.3 | 44.2 | 40.1 | 59.9 | 25.0 | 35.0 |

[a] "n (000)" column does not include a small residual "other race/ethnicity" category (included in the calculations for the "%" column).

*Source:* Authors' calculations from 2000 U.S. Census data.

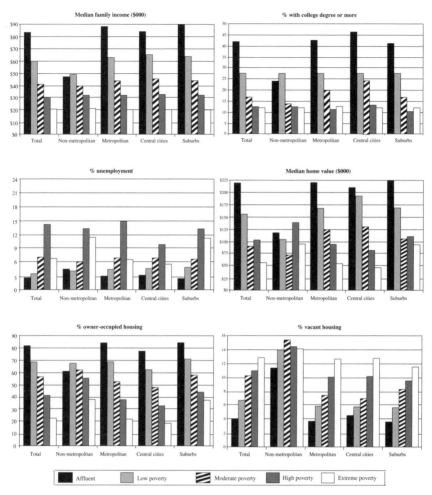

**Figure 9.1**
**Selected Population and Housing Characteristics, by Neighborhood and Urban Area Type, 2000.** *Source:* **Authors' calculations from 2000 U.S. Census data.**

captures the quality of social networks embedded in neighborhoods, networks which enable or retard the ability of youths to find out about employment and educational opportunities. Third, we measure the unemployment rate, which, among other things, has effects on the culture of work to which children are exposed in a neighborhood.[25] We also measure three housing characteristics: median home value and percent owner-occupied housing, which indicate the stake that residents have in their neighborhoods, and the percentage of vacant units, which is correlated with neighbors' and landlords' willingness to invest in the upkeep of property.[26] Each of these measures of housing quality is related to residential stability and the willingness of residents to form social ties and maintain public order.[27]

Figure 9.1 demonstrates that poor neighborhoods on average provide more disadvantaged contexts for children's development. As of 2000, the average affluent neighborhood boasts a median family income of about $82,000, compared to less than $20,000 for the poorest neighborhood type. Affluent neighborhoods have an average of 42 percent of their residents with a college degree or more, against 12 percent for extremely poor neighborhoods. Unemployment rates are shockingly high in extremely poor neighborhoods, averaging about 20 percent. High poverty neighborhoods have an average of 11 percent unemployment rates, while these rates average 6 percent or less in the three "nonpoor" neighborhood types. Children growing up in affluent neighborhoods are surrounded by homes with an average median value of nearly $220,000, compared to just over $70,000 for homes in the poorest type. Fully 82 percent of households in affluent neighborhoods own their own homes, while this percentage drops to an average of 23 percent in extremely poor neighborhoods. Finally, vacancy rates average about 4 percent in affluent neighborhoods, against 13 percent in the poorest neighborhood type.

Figure 9.1 also reveals substantial variation by urban area type in these indicators. Family incomes, levels of human capital, and median home values are appreciably higher on average in metropolitan areas versus nonmetropolitan areas, while vacancy rates are higher in nonmetropolitan areas than in urban areas. Unemployment rates are essentially identical across the urban/nonurban divide. Percent owner-occupied housing presents a unique pattern among the indicators we analyze here. Note that the most affluent tracts in metropolitan areas have dramatically higher rates of homeownership than in the equivalent nonmetropolitan tracts, while the reverse is true for high and extreme poverty neighborhoods. In low and moderate poverty neighborhoods, there is little difference between metropolitan and nonmetropolitan areas on this indicator.

### 2000 Distributions of Neighborhood Types

We turn next to an analysis of the geographic distribution of neighborhood types as of 2000. Figures 2 and 3 present these distributions, first by region and then by urban area type. We present all remaining data in the form of bar graphs, for ease of visual inspection. A full set of tables upon which the figures are based is available upon request.

### Region

The distributions for the Northeast and Midwest are strikingly similar, likely reflecting a relatively common industrial past. Cities in the Northeast were founded and developed earlier than in the Midwest; however, by 1900, industrialization was in full swing in both regions. Owing to its poorer, more rural past, the South has appreciably fewer affluent and low poverty neighborhoods compared to the Northeast and Midwest (about 40% versus about 60%). A plurality of southern census tracts is moderately poor (34.2%), while the South contains the largest percentage of high poverty (22.1%) and extreme poverty (4.4%) neighborhoods of the four census

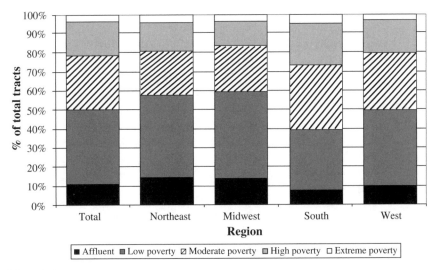

**Figure 9.2**
**Distribution of Neighborhood Types, by Region, 2000.** *Source:* **Authors' calculations from 2000 U.S. Census data.**

regions. The West represents an intermediate case, with a greater percentage of affluent and low poverty tracts, and a lower percentage of the two poorest neighborhood types than the South.

### Urban Area Type

Figure 9.3 shows much more variation in the distribution of neighborhood types than did Figure 9.2. Although the total percentages of "nonpoor" (0 to 20% poor) and "poor" (greater than 20% poor) tracts are virtually identical in nonmetropolitan and metropolitan areas (about a 4:1 ratio for each), the tails of the distribution are much smaller in nonmetropolitan than in metropolitan areas. Small towns and rural areas contain very few of the poorest and richest neighborhood types, with a large plurality (45.7%) of tracts falling in the "moderate poverty" type (rates of 10% to 20%). By contrast, only about 24 percent of metropolitan area tracts are moderately poor. This difference is distributed into a much higher percentage of affluent (13.6% vs. 1.9%), and to a lesser extent, low poverty (41.4% vs. 30.7%), and extremely poor (4.3% vs. 2.4%) tracts.

Within metropolitan areas, we are not surprised to observe dramatic differences in the percentage of affluent and extremely poor neighborhoods. Central cities have nearly 12 times the percentage of the poorest neighborhoods compared to suburbs (9.0% vs. 0.8%), and suburbs have nearly 4 times the percentage of affluent tracts (19.8% vs. 5.4%). Fully 92 percent of all suburban tracts fall in the "nonpoor" aggregate category, against 60 percent for central cities. Within this aggregate grouping,

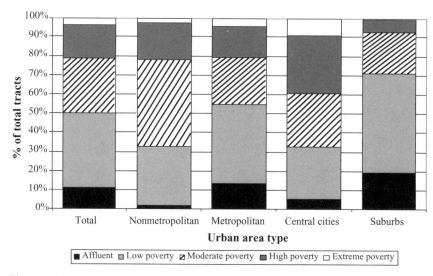

**Figure 9.3**
**Distribution of Neighborhood Types, by Urban Area Type, 2000.** *Source:* **Authors' calculations from 2000 U.S. Census data.**

about 52 percent of suburban tracts are in the "low poverty" category, compared to about 28 percent for central cities.

### 1990 to 2000 Change in the Distribution of Neighborhood Types

We now analyze relative percent changes ([%2000 − %1990] %1990 × 100) in the distribution of neighborhood types, first by region (Figure 9.4) and then by urban area type (Figure 9.5). Figure 9.4 shows that the 1990s were a decade of shrinking tails in the distribution of neighborhood types. Note that the total percentage of affluent neighborhoods declined by about 9 percent from 1990 to 2000, while the percentage of extremely poor neighborhoods declined nearly 25 percent in relative terms. This latter finding was observed by Jargowsky,[28] and likely reflects the long and robust economic recovery during the Clinton administrations. The three intermediate neighborhood types all showed small growth, indicating that the richest and poorest neighborhoods were redistributed somewhat into these three categories.

#### *Region*

These changes were not shared equally across regions, however. The Northeast saw sharp declines in the percentage of affluent tracts (from 19.3 percent in 1990 to 14.6 percent in 2000, yielding a relative decline of almost one-quarter), while the percentage of affluent tracts changed little in the three remaining regions. The 1990s appeared to benefit the Midwest the most, as the percentage of low poverty tracts

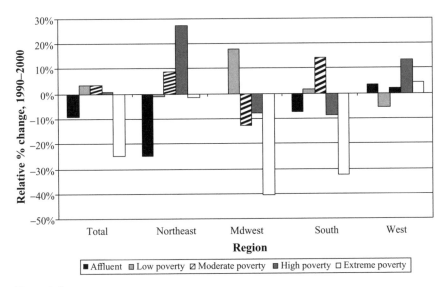

**Figure 9.4**
**Relative Percent Change (1990–2000) in the Distribution of Neighborhood Types, by Region.** *Source:* **Authors' calculations from 1990 to 2000 U.S. Census data.**

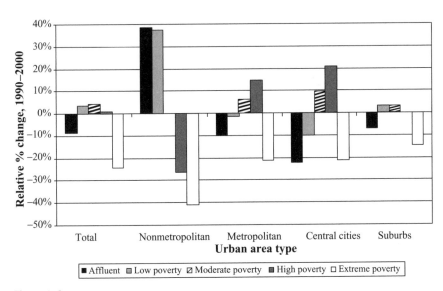

**Figure 9.5**
**Relative Percent Change (1990–2000) in the Distribution of Neighborhood Types, by Urban Area Type.** *Source:* **Authors' calculations from 1990 to 2000 U.S. Census data.**

increased about 19 percent and the percentage of extremely poor tracts declined by over 40 percent. The South experienced a redistribution of the most affluent and the two poorest neighborhood types into the low and especially moderate poverty types, while the West saw increases in the percentage of all neighborhood types except for the low poverty category.

### Urban Area type

Figure 9.5 presents percentage changes in the distribution of neighborhood types across nonmetropolitan and metropolitan areas. Nonmetropolitan areas enjoyed an increase in the proportion of affluent and low poverty tracts and a decline in the percentage of the two poorest neighborhood types. Our data do not permit us to account definitively for these changes, but we suspect that the 1990s benefited nonmetropolitan areas via the continuing tendency of industry to locate in those areas and the resulting attraction of the nonpoor population to these areas. Metropolitan areas and their constituent central cities and suburbs display patterns similar to the overall picture. This is not surprising, given that about 88 percent of all tracts were located in metropolitan areas in 2000. A comparison of central cities and suburbs reveals that the 1990s were a mixed blessing for the former. Central cities experienced sharper relative declines in the proportion of affluent and nonpoor tracts than suburbs, though the percentage of the poorest neighborhood type also declined more in central cities than in the suburbs.

## Distributions of Children across Neighborhood Types

The third stage in our analysis concerns the distribution of children (less than age 18) across neighborhood types. We first examine these distributions by race/ethnicity and poverty status, and these two variables by region and urban area type.

### Race and Ethnicity

Figure 9.6 presents the distribution of all children, and children from five major racial/ethnic groups. As of 2000, about 80 percent of all children live in the three "nonpoor" neighborhood types. Of these, 12 percent live in affluent, 40 percent are in low poverty, and 28 percent are in moderately poor neighborhoods. Children in poor neighborhoods are distributed into high poverty (17%) and extremely poor neighborhoods (about 3%).

Prior research on racial and ethnic inequality in neighborhood context would predict dramatic levels of variation in these distributions across the five racial/ethnic categories. Indeed, our research bears out these predictions. Whereas about 83 percent of Asian and 89 percent of white children live in the three nonpoor neighborhood types, those percentages are about 52 percent for black, 59 percent for Hispanic, and 55 percent for American Indian children. Within the nonpoor category, white and Asian children live in affluent neighborhoods at about five times the rate of the three other groups, about 15 percent compared to 3 or 4 percent. At the other end of the distribution, rates of exposure to extremely poor neighborhoods average 12 percent

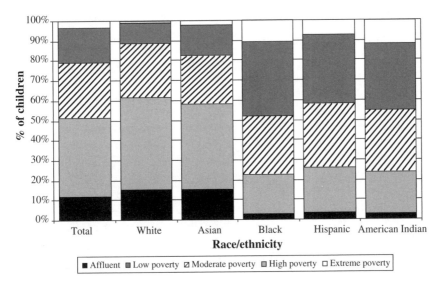

**Figure 9.6**
**Distribution of Children in Neighborhood Types, by Race/Ethnicity, 2000.** *Source:*
**Authors' calculations from 2000 U.S. Census data.**

for American Indian, 10 percent for black, 7 percent for Hispanic, 2 percent for
Asian, and 1 percent for white children. Over 40 percent of black, American Indian,
and Hispanic children can be found in neighborhoods with poverty rates in excess
of 20 percent in 2000, against only 11 percent of white and 17 percent of Asian
children.

Thus, at least on the dimension of children's exposure to neighborhood poverty
and affluence, by 2000 the American racial/ethnic hierarchy has effectively become
bifurcated into a white/Asian component and a black/Hispanic/American Indian
component. Indeed, the graphical method of presenting results employed in this
chapter drives this point home visually. Note that the white and Asian distributions
collectively look starkly different from those of the three remaining groups, which in
turn look remarkably similar.

Counterbalancing this rather gloomy snapshot is Figure 9.7, which shows overall
changes in the distribution of children in neighborhood types, and presents findings
broken down by race and ethnicity. Overall, children's exposure to the poorest neighborhood type declined substantially in the 1990s, from 5.0 percent of all children
in 1990 to 3.2 percent in 2000. These improvements were experienced most dramatically by black children, whose representation in extremely poor neighborhoods
declined 44 percent, from a 1990 rate of 18.3 percent to 10.3 percent in 2000.
American Indian and Hispanic children's exposure to the poorest neighborhood type
declined by about 38 percent, while Asian and white children experienced less dramatic relative declines (32 percent and 29 percent, respectively), from an already very
low 1990 baseline.

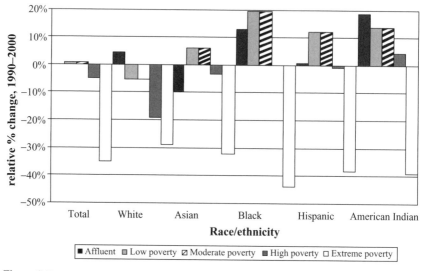

**Figure 9.7**
**Percent Change (1990–2000) in the Distribution of Children in Neighborhood Types, by Race/Ethnicity.** *Source:* **Authors' calculations from 1990 to 2000 U.S. Census data.**

Overall, it appears as though the 1990s were quite beneficial for children from the three most disadvantaged racial and ethnic groups. In addition to the findings regarding changes in exposure to extremely poor neighborhoods already reported, black and American Indian children experienced substantial increases in their exposure to the three nonpoor neighborhood types, and Hispanic children experienced increases in exposure to two of the three. In comparison, Asian children experienced a decline in exposure to the most affluent neighborhood type, and white children experienced increasing exposure to neighborhood affluence and declining exposure to the four other neighborhood types.

### Poverty Status

Figure 9.8 presents the 2000 distributions of poor and nonpoor children in the five neighborhood types, and the relative percent change in those distributions from 1990 to 2000. The left-hand section of the figure shows dramatic differences in the neighborhood contexts to which poor and nonpoor children are exposed. As of 2000, nearly 50 percent of poor children live in neighborhoods with poverty rates of at least 20 percent, compared to only 12 percent of their nonpoor counterparts. At the other end of the distribution, about 59 percent of nonpoor children live in the two least poor neighborhoods, of which 14.4 percent live in neighborhoods we categorize as "affluent." The equivalent percentages for poor children are 19 percent and 1.3 percent, respectively. The right-hand section of Figure 9.8 shows marked improvements in poor children's exposure to neighborhood poverty and affluence. The percentage of poor children living in the three "nonpoor" neighborhood types all increased

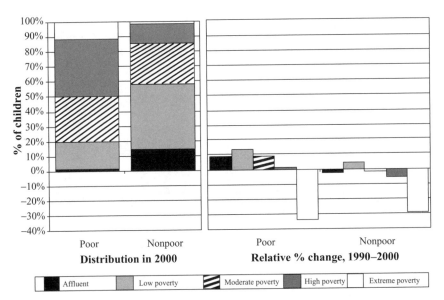

**Figure 9.8**
**Distribution of Children in Neighborhood Types, by Poverty Status, 2000 and Relative Percent Change, 1990–2000.** *Source:* **Authors' calculations from 1990 to 2000 U.S. Census data.**

during the 1990s, and the percentage exposed to extremely poor neighborhoods declined by about one-third, from a 1990 level of 17 percent to about 11 percent in 2000. Nonpoor children experienced almost no change in their neighborhood poverty distributions—the large bar associated with extremely poor neighborhoods represents a small absolute decline in exposure, from 2.2 percent in 1990 to 1.6 percent in 2000.

### Race/Ethnicity and Region

Figure 9.9 presents distributions of children in the five neighborhood types by race/ethnicity and region. In general, the findings in Figure 9.9 conform to those in Figure 9.6; however, several noteworthy regional differences are apparent. First, white children in the Northeast and Midwest are much more likely to live in the most affluent neighborhoods than their southern and western counterparts. About 72 percent of white children from the first two regions live in neighborhoods with less than 10 percent, compared to only 51 percent in the South and 57 percent in the West. White children are about twice as likely to live in the most affluent type in the former compared to the latter two regions (about 20% vs. about 10%). black children, by contrast, experience the lowest exposure to extremely poor neighborhoods in the West—about 7 percent in 2000—compared to the Northeast and Midwest (about 14% and 12%, respectively).

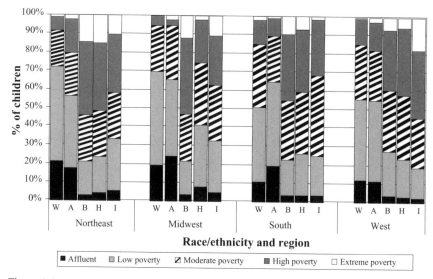

**Figure 9.9**
**Distribution of Children in Neighborhood Types, by Race/Ethnicity and Region, 2000.**
*Source:* **Authors' calculations from 2000 U.S. Census data.**

Hispanic children in the Midwest experience much more advantaged neighborhood contexts compared to their co-ethnics from other regions. Over 40 percent of midwestern Hispanic children live in the two most affluent neighborhood types, compared to about 25 percent in the Northeast, South, and West. At the other end of the distribution, about 25 percent of midwestern Hispanic children live in the two poorest neighborhood types, including only 2 percent in extremely poor neighborhoods. This latter figure declined from 7 percent in 1990, representing a relative decrease of about 72 percent (data not shown). In contrast, exposure to the two poorest neighborhood types combined averages 52 percent in the Northeast (of which 15% are in extremely poor neighborhoods), 41 percent in the South, and 43 percent in the West.

Asian children in the Midwest are twice as likely to live in affluent neighborhoods than their western counterparts (24% vs. 12%) and southern Asian children are substantially less likely to live in the two poor neighborhood types compared to Asian children in the Northeast and West (11% versus 21% and 19%, respectively). Finally, about 56 percent of western American Indian children live in the two poorest neighborhood types, of which about 18 percent live in tracts with greater than 40 percent poverty rates. This represents the largest single race/ethnicity by region concentration we observed in 2000. Only 2 percent of western American Indian children live in affluent neighborhoods, one-half to one-third the rate of American Indian children in the three other regions.

What accounts for the regional variation we observe? We suspect it is largely due to class-selective internal migration, at least for the four non-White groups. Note

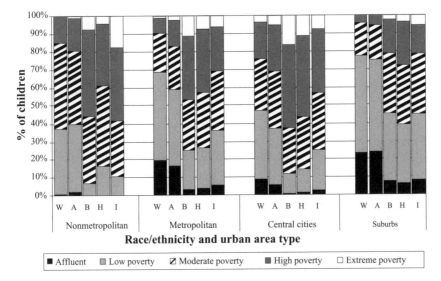

**Figure 9.10**
**Distribution of Children in Neighborhood Types, by Race/Ethnicity and Urban Area Type, 2000.** *Source:* **Authors' calculations from 2000 U.S. Census data.**

that in each case outlined above, children experienced their most advantaged contexts in regions that have historically been destinations for internal migrants. For blacks, historically concentrated in the South, and following the Great Migration in the Northeast and Midwest, children experience the least neighborhood disadvantage in the West, a more recent destination for black migrants. For Hispanic children, the largest ports of entry for immigrants are in the South (including Florida and Texas), the West (including Arizona and California), and the Northeast (including New York and New Jersey). Thus, midwestern Hispanic children are likely to be children of internal migrants, who may be selected for income, education, or other class factors. Asian immigrants largely enter the United States through gateway cities in the West and Northeast; hence, children in the South and West are likely also children of more advantaged internal migrants. Therefore, regional variation in children's exposure to neighborhood poverty and affluence may have less to do with variation in the treatment of different racial/ethnic groups than with the class composition of members of those groups.

### Race/Ethnicity and Urban Area Type

Figure 9.10 presents distributions of children in the five neighborhood types by race/ethnicity and urban area type.   Figure 9.10 shows that children in small towns and rural areas tend to experience much poorer neighborhood contexts than their urban counterparts. Whereas 70 percent of white and 60 percent of Asian children in metropolitan areas live in neighborhoods with poverty rates of less than 10 percent, the equivalent figures for nonmetropolitan areas are 38 percent and 40 percent.

black and American Indian children are much more likely to live in these two types of neighborhoods in metropolitan areas (25% and 37%, respectively) than in rural areas and small towns (8% and 11%, respectively). At the other end of the distribution, 56 percent of black children live in the two poorest neighborhood types in nonmetropolitan areas. In metropolitan areas this figure is about 47 percent, although urban black children are more likely than rural and small town children to live in the poorest neighborhood type (11% vs. 7%, respectively). American Indian children are nearly twice as likely to live in the two combined poor neighborhoods in nonmetropolitan relative to metropolitan areas (59% vs. 31%, respectively), and almost three times more likely to live in the poorest neighborhood type in rural areas and small towns relative to urban areas (17% vs. 6%). Hispanic children are a somewhat anomalous case, experiencing less exposure to neighborhood affluence and about the same exposure to neighborhood poverty in metropolitan relative to nonmetropolitan areas.

Within metropolitan areas, we observe substantial variation in the distributions of children between central cities and suburbs, and substantial racial/ethnic variation within each of these components. This is not surprising, given that a vast literature details the increasing concentration of poverty in central city neighborhoods in the 1970s and 1980s,[29] as well as racial/ethnic inequality in both the propensity of groups to reside in the suburbs and the attainment of high-SES neighborhoods within suburbs.[30]

Indeed, the two right-hand sets of bars in Figure 9.10 reveal that central city children experience far more disadvantaged neighborhood contexts than suburban children, and that, as shown in Figure 9.6, there are essentially two racial/ethnic patterns: one for whites and Asians, and one for blacks, Hispanics and American Indians. The one exception to this latter rule is that American Indian children in central cities evince substantially more exposure to nonpoor neighborhoods—especially the low poverty type—and substantially less exposure to neighborhood poverty than either blacks or Hispanics. Note also the similarity between the central city distributions for white and Asian children and the suburban distributions for black, Hispanic, and American Indian children. If neighborhood conditions are one source of mobilization for political coalitions that cross-racial and ethnic lines,[31] the findings in Figure 9.10 suggest that central city whites and Asians and suburban blacks, Hispanics, and American Indians would be natural allies. However, given the separation between these groups by physical distance and municipal boundaries, such a coalition would seem unlikely to form or persist over time.

### Poverty Status, Region, and Urban Area Type

Figure 9.11 presents distributions of children in the five neighborhood types by poverty status, region (the left-hand section), and urban area type (the right-hand section). For poor children, about half live in each of the aggregated nonpoor and poor categories, and within those types there are nearly identical distributions of children in the disaggregated neighborhood types. In the Northeast, a slightly larger percentage of children live in the low poverty and extreme poverty types than in the South and West.

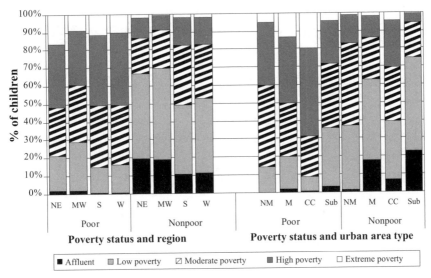

**Figure 9.11**
**Distribution of Children in Neighborhood Types, by Poverty Status, Region, and Urban Area Type, 2000.** *Source*: **Authors' calculations from 2000 U.S. Census data.**

In the Midwest, children are twice as likely to live in low poverty neighborhoods as in the South and West (about 30% vs. about 15%, respectively), with the distributions in each of the other four neighborhood types being about equal in these three regions. For nonpoor children, there is a split between the distributions in the Northeast and Midwest, and in the South and West. These differences are driven primarily by larger representations of children in the most affluent neighborhood type and smaller percentages of children in high poverty neighborhoods in the former relative to the latter two regions.

With respect to variation across urban area types, the most striking finding concerns the distribution of poor children in central cities. As of 2000, nearly 70 percent of poor central city children live in the two poorest neighborhood types, of which fully 20 percent live in extremely poor neighborhoods. As shown in Figure 9.1, these are neighborhoods with low median incomes, percentages of residents with a college degree, median home values, and percentages of owner-occupied housing, and extremely high rates of unemployment and vacant housing. If growing up in such neighborhood contexts has deleterious effects on children, then it is clear from Figure 9.11 that a great majority of poor urban children are at a disadvantage relative to their poor nonmetropolitan and suburban counterparts. Indeed, poor children in suburbs experienced about two-fifths the rate of exposure to high and extreme poverty neighborhoods as poor children in central cities. Finally, to take the most extreme cross-group comparison, note that less than *6 percent* of nonpoor suburban children live in the two poorest neighborhood types (compared to the previously reported

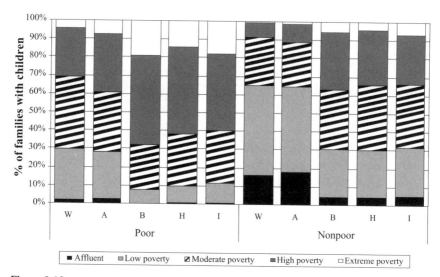

**Figure 9.12**
**Distribution of Families with Children in Neighborhood Types, by Poverty Status and Race/Ethnicity, 2000.** *Source:* **Authors' calculations from 2000 U.S. Census data.**

70%), and nearly a quarter live in the most affluent type, compared to four-tenths of 1 percent among poor central city children.

## Distributions of Families with Children Across Neighborhood Types

As noted previously, the NCDB does not provide breakdowns of children by race/ethnicity and poverty status; hence, we use a proxy measure—poor and nonpoor families with children.

### Race/Ethnicity and Poverty Status

Figure 9.12 presents the 2000 distributions of families with children in the five neighborhood poverty types, by race/ethnicity and poverty status. As with Figure 9.6, note the remarkable similarity in the distributions of white and Asian families versus black, Hispanic, and American Indian families, a finding that holds for both poor and nonpoor families alike. Among the poor, nearly 70 percent of white families with children live in the three nonpoor neighborhood types, while about 60 percent of poor Hispanic and American Indian families and nearly 70 percent of black families with children live in the two poorest neighborhood types. Nearly half of black poor families live in high poverty neighborhoods, with the remaining 20 percent living in extremely poor neighborhoods. The equivalent percentages for poor white families are 25 percent and 5 percent. Poor Asian families experience about the same exposure to nonpoor neighborhoods as whites, but are more heavily represented in high poverty neighborhoods than are whites. Among the nonpoor, nearly 90 percent of white and Asian families live in nonpoor neighborhoods, compared to about 65 percent of families from the three other groups. As in Figure 9.10, note that the distributions

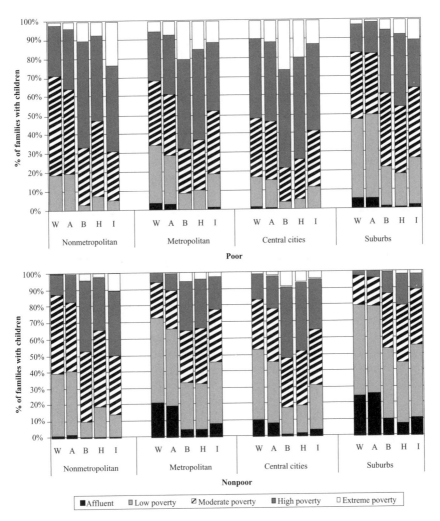

**Figure 9.13**
**Distribution of Families with Children in Neighborhood Types, by Poverty Status, Race/Ethnicity, and Urban Area Type, 2000.** *Source:* **Authors' calculations from 2000 U.S. Census data.**

of nonpoor black, Hispanic, and American Indian families look virtually identical to the distributions for poor white and Asian families. Thus, in terms of exposure to neighborhood poverty and affluence in the United States, poverty for whites and Asians is more or less equivalent to nonpoverty for the three other racial/ethnic groups.

### Race/Ethnicity, Poverty Status, and Urban Area Type

Figure 9.13 presents the neighborhood poverty distributions for poor and nonpoor families, by race/ethnicity and urban area type. This three-way cross-classification of independent variables produce a large number of data points, so we focus our discussion on poor central city black and Hispanic families—the "truly disadvantaged" families on whom much scholarly attention has been focused over the past two decades—and on nonpoor suburban white and Asian families with children. This latter set of groups is sometimes thought to be the American "mainstream"—groups that face little discrimination in the labor market and who have achieved both nonpoor economic status and residence in American suburbs.

Figure 9.13 shows that as of 2000, nearly 80 percent of poor central city black families live in neighborhoods with poverty rates of at least 20 percent. About 27 percent of black poor central city families reside in the poorest neighborhood type, those with poverty rates in excess of 40 percent. The corresponding figures for Hispanic families are 74 percent and 20 percent. These figures correspond to about 237,000 poor black families (5.1% of all black families) and 138,000 poor Hispanic families (2.8% of all Hispanic families) living in the poorest central city neighborhoods. In contrast, between 50 percent and 60 percent of poor central city families from the three other groups live in the two poorest neighborhood types, of which 10 percent to 12 percent live in the poorest type. For whites, only about 75,000 poor families live in extremely poor central city neighborhoods, about 0.3 percent of all white families. Thus, in proportionate terms, there are 17.3 times as many poor black central city families living in the poorest neighborhoods as equivalent white families (0.051 0.003 = 17.3). As astounding as these levels of inequality are, they represent some improvement from 1990 to 2000. The share of poor black and Hispanic central city families in the poorest neighborhood type declined by about one-third during this decade, compared to about one-quarter for white families (data not shown).

At the other end of the distribution, nearly every nonpoor suburban white and Asian family (96%) lived in one of the three "nonpoor" neighborhood types. These rates for the three other groups were 85 percent for black, 78 percent for Hispanic, and 86 percent for American Indian families. However, here is another instance where disaggregating the nonpoor category reveals more inequality than would otherwise be observed—about 25 percent of white and Asian nonpoor suburban families lived in "affluent" neighborhoods, compared to only 10 percent, 8 percent, and 11 percent for black, Hispanic, and American Indian families, respectively. Note finally from Figure 9.13 that the "moderate poverty" bars are much larger for the latter three groups compared to whites and Asians. This indicates that a substantial fraction of nonpoor suburban black, Hispanic, and American Indian families are living in neighborhoods with 10 percent to 20 percent of their residents in poverty. In short, even when they are nonpoor, and even when they are suburbanized, black, Hispanic, and American Indian families with children face much greater exposure to neighborhood poverty than their white and Asian counterparts.

We find that about 46 percent of all nonpoor white and Asian families live in the two most affluent neighborhood types in the suburbs. These figures correspond to about 40 percent of all white and Asian families. This datum deserves special emphasis: *about 40 percent of all white and Asian families are nonpoor and reside in suburban neighborhoods with poverty rates of 10 percent or less.* The corresponding figures for black, Hispanic, and American Indian families are 15 percent, 16 percent, and

13 percent, respectively. Returning to our analysis of exposure to central city neighborhood poverty, 15 percent of all black families and 11 percent of all Hispanic families are poor and reside in central city neighborhoods with poverty rates of 20 percent or more. The corresponding figures for whites and Asians are 2 percent and 4 percent. Irrespective of poverty status and central city/suburban residence, fully 39 percent of black and 38 percent of Hispanic urban families with children live in the two poorest neighborhood types, compared to 7 percent for white and 14 percent for Asian families.

## CONCLUSIONS

Our goal in this chapter was to present descriptive data on the levels of and changes in the exposure of children from five major racial and ethnic groups to neighborhoods with drastically different socioeconomic profiles. We showed that many important indicators of neighborhood SES vary dramatically across neighborhood poverty types, and that in general nonmetropolitan areas are less well off on the six indicators analyzed than metropolitan areas. We then presented changes in the geographic distribution of poor and nonpoor neighborhoods, finding scant variation by region and much more substantial variation by urban area type. We argued that although American Indian, black, and Hispanic children continue to suffer much higher rates of exposure to neighborhood poverty than their white and Asian counterparts, the 1990s was also a decade of hopeful improvements in the neighborhood conditions of children from the more disadvantaged groups. Finally, we demonstrated that although poor and nonpoor children and families with children from the five racial/ethnic groups may nominally share residential space in metropolitan areas, black, Hispanic, and American Indian children continue to be exposed to dramatically higher rates of neighborhood poverty than their white and Asian counterparts.

Over a decade ago, Douglas Massey and Nancy Denton demonstrated that the spatial segregation of a racial or ethnic group with high poverty rates has the mathematical effect of concentrating poverty in the neighborhoods of that group.[32] In subsequent work, Massey and Mary Fischer noted that just as segregation and increasing poverty interact to generate ever-growing poverty concentrations, the reverse occurs if either segregation or the poverty rate of a segregated group declines.[33] For at least 30 years, blacks and Hispanics have been both residentially segregated and suffered dramatically higher rates of poverty than their white counterparts. And, *ipso facto*, for at least 30 years, poverty has been highly concentrated in black and Hispanic neighborhoods. However, during the 1990s segregation declined appreciably for African Americans, and the U.S. economy showed nearly unprecedented levels of economic growth and prosperity. We believe we have detected at least one of the effects of these changes; namely, black, Hispanic, and American Indian children's exposure to neighborhood poverty declined appreciably in the 1990s.

The results of this analysis, along with those of Jargowsky,[34] suggest that neighborhood conditions for children, at least along various socioeconomic dimensions, are dramatically affected by the health of the national, regional, state, and local economies. As such, the findings of this analysis would prescribe prolonged and robust economic development for improving the neighborhood conditions of America's children. Of course, such development is not always subject to the whims of policy makers, given normal business cycle fluctuations over time. What is more under the control of policy makers are antipoverty policies, specifically job growth policies, that would target residents of poor neighborhoods. Finally, although residential desegregation policies have rarely been given serious consideration, it is clear that dispersing poor and minority group members throughout American metropolitan would serve to reduce the stark levels of inequality in exposure to neighborhood poverty and affluence observed in this chapter.

## NOTES

\* Direct correspondence to Jeff Timberlake, University of Cincinnati Department of Sociology, PO Box 210378, Cincinnati, OH 45221-0378 (jeffrey.timberlake@uc.edu). The authors gratefully acknowledge research support from the Charles Phelps Taft Research Center at the University of Cincinnati.

1. Lee Rainwater and Timothy M. Smeeding, *Poor Kids in a Rich Country: America's Children in Comparative Perspective* (New York: Russell Sage Foundation, 2003).

2. Luxembourg Income Study [LIS], "Key Figures," accessed April 24, 2006, http://www.lisproject.org/keyfigures.htm. Data from Census 2000 estimates the U.S. rate to be 16.6 percent (See Table 1). This discrepancy is due to variation in the definition of poverty status. See LIS for details on measurement.

3. Ibid.

4. Mary Corcoran, "Rags to Rags: Poverty and Mobility in the United States," *Annual Review of Sociology* 21 (1995); Robert Haveman and Barbara Wolfe, "The Determinants of Children's Attainments: A Review of Methods and Findings," *Journal of Economic Literature* 33 (1995); Greg J. Duncan, W. Jean Yeung, Jeanne Brooks-Gunn, and Judith R. Smith, "How Much Does Childhood Poverty Affect the Life Chances of Children?" *American Sociological Review* 63(1997); Susan E. Mayer, *What Money Can't Buy: Family Income and Children's Life Chances* (Cambridge, MA: Harvard University Press, 1997).

5. Ibid, 42.

6. In 1960 the black poverty rate was about 55 percent compared to only about 18 percent for whites. Black poverty rates declined dramatically in the 1960s, reaching about 32 percent in 1970, compared to about 10 percent for whites. For most of the 1970 to 2000 period, Black poverty rates have averaged about 30 percent, compared to about 10 percent for whites, 25 percent for Hispanics, and 12 percent for Asians. See U.S. Bureau of the Census, "Historical Poverty Tables," accessed May 10, 2006, http://www.census.gov/hhes/www/poverty/histpov/hstpov2.html. In 2003, poverty rates for blacks, Hispanics, whites, and Asians were estimated to be 24 percent, 23 percent, 8 percent, and 12 percent, respectively. See U.S. Bureau of the Census, "Income Stable, Poverty Up, Numbers of Americans With and Without Health Insurance Rise, Census Bureau Reports," accessed April 21, 2006, http://www.census.gov/Press-Release/www/releases/archives/income_wealth/002484.html>.

7. Christopher Jencks and Susan E. Mayer, "The Social Consequences of Growing up in a Poor Neighborhood," in *Inner-City Poverty in the United States*, ed. Laurence E. Lynn, Jr. and Michael G. H. McGeary (Washington, DC: National Academy Press, 1990): 111; Robert J. Sampson, Jeffrey D. Morenoff, and Thomas Gannon-Rowley, "Assessing 'Neighborhood Effects:' Social Processes and New Directions in Research," *Annual Review of Sociology* 28(2002): 446.

8. William J. Wilson, *The Truly Disadvantaged: The Inner City, the Underclass, and Public Policy* (Chicago: The University of Chicago Press, 1987), 57.

9. Sampson, Morenoff, and Gannon-Rowley, "Assessing 'Neighborhood Effects:' Social Processes and New Directions in Research."

10. James P. Connell and Bonnie L. Halpern-Felsher, "How Neighborhoods Affect Educational Outcomes in Middle Childhood and Adolescence: Conceptual Issues and an Empirical Example," in *Neighborhood Poverty Volume I: Context and Consequences for Children*, ed. Jeanne Brooks-Gunn, Greg J. Duncan, and J. Lawrence Aber (New York: Russell Sage Foundation, 1997); David J. Harding, "Counterfactual Models of Neighborhood Effects: The Effect of Neighborhood Poverty on Dropping Out and Teenage Pregnancy," *American Journal of Sociology* 109 (2003).

11. Harding, "Counterfactual Models of Neighborhood Effects"; Christopher R. Browning, Tama Leventhal, and Jeanne Brooks-Gunn, "Neighborhood Context and Racial Differences in Early Adolescent Sexual Activity," *Demography* 41 (2004).

12. Greg J. Duncan, Johanne Boisjoly, and Kathleen Mullan Harris, "Sibling, Peer, Neighbor, and Schoolmate Correlations as Indicators of the Importance of Context for Adolescent Development," *Demography* 38 (2001); Bruce H. Rankin and James M. Quane, "Social Contexts and Urban Adolescent Outcomes: The Interrelated Effects of Neighborhoods, Families, and Peers on African American Youth," *Social Problems* 49 (2002).

13. Jencks and Mayer, *Inner-City Poverty in the United States*; Delbert S. Elliott, William Julius Wilson, David Huizinga, Robert J. Sampson, Amanda Elliott, and Bruce Rankin, "The Effects of Neighborhood Disadvantage on Adolescent Development," *Journal of Research in Crime and Delinquency* 33 (1996).

14. See, e.g., Richard D. Alba and John R. Logan, "Variations on Two Themes: Racial and Ethnic Patterns in the Attainment of Suburban Residence," *Demography* 28 (1991); Emily Rosenbaum and Samantha Friedman, "Differences in the Locational Attainment of Immigrant and Native-Born Households with Children in New York City," *Demography* 38 (2001); Craig St. John and Shana M.B. Miller, "The Exposure of Black and Hispanic Children to Urban Ghettos: Evidence from Chicago and the Southwest," *Social Science Quarterly* 76 (1995).

15. Paul A. Jargowsky, *Poverty and Place: Ghettoes, Barrios, and the American City* (New York: Russell Sage Foundation, 1997); Paul A. Jargowsky, "Stunning Progress, Hidden Problems: The Dramatic Decline of Neighborhood Poverty in the 1990s," Living Cities Census Series Report, Center on Urban and Metropolitan Policy (Washington, DC: The Brookings Institution, 2003).

16. St. John and Miller, "The Exposure of Black and Hispanic Children to Urban Ghettos."

17. GeoLytics, Inc., "Census CD Neighborhood Change Database 1970–2000 Tract Data," Machine-readable data file (East Brunswick, NJ, 2003).

18. The Census Bureau defines census tracts as "small, relatively permanent statistical subdivisions of a county . . . [with] between 2,500 and 8,000 persons and, when first delineated, are designed to be homogeneous with respect to population characteristics, economic status, and living conditions" (U.S. Bureau of the Census, *Census of Population and Housing, 1990 United States: Summary Tape File 3A, Technical Documentation, Appendix A*, (Washington, DC: U.S. Department of Commerce, Bureau of the Census, 1992). While tracts may not perfectly replicate the subjective definitions citizens have of their "neighborhoods," many researchers have used tracts as the best available proxy.

19. Because the sociological concept of "neighborhood" generally requires at least a moderate degree of propinquity among residents, it isn't evident that rural or small town census tracts

have sociologically meaningful levels of "neighborhood" poverty. Nevertheless, because the distribution of neighborhood types and racial/ethnic groups in those types differs dramatically in nonmetropolitan relative to metropolitan areas, we include nonmetropolitan areas in the analysis for comparison's sake.

20. Paul A. Jargowsky and Mary Jo Bane, "Ghetto Poverty in the United States, 1970-1980," in *The Urban Underclass*, ed. Christopher Jencks and Paul Peterson (Washington, DC: The Brookings Institution, 1991).

21. This neighborhood type might be more precisely labeled "extremely nonpoor," since it is not necessarily true that neighborhoods with low poverty rates are affluent in other respects. Our analysis of 2000 census data reveals that the average 1999 median family income in "affluent" neighborhoods fell between the 91st and 92nd percentiles of the entire family income distribution. Although there is obviously variation around that average (i.e., not all "extremely nonpoor" neighborhoods also have high median family incomes), this fact, combined with the findings we present in Figure 9.1, suggest that this neighborhood type corresponds well to a reasonable definition of "affluent."

22. The findings presented using this proxy measure are conservative estimates of the true level of racial and ethnic inequality, because the average black or Hispanic family has more children than the average white or Asian family (about 1.31 and 1.64 versus 0.88 and 1.05 children per family, respectively [authors' calculations from U.S. Census data, 2000]).

23. $8.6\% = 0.16$ (proportion of Black central city children in extremely poor neighborhoods from Figure 10) $\times 0.53$ (proportion of black children in central cities from Table 9.1) $\times 100$, and $0.086 \times 10.75$ million Black children $\approx 927{,}000$ black children.

24. Douglas S. Massey and Nancy A. Denton, *American Apartheid: Segregation and the Making of the Underclass* (Cambridge, MA: Harvard University Press, 1993), 135.

25. William J. Wilson, *When Work Disappears: The World of the New Urban Poor* (New York: Alfred A. Knopf, 1996).

26. Massey and Denton, *American Apartheid*, 133.

27. Robert J. Sampson, Jeffrey D. Morenoff, and Felton Earls, "Beyond Social Capital: Spatial Dynamics of Collective Efficacy for Children," *American Sociological Review* 64 (1999).

28. Jargowsky, "Stunning Progress."

29. Wilson, *Truly Disadvantaged*; Jargowsky, *Poverty and Place*.

30. Alba and Logan; Scott J. South, and Kyle D. Crowder, "Residential Mobility between Cities and Suburbs: Race, Suburbanization, and Back-to-the-city Moves," *Demography* 34 (1997).

31. John R. Logan and Harvey L. Molotch, *Urban Fortunes: The Political Economy of Place* (Berkeley, CA: University of California Press, 1987).

32. Massey and Denton, *American Apartheid*.

33. Douglas S. Massey and Mary J. Fischer, "How Segregation Concentrates Poverty," *Ethnic and Racial Studies* 23 (2000).

34. Jargowsky, "Stunning Progress."

## REFERENCES

Alba, Richard D. and John R. Logan. "Variations on Two Themes: Racial and Ethnic Patterns in the Attainment of Suburban Residence." *Demography* 28 (1991): 431–53.

Browning, Christopher R., Tama Leventhal, and Jeanne Brooks-Gunn. "Neighborhood Context and Racial Differences in Early Adolescent Sexual Activity." *Demography* 41 (2004): 697–720.

Connell, James P. and Bonnie L. Halpern-Felsher. "How Neighborhoods Affect Educational Outcomes in Middle Childhood and Adolescence: Conceptual Issues and an Empirical Example." In *Neighborhood Poverty Volume I: Context and Consequences for Children*, ed. by J. Brooks-Gunn, G. J. Duncan, and J. L. Aber. New York: Russell Sage Foundation, 1997.

Corcoran, Mary. "Rags to Rags: Poverty and Mobility in the United States." *Annual Review of Sociology* 21 (1995): 237–267.

Duncan, Greg J., Johanne Boisjoly, and Kathleen Mullan Harris. "Sibling, Peer, Neighbor, and Schoolmate Correlations as Indicators of the Importance of Context for Adolescent Development." *Demography* 38 (2001): 437–447.

Duncan, Greg J., W. Jean Yeung, Jeanne Brooks-Gunn, and Judith R. Smith. "How Much Does Childhood Poverty Affect the Life Chances of Children?" *American Sociological Review* 63 (1997): 406–223.

Elliott, Delbert S., William Julius Wilson, David Huizinga, Robert J. Sampson, Amanda Elliott, and Bruce Rankin. "The Effects of Neighborhood Disadvantage on Adolescent Development." *Journal of Research in Crime and Delinquency* 33 (1996): 389–426.

GeoLytics, Inc. "Census CD Neighborhood Change Database 1970–2000 Tract Data." Machine-readable data file. East Brunswick, NJ, 2003.

Harding, David J. "Counterfactual Models of Neighborhood Effects: The Effect of Neighborhood Poverty on Dropping Out and Teenage Pregnancy." *American Journal of Sociology* 109 (2003): 676–719.

Haveman, Robert and Barbara Wolfe. "The Determinants of Children's Attainments: A Review of Methods and Findings." *Journal of Economic Literature* 33 (1995): 1829–1878.

Jargowsky, Paul A. *Poverty and Place: Ghettoes, Barrios, and the American City*. New York: Russell Sage Foundation, 1997.

———. "Stunning Progress, Hidden Problems: The Dramatic Decline of Neighborhood Poverty in the 1990s." *Living Cities Census Series Report*, Center on Urban and Metropolitan Policy. Washington, DC: The Brookings Institution, 2003.

Jargowsky, Paul A. and Mary Jo Bane. "Ghetto Poverty in the United States, 1970–1980." In *The Urban Underclass*, ed. by C. Jencks and P. Peterson. Washington, DC: The Brookings Institution, 1991.

Jencks, Christopher and Susan E. Mayer. The Social Consequences of Growing up in a Poor Neighborhood." In *Inner-City Poverty in the United States*, ed. by L. E. Lynn, Jr. and M. G. H. McGeary. Washington, DC: National Academy Press, 1990.

Logan, John R. and Harvey L. Molotch. *Urban Fortunes: The Political Economy of Place*. Berkeley, CA: University of California Press, 1990.

Luxembourg Income Study (LIS). "Key Figures." Accessed on April 24, 2006. Available at http://www.lisproject.org/keyfigures.htm

Massey, Douglas S. and Nancy A. Denton. *American Apartheid: Segregation and the Making of the Underclass*. Cambridge, MA: Harvard University Press, 1993.

Massey, Douglas S. and Mary J. Fischer. "How Segregation Concentrates Poverty." *Ethnic and Racial Studies* 23 (2000): 670–691.

Mayer, Susan E. *What Money Can't Buy: Family Income and Children's Life Chances*. Cambridge, MA: Harvard University Press, 1997.

Rainwater, Lee and Timothy M. Smeeding. *Poor Kids in a Rich Country: America's Children in Comparative Perspective*. New York: Russell Sage Foundation, 2003.

Rankin, Bruce H. and James M. Quane. "Social Contexts and Urban Adolescent Outcomes: The Interrelated Effects of Neighborhoods, Families, and Peers on African American Youth." *Social Problems* 49 (2002): 79–100.

Rosenbaum, Emily and Samantha Friedman. "Differences in the Locational Attainment of Immigrant and Native-Born Households with Children in New York City." *Demography* 38 (2001): 337–348.

Sampson, Robert J., Jeffrey D. Morenoff, and Felton Earls. "Beyond Social Capital: Spatial Dynamics of Collective Efficacy for Children." *American Sociological Review* 64 (1999): 633–660.

Sampson, Robert J., Jeffrey D. Morenoff, and Thomas Gannon-Rowley. "Assessing 'Neighborhood Effects:' Social Processes and New Directions in Research." *Annual Review of Sociology* 28 (2002): 443–478.

South, Scott J. and Kyle D. Crowder. "Residential Mobility between Cities and Suburbs: Race, Suburbanization, and Back-to-the-city Moves." *Demography* 34 (1997): 525–538.

St. John, Craig and Shana M.B. Miller. "The Exposure of Black and Hispanic Children to Urban Ghettos: Evidence from Chicago and the Southwest." *Social Science Quarterly* 76 (1995): 562–576.

U.S. Bureau of the Census. *Census of Population and Housing, 1990 United States: Summary Tape File 3A.* Technical Documentation. Washington, DC: U.S. Department of Commerce, Bureau of the Census, producer. Ann Arbor, MI: Inter-university Consortium for Political and Social Research, distributor, 1992.

———. "Income Stable, Poverty Up, Numbers of Americans With and Without Health Insurance Rise, Census Bureau Reports." Accessed April 21, 2006. Available at http://www.census.gov/Press-Release/www/releases/archives/income_wealth/002484.html.

———. "Historical Poverty Tables." Accessed May 10, 2006. Available at http://www.census.gov/hhes/www/poverty/histpov/hstpov2.html

Wilson, William J. *The Truly Disadvantaged: The Inner City, the Underclass, and Public Policy.* Chicago: The University of Chicago Press, 1987.

———. *When Work Disappears: The World of the New Urban Poor.* New York: Alfred A. Knopf, 1996.

CHAPTER 10

# CHILDREN AND THE CHANGING SOCIAL ECOLOGY OF ECONOMIC DISADVANTAGE IN URBAN AMERICA

*Robert L. Wagmiller, Jr.*

Children living in high-poverty neighborhoods, regardless of their own family economic circumstances, face challenges that children residing in more affluent neighborhoods do not. They experience poorer home environments, less maternal warmth, and less cognitive stimulation from their mothers.[1] They encounter greater social and physical disorder and lower levels of child-centered control in their neighborhoods.[2] They see fewer stably employed men and women in their neighborhoods and their parents have fewer friends who are stably employed or college graduates and more friends and neighbors who are on public assistance.[3] A culture of despair that further impedes achievement and fosters delinquency oftentimes arises in their neighborhoods.[4]

Consequently, children in these neighborhoods typically fare worse than similarly situated children in more affluent neighborhoods.[5] They score lower on IQ and educational achievement tests.[6] They have higher rates of behavior problems.[7] They are more likely to experience depression, anxiety, oppositional defiant disorder, and conduct disorder.[8] They are more likely to drop out of high school.[9] They engage in riskier sexual behavior, resulting in higher teenage pregnancy rates.[10] They commit more delinquent acts and more serious delinquent acts.[11]

Although exposure to extreme levels of neighborhood poverty has many harmful consequences for children, no study has comprehensively examined children's exposure to extreme levels of neighborhood poverty. Previous studies have documented trends for the entire population,[12] but no study has reported trends for children separately. There are, however, several reasons to believe that levels of exposure and trends for children may differ from those for adults and the population as a whole. First, poverty rates for families with children are much higher than for families without children, which may make it more difficult for families with children to escape high-poverty neighborhoods.[13] Second, growing segregation by life course cycle in the metropolis, with childless individuals and couples increasingly inhabiting city neighborhoods, may lead to greater racial and ethnic disparities in exposure to concentrated disadvantage for children because of the overrepresentation of poor, minority children in those families that remain in the city.[14] Third, while segregation by race and ethnicity declined for adults between 1990 and 2000, it increased for children.[15] Consequently, the exposure of minority children to extreme levels of neighborhood poverty may not have declined as dramatically in the 1990s as did overall levels of exposure for minority group members.[16] Jargowsky, in the only study that has examined children's levels of exposure to high-poverty neighborhoods, reports that in 1990 poor children and black and Hispanic children were more likely to live in high-poverty neighborhoods than poor adults and black and Hispanic adults.[17]

This chapter makes several contributions to the growing literature on neighborhood poverty. First, it develops a comprehensive, multidimensional framework for assessing the social ecology of children's economic disadvantage. Second, it uses this framework to investigate racial and ethnic group disparities in children's exposure to economic disadvantage in urban America. Levels and trends in children's exposure to neighborhood poverty, presented separately by race and ethnicity, are reported for all U.S. metropolitan areas over the last 30 years using aggregate data from the U. S. Census of Population and Housing.

## THE CHANGING SOCIAL ECOLOGY OF DISADVANTAGE IN URBAN AMERICA AND CHILDREN'S EXPOSURE TO NEIGHBORHOOD POVERTY

The social ecology of disadvantage in urban America has changed dramatically over the last three decades, "creating a social milieu significantly different from the environment that existed in these communities [low-income neighborhoods] several decades ago."[18] In his now classic study of the predominately African American neighborhoods on the south side of Chicago, Wilson first noted that the geography of urban poverty was changing. Industrial restructuring, suburbanization of population and employment, and the migration of middle-class African Americans out of traditionally black neighborhoods, Wilson argued, was causing poverty and other forms of social and economic disadvantage to become increasingly concentrated in a small but growing number of intensely disadvantaged and progressively more isolated inner-city neighborhoods.

While Wilson's explanations for this new geography of urban poverty continue to be debated,[19] many studies have documented an increasing geographic concentration of poverty in U.S. metropolitan areas.[20] Jargowsky, for example, reports that during the 1970s the number of high-poverty neighborhoods[21] in American metropolitan areas increased 50.1 percent and the population of high-poverty neighborhoods rose 24.7 percent.[22] During the 1980s, the geographic concentration of poverty increased even more sharply, with the number of high-poverty neighborhoods increasing 54.3 percent and the population of these neighborhoods rising by 54.1 percent. By

1990, there were 2,726 high-poverty neighborhoods with a population of nearly 8 million people.

As the number and population of high-poverty neighborhoods rose dramatically in the 1970s and 1980s, the racial and ethnic composition of these neighborhoods also began to change.[23] While the absolute number of blacks living in high-poverty neighborhoods increased sharply during this period and a much higher percentage of blacks than whites or Hispanics continued to live in these deeply disadvantaged neighborhoods, the number of Hispanics and whites living in high-poverty neighborhoods rose more sharply than did the number of blacks. As a result, blacks represented a declining proportion of the population of high-poverty neighborhoods during the 1970s and 1980s. By 1990, 17.4 percent of blacks, 10.5 percent of Hispanics, and 1.4 percent of whites resided in high-poverty neighborhoods.

Recent studies by Jargowsky, and Kingsley and Pettit indicate that during the 1990s this ecological shift in the geographic distribution of poverty unexpectedly reversed.[24] The number of high-poverty neighborhoods declined by 20 percent and the total population of these neighborhoods fell by 23 percent.[25] As the number and population of high-poverty neighborhoods declined dramatically in the 1990s, the proportion of the population of high-poverty neighborhoods that is African American continued to fall and the proportion that is Hispanic continued to rise.[26] By 2000, less than 40 percent of the population of high-poverty neighborhoods was black, 29 percent was Hispanic, and 24 percent was white.

While recent studies have extensively documented levels and trends in exposure to high-poverty neighborhoods for the population and specific racial and ethnic subgroups, little is known about how levels and trends for children may differ from those for the population or subgroup as a whole. There are, however, several reasons to believe that levels of exposure and trends for children, particularly racial and ethnic minority children, may differ from those for the population or subgroup as a whole. First, poverty rates for children, especially young children, are much higher than for adults and a much higher percentage of children live in families experiencing extreme poverty (<50% of federal poverty threshold).[27] As a result, children, particularly young children, may be more likely to live in high-poverty neighborhoods. Second, racial and ethnic group disparities in levels of exposure to high-poverty neighborhoods may be greater for children than for the group as a whole because minority children experience greater residential segregation than do adult group members.[28] Third, trends for children, particularly for children from racial and ethnic minority groups, may diverge from overall trends both because of growing residential segregation by life course stage[29] and diverging patterns of racial residential segregation for adults and children.[30]

## A MULTIDIMENSIONAL FRAMEWORK FOR ASSESSING CHILDREN'S EXPOSURE TO NEIGHBORHOOD POVERTY

Children's exposure to neighborhood poverty varies across multiple analytic dimensions. Children can live in neighborhoods in which many residents are poor (*resident high-poverty neighborhoods*). They can reside in neighborhoods in which many group members are poor (*group high-poverty neighborhoods*). They can live in communities in which many children are poor (*child high-poverty neighborhoods*). Each of these dimensions can have different and independent effects on children's experiences, opportunities, and outcomes. Resident poverty, for example, can drain from a community the resources necessary to sustain local organizations and institutions and reduce the number of mainstream role models available in a community.[31] Because even in integrated environments social interactions tend to be highly segregated,[32] group poverty can limit children's access to social capital and race-specific role models. Child poverty can foster the development of a youth subculture that impedes achievement and nurtures delinquency.[33] When multiple dimensions overlap, children in a neighborhood or racial and ethnic subgroup confront even greater challenges.

Children's exposure to poverty in their community environment is examined across three dimensions:

*Resident Poverty Rate:* The percentage of children in a geographic unit (county, region, metropolitan area, etc.) that live in neighborhoods in which more than 40 percent of persons are poor.

*Group Poverty Rate:* The percentage of children in a racial or ethnic subgroup in a geographic unit (county, region, metropolitan area, etc.) that live in neighborhoods in which more than 40 percent of subgroup members are poor.

*Child Poverty Rate:* The percentage of children in a geographic unit (county, region, metropolitan area, etc.) that live in neighborhoods in which more than 40 percent of children are poor.

Neighborhoods are defined as high-poverty neighborhoods when 40 percent or more of residents are poor. Previous studies have shown that this threshold most closely matches local individuals' perceptions of the neighborhoods in their city that are most deeply disadvantaged. Ethnographic observation has confirmed that these neighborhoods "look and feel" like underclass neighborhoods (i.e., they are characterized by dilapidated housing, vacant units with broken and boarded-up windows, abandoned and burned-out cars, young men loitering, etc.).[34]

## DATA AND METHODS

### Sample and Data

Children's exposure to extreme levels of neighborhood poverty as well as racial and ethnic disparities in exposure is investigated using tract-level Census data for U.S. metropolitan areas between 1970 and 2000. Census tracts are employed because they represent the closest approximation to neighborhoods available in official statistics, with populations typically ranging between 2,500 and 8,000 inhabitants and boundaries initially drawn to construct geographic units with relatively homogenous population characteristics, economic status, and living conditions. The sample employed in this study includes all tracts in the 204 metropolitan areas defined by the U.S. Bureau of the Census in 1970.[35] Data were drawn from the Neighborhood Change Database (NCDB), which integrates information on population and housing characteristics from the 1970, 1980, 1990, and 2000 Decennial Census of Population and Housing into a single database. All 42,178 tracts in the counties and towns comprising the 204 metropolitan areas selected for inclusion in this sample are employed in the analyses to follow.

Tract and metropolitan area boundaries are periodically redrawn in response to population shifts, making geographic comparability an important concern in any longitudinal study of neighborhoods. Tract boundaries are redrawn in order to maintain their size and geographic integrity and new tracts are added as the population of a metropolitan area migrates into previously untracted areas. Relatively few tracts maintain stable boundaries over the entire 1970–2000 time span.[36] Because the principal focus of this study is change in children's exposure to high-poverty neighborhoods, it is important that temporally consistent geographic units are used. Otherwise, it is impossible to determine whether apparent changes in children's exposure to concentrated poverty are attributable to changes in the spatial distribution of children and poverty or to changes in the geographic boundaries of spatial units. To avoid this problem, this study computes measures of children's exposure to high levels of neighborhood poverty using census tract data normalized to Census 2000 tract boundaries.

The boundaries of metropolitan areas also change over time. Much as tract boundaries are redrawn as population distributions shift, metropolitan area boundaries shift as the size, distribution, and social and economic integration of core and outlying areas change. Because changes in metropolitan area boundaries reflect the spatial expansion or contraction of the metropolis, some researchers prefer to use contemporaneous boundaries.[37] However, researchers whose primary interest is change in the geographic distribution of the population often prefer to use temporally consistent metropolitan area definitions that avoid confounding distribution and boundary changes.[38] For this reason, this study applies 1970 metropolitan area boundaries to the 1980, 1990, and 2000 data to create temporally consistent metropolitan area definitions.

Although the creation of temporally consistent tract and metropolitan area boundaries greatly reduces the possibility that arbitrary changes in geographic boundaries distort conclusions about changes in the social ecology of child poverty, the use of these boundaries is not without its drawbacks. The application of 2000 tract definitions to earlier census years results in the creation of a few tracts with unusually small populations and a few tracts with unusually large populations.[39] More problematically, the application of 1970 metropolitan area boundaries to subsequent decades ignores the spatial expansion or contraction of the metropolis since 1970. Regrettably, this is unavoidable if temporally consistent geographic boundaries are to be used.[40] Because few high-poverty neighborhoods are located in these mainly outlying regions of the metropolis, the exclusion of these neighborhoods has a negligible effect on the trends discussed in this chapter.

## RESULTS

Overall trends in children's exposure to extreme levels of neighborhood poverty are presented for each dimension in order to provide a comprehensive picture of the changing social ecology of child poverty in the United States. To gain a better understanding of racial and ethnic group disparities in children's exposure, measures are reported separately by race and ethnicity. Racial and ethnic group differences in the extent of overlap between dimensions are also discussed at the conclusion of this section.

### Resident Poverty

Table 10.1 presents for each census year resident poverty rates—the percentage of persons who live in neighborhoods in which 40 percent or more of persons are poor (*resident high-poverty neighborhoods*)—by age, poverty status, and race and ethnicity. Percentage change between 1970 and 1990 and 1990 and 2000 are also reported. Data for Hispanics, Native Americans, and Asians, Native Hawaiians, and Pacific Islanders are unavailable for 1970. Data on children's poverty statuses are unavailable for 1970 and 1980.

Overall levels and trends in children's exposure to resident high-poverty neighborhoods parallel those previously reported for the entire population.[41] Children's exposure rose sharply in the 1970s and 1980s and fell dramatically in the 1990s. Between 1970 and 1990, resident poverty rates for children increased by 80 percent to 90 percent, which is comparable to the rate of increase for working-age adults and moderately higher than the rate of increase for the elderly population. In the 1990s, resident poverty rates for children fell by 30–35 percent, which again parallels the experiences of working-age and older adults. Resident poverty rates decline with age, with the youngest children experiencing the highest rates of exposure to resident high-poverty neighborhoods. One notable exception to this general pattern is the high rate of exposure for young adults, which increased more sharply in the 1970s and 1980s and declined less sharply in the 1990s than did exposure rates for other age groups, even young children. On average, children's rates of exposure to resident high-poverty neighborhoods are 50 to 70 percent higher than those for working-age and elderly adults, but nonetheless remain relatively low (3–6%).

While overall age differences in exposure to resident high-poverty neighborhoods are modest, racial and ethnic disparities in children's exposure are quite large. Only 1 to 2 percent of white children in any given year reside in resident high-poverty neighborhoods. Moreover, resident poverty rates for white children are nearly identical to those for working-age whites. Resident poverty rates for black children, by comparison, are 10 to 16 times higher than those for white children, with rates ranging from 13 to 27 percent, and are noticeably higher for black children (particularly young black children) than for black adults. Resident poverty rates for children from other racial and ethnic minority groups are generally higher than for

**Table 10.1**
**Resident Poverty Rates by Year and Age, 1970–2000: All U.S. Metropolitan Areas**

| | 1970 | 1980 | 1990 | 2000 | Percent Change 1970–1990 | Percent Change 1990–2000 |
|---|---|---|---|---|---|---|
| Age | | | | | | |
| 0–4 years | 3.60 | 4.88 | 6.80 | 4.63 | 88.81 | −31.94 |
| 5–9 years | 3.58 | 4.60 | 6.46 | 4.60 | 80.33 | −28.80 |
| 10–14 years | 3.40 | 4.39 | 6.37 | 4.14 | 87.17 | −34.95 |
| 15–17 years | 3.27 | 4.39 | 6.28 | 4.00 | 92.08 | −36.24 |
| 18–24 years | 2.60 | 5.22 | 8.84 | 8.10 | 239.36 | −8.39 |
| 25–64 years | 2.15 | 2.76 | 4.04 | 2.81 | 88.19 | −30.50 |
| 65 years or older | 2.61 | 3.21 | 4.26 | 2.53 | 63.22 | −40.57 |
| Children by poverty status | | | | | | |
| Poor Children | – | – | 21.65 | 14.65 | – | −32.33 |
| Nonpoor Children | – | – | 2.66 | 2.04 | – | −23.41 |
| Children by race | | | | | | |
| White | | | | | | |
| 0–5 years | 1.55 | 1.28 | 2.02 | 1.80 | 30.43 | −10.83 |
| 6–14 years | 1.40 | 1.12 | 1.95 | 1.56 | 39.43 | −19.91 |
| 15–64 years | 1.06 | 1.27 | 2.20 | 1.93 | 108.64 | −12.55 |
| 65+ years | 1.26 | 1.24 | 1.87 | 1.12 | 48.31 | −40.06 |
| Black | | | | | | |
| 0–5 years | 16.72 | 20.42 | 26.85 | 14.14 | 60.65 | −47.34 |
| 6–14 years | 17.17 | 18.97 | 24.61 | 12.99 | 43.30 | −47.23 |
| 15–64 years | 13.69 | 16.07 | 19.52 | 10.52 | 42.63 | −46.13 |
| 65+ years | 20.85 | 24.36 | 29.53 | 13.86 | 41.64 | −53.08 |
| Hispanic | | | | | | |
| 0–5 years | – | 10.32 | 12.86 | 8.26 | – | −35.80 |
| 6–14 years | – | 11.39 | 13.62 | 8.53 | – | −37.36 |
| 15–64 years | – | 9.07 | 11.24 | 7.37 | – | −34.44 |
| 65+ years | – | 11.24 | 15.26 | 8.45 | – | −44.62 |
| Native American | | | | | | |
| 0–5 years | – | 7.02 | 9.81 | 7.31 | – | −25.48 |
| 6–14 years | – | 6.74 | 8.98 | 6.70 | – | −25.42 |
| 15–64 years | – | 5.55 | 7.24 | 5.35 | – | −26.02 |
| 65+ years | – | 7.35 | 8.52 | 6.35 | – | −25.47 |
| Asian, Native Hawaiian, and Pacific Islander | | | | | | |
| 0–5 years | – | 1.70 | 4.46 | 2.34 | – | −47.42 |
| 6–14 years | – | 1.56 | 3.72 | 2.71 | – | −26.95 |
| 15–64 years | – | 1.72 | 3.32 | 2.87 | – | −13.51 |
| 65+ years | – | 1.99 | 2.73 | 2.37 | – | −13.04 |

white children, but are universally much lower than for black children, highlighting the exceptional nature of black poverty.[42] For Hispanic children, resident poverty rates for this period range from 8 percent to 14 percent. For Native American children, they range from 7 percent to 10 percent. For Asian, Native Hawaiian, and Pacific Islander children, they range from 1.5 percent to 4.5 percent.

Not only are racial and ethnic disparities in children's exposure to extreme levels of neighborhood poverty great, but they have expanded significantly over the last three decades. Between 1970 and 1990, the percentage of black children between the ages of birth and 5 years old living in resident high-poverty neighborhoods increased from 16.7 percent to 26.9 percent and the percentage of black children between the ages of 6 and 14 years old living in resident high-poverty neighborhoods increased from 17.2 percent to 24.6 percent. Over this same period, the percentages of white children between the ages of birth and 5 years old and 6 and 14 years old living in resident high-poverty neighborhoods increased only from, respectively, 1.5 percent to 2.0 percent and 1.4 percent to 2.2 percent. During the 1980s, Hispanic, Native American, and Asian children experienced similarly modest increases. As a result, black children represented a slightly increasing proportion of the population of children in resident high-poverty neighborhoods in the 1970s and 1980s and white children represented a rapidly declining proportion of residents in these neighborhoods. In sharp contrast, black adults represented a persistently declining proportion of the population of resident high-poverty neighborhoods during this period and the proportion of white adults in these neighborhoods remained stable.

While the increase in the number of resident high-poverty neighborhoods in the 1970s and 1980s disproportionately disadvantaged black children, the dramatic and unexpected decline in the number of high-poverty neighborhoods in the 1990s disproportionately benefited black children. Between 1990 and 2000, the percentage of young black children living in resident high-poverty neighborhoods fell from 26.9 percent to 14.1 percent and the percentage of older black children living in these neighborhoods fell from 24.6 percent to 13.0 percent. By contrast, the percentage of young white children living in resident high-poverty neighborhoods fell only from 2.0 percent to 1.8 percent and the percentage of older white children living in these neighborhoods fell from 2.0 percent to 1.6 percent. Hispanic, Native American, and Asian children also experienced more modest declines during this period than did black children. As a result, the proportion of the child population of resident high-poverty neighborhoods that is black fell sharply in the 1990s, declining from 59.1 percent to 49.5 percent. Meanwhile, the proportion of the child population that is white increased for the first time, rising from 22.0 percent to 23.4 percent. In the 1970s and 1980s, the changing social ecology of economic disadvantage disproportionately disadvantaged black children, particularly young black children, greatly increasing their exposure to extreme levels of neighborhood poverty. In the 1990s, the unexpected reversal of these trends largely benefited black children, greatly reducing their exposure to resident high-poverty neighborhoods and moderating their overrepresentation in these deeply disadvantaged neighborhoods.

**Table 10.2**
**Group Poverty Rates by Year and Age. 1970–2000: All U.S. Metropolitan Areas**

| | 1970 | 1980 | 1990 | 2000 | Percent Change 1970–1990 | Percent Change 1990–2000 |
|---|---|---|---|---|---|---|
| White | | | | | | |
| 0–5 years | 1.39 | 1.06 | 1.50 | 1.70 | 8.45 | 13.25 |
| 6–14 years | 1.23 | 0.92 | 1.48 | 1.45 | 20.22 | −2.09 |
| 15–64 years | 0.87 | 1.05 | 1.65 | 1.68 | 89.87 | 1.72 |
| 65+ years | 0.95 | 0.86 | 1.17 | 0.86 | 23.26 | −26.61 |
| Black | | | | | | |
| 0–5 years | 30.19 | 29.64 | 40.29 | 22.37 | 33.44 | −44.48 |
| 6–14 years | 31.14 | 26.90 | 36.34 | 20.08 | 16.70 | −44.74 |
| 15–64 years | 24.46 | 22.38 | 27.82 | 16.02 | 13.72 | −42.41 |
| 65+ years | 27.47 | 24.52 | 27.74 | 15.49 | 0.96 | −44.16 |
| Hispanic | | | | | | |
| 0–5 years | – | 16.72 | 18.43 | 11.53 | – | −37.44 |
| Poor children | – | 17.34 | 18.75 | 11.54 | – | −38.49 |
| Nonpoor children | – | 14.41 | 15.81 | 10.19 | – | −35.51 |
| 65+ years | – | 15.20 | 18.09 | 10.42 | – | −42.42 |
| Native American | | | | | | |
| 0–5 years | – | 28.77 | 34.07 | 25.34 | – | −25.63 |
| 6–14 years | – | 25.69 | 29.53 | 23.60 | – | −20.09 |
| 15–64 years | – | 20.86 | 22.84 | 19.00 | – | −16.81 |
| 65+ years | – | 22.95 | 23.45 | 19.03 | – | −18.84 |
| Asian, Native Hawaiian, and Pacific Islander | | | | | | |
| 0–5 years | – | 8.66 | 11.79 | 6.06 | – | −48.64 |
| 6–14 years | – | 8.11 | 10.55 | 6.76 | – | −35.90 |
| 15–64 years | – | 6.83 | 8.67 | 6.35 | – | −26.72 |
| 65+ years | – | 4.51 | 5.81 | 4.32 | – | −25.65 |

## Group Poverty Rates

Resident poverty rates reveal the distinctive nature of black children's exposure to high-poverty neighborhoods. However, as stark as racial disparities in children's exposure to extreme levels of neighborhood poverty are, resident poverty rates alone understate the distinctive disadvantage experienced by black children. For racial and ethnic group disparities in group poverty rates, which indicate the percentage of persons who live in neighborhoods in which 40 percent or more of their group members are poor (*group high-poverty neighborhoods*), are even greater. Group poverty rates for white, black, Hispanic, Native American, and Asian children and adults are reported in Table 10.2.

Group poverty rates for white children are universally low, ranging from less than 1.0 percent to 1.7 percent, and have changed very little over the past 30 years. Very few white children live in neighborhoods in which 40 percent or more of whites are poor.

Even when white children live in resident high-poverty neighborhoods, their neighborhoods frequently are not group high-poverty neighborhoods. Typically between 20 percent and 30 percent of white children in resident high-poverty neighborhoods reside in neighborhoods in which less than 40 percent of whites are poor.

Nearly all black children who reside in high-poverty neighborhoods, by contrast, live in neighborhoods in which 40 percent or more of the black population is poor. Even when black children escape living in a resident high-poverty neighborhood, there is a 1 in 10 chance that their neighborhood is a group high-poverty neighborhood for them. Consequently, group poverty rates for black children are exceptionally high, ranging from 20 percent to 40 percent over this period.

Group poverty rates for black children follow a somewhat different trajectory over the 1970-2000 time period than did resident poverty rates for these children. In the 1970s, while resident poverty rates for black children were generally rising, group poverty rates were declining. In the 1980s, both resident poverty rates and group poverty rates for black children increased sharply. In the 1990s, both resident poverty rates and group poverty rates for black children decreased dramatically. This pattern suggests that the increase in black children's exposure to resident high-poverty neighborhoods in the 1970s was either a reflection of these children's non-black neighbors becoming poorer or moving out of their neighborhoods in large numbers, while in the 1980s the increase in their exposure was largely a consequence of their black neighbors becoming poorer. In the 1990s, the dramatic decline in their exposure was primarily a reflection of their black neighbors becoming less poor.

Group poverty rates for the other racial and ethnic minority groups highlight the exceptionally disadvantaged ecological niche that black children occupy relative to other children. Not only are Hispanic and Asian children much less likely than black children to live in resident high-poverty neighborhoods, they are also much less likely to live in neighborhoods in which a large proportion of their group members are poor. Group poverty rates for Native American children are comparable to those for black children, but they are much less likely to reside in resident high-poverty neighborhoods. Only black children are likely to live in neighborhoods in which both high levels of poverty drain community social and economic resources and high levels of subgroup poverty limit access to group-specific social capital and role models.

### Child Poverty Rates

Table 10.3 presents child poverty rates—which represent the percentage of persons who live in neighborhoods in which 40 percent or more of children are poor (*child high-poverty neighborhoods*)—by age, poverty status, and race and ethnicity. Because poverty status is only available by age after 1990, child poverty rates can only be computed for 1990 and 2000.

Poor children are more geographically concentrated than poor adults. Consequently, children are much more likely to live in communities in which many children are poor than they are to live in neighborhoods in which many residents are poor.

**Table 10.3**
**Child Poverty Rates by Year and Age, 1990-2000: All U.S. Metropolitan Areas**

| | 1990 | 2000 | Percent change 1990–2000 |
|---|---|---|---|
| Age | | | |
|   0–4 years | 14.09 | 11.26 | −20.09 |
|   5–9 years | 13.44 | 11.24 | −16.33 |
|   10–14 years | 13.23 | 10.32 | −22.00 |
|   15–17 years | 13.04 | 9.91 | −24.04 |
|   18–24 years | 13.49 | 11.72 | −13.15 |
|   25–64 years | 9.51 | 7.58 | −20.21 |
|   65 years or older | 10.22 | 7.28 | −28.79 |
| Children by Poverty Status | | | |
|   Poor children | 41.1 | 32.7 | −20.60 |
|   Nonpoor children | 7.38 | 6.27 | −15.07 |
| Children by Race | | | |
|   White | | | |
|     0–5 years | 5.77 | 5.09 | −11.82 |
|     6–14 years | 5.35 | 4.44 | −17.00 |
|     15–64 years | 5.16 | 4.18 | −19.00 |
|     65+ years | 6.01 | 3.95 | −34.32 |
|   Black | | | |
|     0–5 years | 40.07 | 28.63 | −28.56 |
|     6–14 years | 38.13 | 27.66 | −27.45 |
|     15–64 years | 33.14 | 23.43 | −29.31 |
|     65+ years | 44.78 | 30.99 | −30.80 |
|   Hispanic | | | |
|     0–5 years | 26.44 | 19.55 | −26.06 |
|     6–14 years | 26.79 | 19.66 | −26.63 |
|     15–64 years | 23.21 | 17.52 | −24.53 |
|     65+ years | 27.29 | 19.45 | −28.74 |
|   Native American | | | |
|     0–5 years | 21.53 | 15.34 | −28.74 |
|     6–14 years | 18.83 | 14.82 | −21.31 |
|     15–64 years | 14.97 | 13.59 | −9.26 |
|     65+ years | 21.39 | 13.93 | −34.89 |
|   Asian, Native Hawaiian, and Pacific Islander | | | |
|     0–5 years | 11.06 | 6.52 | −41.08 |
|     6–14 years | 9.82 | 7.35 | −25.13 |
|     15–64 years | 7.40 | 5.95 | −19.54 |
|     65+ years | 8.55 | 7.25 | −15.28 |

While only 4.0 percent to 6.8 percent of children reside in resident high-poverty neighborhoods, 11.2–14.1 percent of children reside in child high-poverty neighborhoods. As a result, a significant proportion of children live in communities in which many of the children they will encounter and befriend are likely to be poor.

As black children are much more likely than other children to reside in resident and group high-poverty neighborhoods, they are also much more likely to reside in child high-poverty neighborhoods. In 1990, 40 percent of black children resided in a neighborhood in which in at least 40 percent of children were poor. By comparison, only 5 percent of white children, 26 percent of Hispanic children, 20 percent of Native American children, and 10 percent of Asian children lived in such neighborhoods. The shifting social ecology of urban poverty in the 1990s, which dramatically decreased children's, particularly black children's, exposure to resident and group high-poverty neighborhoods also sharply reduced children's exposure to child high-poverty neighborhoods. By 2000, child poverty rates for black children had dropped by a quarter, to 28.6 percent. Child poverty rates for other racial and ethnic minority children also dropped dramatically in the 1990s, with rates for Hispanic children falling to 20 percent, rates for Native American children falling to 15 percent, and rates for Asian children declining to 7 percent. Child poverty rates for white children fell moderately, from 5.8 percent in 1990 to 5.1 percent in 2000. As a consequence, the proportion of the child population in child high-poverty neighborhoods that is black declined and the proportion that is white increased in the 1990s.

### Overlap between Dimensions

Racial and ethnic disparities in children's exposure to different forms of neighborhood poverty are even more evident when the overlap between dimensions is examined. Table 10.4 presents the percentage of children by racial and ethnic group that live in neighborhoods that are classified as high-poverty on all three dimensions and no dimensions.

Black children are both much more likely than children from other racial and ethnic subgroups to reside in neighborhoods that are simultaneously classified as resident, group, and child high-poverty neighborhoods and are much less likely to reside in neighborhoods that are neither classified as resident, group, nor child high-poverty neighborhoods. By 1990, nearly 1 in every 5 black children lived in a neighborhood that was classified as high-poverty on all three dimensions, while only slightly more than half of black children resided in a neighborhood that was not classified as high poverty on any of the dimensions. The sharp decline in neighborhood poverty rates in the 1990s both dramatically decreased the share of black children residing in neighborhoods classified as high-poverty on all three dimensions (10–11%) and sharply increased the share of black children residing in neighborhoods not classified as high poverty on any of the three dimensions (68–70%).

Nearly all white children (94%) reside in neighborhoods that are not classified as high-poverty on any dimension and very few white children live in neighborhoods that are classified as high-poverty on all three dimensions (1%). Asian children are almost as unlikely as white children to reside in a neighborhood that is classified as

**Table 10.4**
**Percentage Living in Neighborhoods That Are High and Low on All Three Dimensions, by Race, Age, and Year**

| | % in Neighborhoods High on All Three Dimensions | | | % in Neighborhoods Low on All Three Dimensions | |
|---|---|---|---|---|---|
| | 1990 | 2000 | | 1990 | 2000 |
| White | | | White | | |
| 0–5 years | 1.24 | 1.21 | 0–5 years | 94.12 | 94.75 |
| 6–14 years | 1.24 | 1.05 | 6–14 years | 94.56 | 95.43 |
| Black | | | Black | | |
| 0–5 years | 19.91 | 11.32 | 0–5 years | 56.21 | 68.19 |
| 6–14 years | 18.54 | 10.42 | 6–14 years | 58.46 | 69.54 |
| Hispanic | | | Hispanic | | |
| 0–5 years | 10.69 | 6.83 | 0–5 years | 71.18 | 78.63 |
| 6–14 years | 11.29 | 7.10 | 6–14 years | 71.04 | 78.78 |
| Native American | | | Native American | | |
| 0–5 years | 7.28 | 4.90 | 0–5 years | 59.72 | 68.25 |
| 6–14 years | 6.84 | 4.70 | 6–14 years | 65.34 | 70.18 |
| Asian, Native Hawaiian, and Pacific Islander | | | Asian, Native Hawaiian, and Pacific Islander | | |
| 0–5 years | 3.31 | 1.49 | 0–5 years | 84.35 | 90.37 |
| 6–14 years | 2.86 | 1.95 | 6–14 years | 85.98 | 89.63 |

high-poverty on all three dimensions (3%), but are noticeably more likely to live in a neighborhood that is classified as high-poverty on at least one-dimension (10–15%). Native American children are almost as likely as black children to reside in a neighborhood that is classified as high-poverty on at least one dimension (30–40%), but as much less likely to live in a neighborhood that is classified as high-poverty on all three dimensions (5–7%). Hispanic children's exposure to neighborhood poverty falls between the extremes of black children on one hand and white and Asian children on the other hand. A relatively high percentage of Hispanic children live in neighborhoods that are classified as high-poverty on all three dimensions (7–11%), but a relatively high percentage also lives in neighborhoods that are not classified as high-poverty on any dimension (70–80%).

Black children occupy a uniquely disadvantaged ecological niche in the metropolis. They are more likely than children in other racial and ethnic subgroups to reside in neighborhoods in which large shares of residents, group members, and children are poor. They are much more likely to live in neighborhoods in which the three dimensions of neighborhood poverty overlap. They are much less likely to live in neighborhoods that are not classified as high-poverty on any dimension. At the other extreme, white children, and to somewhat lesser extent Asian children, occupy a distinctively advantaged ecological niche in which they tend to experience relatively little exposure to neighborhood poverty. Hispanic and Native American children neither experience the ecological disadvantages that black children experience nor enjoy the ecological advantages that white and Asian children enjoy.

## CONCLUSION

On a diverse set of indicators African American children and adolescents fare worse than other children and adolescents. They exhibit more behavioral and cognitive problems and score lower on academic achievement tests.[43] They are less likely to graduate high school[44] and enroll in college.[45] They are more likely to be unemployed or drop out of the labor force after leaving school.[46] When employed, they tend to work fewer hours and earn less.[47] They are more likely to be arrested and incarcerated.[48] They engage in riskier sexual behavior at earlier ages, resulting in higher teenage pregnancy rates.[49]

One reason that black children are worse off than other children is that they occupy a uniquely disadvantaged ecological niche in the metropolis. They are much more likely than children from other racial and ethnic subgroups to reside in neighborhoods in which large numbers of residents, group members, and children are poor. Moreover, they are more likely to live in neighborhoods in which the different dimensions of neighborhood poverty overlap and much less likely to live in neighborhoods that are not classified as disadvantaged on any dimension. Children from no other racial and ethnic group experience this multidimensional layering of ecological disadvantage.

Given the well-known harmful effects of residence in economically disadvantaged neighborhoods it is not surprising that black children fare worse than other children.[50] Yet, the findings presented in this chapter suggest some cause for optimism. After decades of deterioration, the ecological position of black children unexpectedly and dramatically improved in the 1990s. By 2000, a smaller percentage of black children resided in neighborhoods in which a large share of their neighbors, group members, and children were poor than at any time since the early 1970s. Though black children continue to be much more exposed to neighborhood poverty than children from other racial and ethnic groups, a much smaller proportion of black children today reside in these deeply disadvantaged neighborhoods than did at their zenith in the early 1990s. If, as a growing body of research documents, residence in high-poverty neighborhoods negatively affects child outcomes, racial and ethnic disparities in children's outcomes may at long last begin to decline as the shifting social ecology of urban poverty lessens black children's exposure to geographically concentrated disadvantage.

## NOTES

1. P. K. Klebanov, J. Brooks-Gunn, P. L. Chase-Landsdale, and R. A. Gordon, "Are Neighborhood Effects on Young Children Mediated by Features of the Home Environment?" In *Neighborhood Poverty: Context and Consequences for Development*, ed. J. Brooks-Gunn, G. Duncan, and J. L. Aber (New York: Russell Sage Foundation, 1997), 119–145; and P. K. Klebanov, J. Brooks-Gunn, and G. J. Duncan, "Does Neighborhood and Family Poverty Affect

Mothers' Parenting, Mental Health and Social Support?" *Journal of Marriage and the Family* 56 (1994): 441–455.

2. K. J. Geis and C. E. Ross, "A New Look at Urban Alienation: The Effect of Neighborhood Disorder on Perceived Powerlessness," *Social Psychology Quarterly* 61 (1998): 232–246; C. E. Ross, "Neighborhood Disadvantage and Adult Depression," *Journal of Health and Social Behavior* 41 (2000): 177–187; and R. J. Sampson, J. D. Morenoff, and F. Earls, "Beyond Social Capital: Spatial Dynamics of Collective Efficacy for Children," *American Sociological Review* 64 (1999): 633–660.

3. L. Quillian, "The Decline of Male Employment in Low-Income Black Neighborhoods, 1950–1990," *Social Science Research* 32 (2003): 220–250; B. H. Rankin and J. M. Quane, "Neighborhood Poverty and the Social Isolation of Inner-City African American Families," *Social Forces* 79 (2000): 139–164; W. J. Wilson, *The Truly Disadvantaged: The Inner City, the Underclass, and Public Policy* (Chicago: University of Chicago Press, 1987); and W. J. Wilson, *When Work Disappears: The World of the New Urban Poor* (New York: Random House, 1996).

4. E. Anderson, *Codes of the Street: Decency, Violence, and the Moral Life of the Inner City* (New York: W. W. Norton and Company, Inc., 1999); D. S. Massey and N. A. Denton, *American Apartheid: Segregation and the Making of the Underclass* (Cambridge: Harvard University Press, 1993); and Wilson, *The Truly Disadvantaged*.

5. J. L. Aber, M. Gephart, J. Brooks-Gunn, J. Connell, and M. B. Spencer, "Neighborhood, Family and Individual Processes As They Influence Child and Adolescent Outcomes," in *Neighborhood Poverty: Context and Consequences for Development*, ed. J. Brooks-Gunn, G. Duncan, and J. L. Aber (New York: Russell Sage Foundation, 1997), 44–61.

6. J. Brooks-Gunn, G. J. Duncan, P. K. Klebanov, and N. Sealand, "Do Neighborhoods Affect Child and Adolescent Development?" *American Journal of Sociology* 99 (1993): 353–395; P. L. Chase-Lansdale, R. Gordon, J. Brooks-Gunn, and P. K. Klebanov, "Neighborhood and Family Influences on the Intellectual and Behavioral Competence of Preschool and Early School-Age Children," in *Neighborhood Poverty: Context and Consequences for Development*, ed. J. Brooks-Gunn, G. Duncan, and J. L. Aber (New York: Russell Sage Foundation, 1997), 79–118; G. Duncan, J. Brooks-Gunn, and P. Klebanov, "Economic Deprivation and Early Childhood Development," *Child Development* 65 (1994): 296–318; C. Garner and S. Raudenbush, "Neighborhood Effects on Educational Attainment: A Multilevel Analysis," *Sociology of Education* 64 (1991): 251–262; P. K. Klebanov, J. Brooks-Gunn, C. McCarton, and M. C. McCormick, "The Contribution of Neighborhood and Family Income to Developmental Test Scores Over the First Three Years of Life," *Child Development* 69 (1998): 1420–1436; and T. Leventhal and J. Brooks-Gunn, "The Neighborhoods They Live In: the Effects of Neighborhood Residence on Child and Adolescent Outcomes," *Psychological Bulletin* 126 (2000): 309–337.

7. Chase-Lansdale et al., *Neighborhood Poverty: Context and Consequences for Development*; Duncan, Brooks-Gunn, and Klebanov, "Economic Deprivation and Early Childhood Development"; Leventhal and Brooks-Gunn, "The Neighborhoods They Live In."

8. C. S. Aneshensel and C. A. Sucoff, "The Neighborhood Context of Adolescent Mental Health," *Journal of Health and Social Behavior* 37 (1996): 293–310.

9. Brooks-Gunn et al., "Do Neighborhoods Affect Child and Adolescent Development?"; R. L. Clark, *Neighborhood Effects on Dropping Out of School among Teenage Boys* (Washington: The Urban Institute, 1992); J. Crane, "Effects of Neighborhood on Dropping Out of School and Teenage Childbearing," in *The Urban Underclass*, ed. C. Jencks and P. Peterson (Washington: Brookings Institution Press, 1991), 299–320; J. Connell and B. Halpern-Felsher. "How Neighborhoods Affect Educational Outcomes in Middle Childhood

and Adolescence: Conceptual Issues and an Empirical Example," in *Neighborhood Poverty: Context and Consequences for Development*, ed. J. Brooks-Gunn, G. Duncan, and J. L. Aber (New York: Russell Sage Foundation, 1997), 174–199; and B. Halpern-Flesher, J. P. Connell, M. Beale Spencer, J. L. Aber, G. Duncan, E. Clifford, W. Crichlow, P. Usinger, S. Cole, L. Allen, and E. Seidman, "Neighborhood and Family Factors Predicting Educational Risk and Attainment in African-American and White Children and Adolescence," in *Neighborhood Poverty: Context and Consequences for Development*, ed. J. Brooks-Gunn, G. Duncan, and J. L. Aber (New York: Russell Sage Foundation, 1997), 146–173.

10. J. O. Billy, K. L. Brewster, and W. R. Grady, "Contextual Effects on the Sexual Behavior of Adolescent Women," *Journal of Marriage and the Family* 56 (1994): 387–404; K. L. Brewster, "Neighborhood Context and the Transition to Sexual Activity among Young Black Women," *Demography* 31 (1994): 603–614; K. L. Brewster, "Race Differences in Sexual Activity among Adolescent Women: The Role of Neighborhood Characteristics," *American Sociological Review* 59 (1994): 408–424; C. R. Browning, "Neighborhood Context and Racial Differences in Early Adolescent Sexual Activity," *Demography* 41 (2004): 697–720; J. Crane, *The Urban Underclass*; D. P. Hogan and E. M. Kitagawa, "The Impact of Social Status, Family Structure, and Neighborhood on the Fertility of Black Adolescents," *American Journal of Sociology* 90 (1985): 825–855; D. S. Massey, A. B. Gross, and M. L. Eggers, "Segregation, the Concentration of Poverty, and the Life Chances of Individuals," *Social Science Research* 20 (1991): 397–420; J. Ramirez-Valles, M. A. Zimmerman, and M. D. Newcomb, "Sexual Risk Behavior among Youth: Modeling the Influence of Prosocial Activities and Socioeconomic Factors," *Journal of Health and Social Behavior* 39 (1998): 237–253; and S. J. South and K. D. Crowder, "Neighborhood Effects on Family Formation: Concentrated Poverty and Beyond," *American Sociological Review* 64 (1999): 113–132.

11 J. Ludwig, G. J. Duncan, and P. Hirschfield, "Urban Poverty and Juvenile Crime: Evidence from a Randomized Housing-Mobility Experiment," (Chicago: Joint Center for Poverty Research, Northwestern University, 1998); and F. Peeples and R. Loeber, "Do Individual Factors and Neighborhood Context Explain Ethnic Differences in Juvenile Delinquency?" *Journal of Quantitative Criminology* 10 (1994): 141–157.

12. A. J. Abramson, M. S. Tobin, and M. R. VanderGoot, "The Changing Geography of Metropolitan Opportunity: The Segregation of the Poor in U.S. Metropolitan Areas: 1970 to 1990," *Housing Policy Debate* 6 (1995): 45–72; P. Jargowsky, *Poverty and Place: Ghettos, Barrios, and the American City* (New York: Russell Sage Foundation, 1997); P. Jargowsky, *Stunning Progress, Hidden Problems: the Dramatic Decline of Concentrated Poverty in the 1990s* (Washington: Brookings Institution, 2003); P. A. Jargowsky and M. J. Bane, "Ghetto Poverty in the United States, 1970–1980," in *The Urban Underclass*, ed. C. Jencks and P. Peterson (Washington: Brookings Institution Press, 1991), 235–273; J. D. Kasarda, "Inner-city Concentrated Poverty and Neighborhood Distress: 1970 to 1990," *Housing Policy Debate* 4 (1993): 253–302; and D. S. Massey and M. L. Eggers, "The Ecology of Inequality: Minorities and the Concentration of Poverty, 1970-1980," *American Journal of Sociology* 95 (1990): 1153–1188.

13. C. DeNavas-Walt, B. D. Proctor, and C. H. Lee, "Income, Poverty, and Health Insurance Coverage in the United States: 2004," *Current Population Reports P60-229* (Washington: U.S. Census Bureau, 2005).

14. C. S. Fischer, G. Stockmayer, J. Stiles, and M. Hout, "Distinguishing the Geographic Levels and Social Dimensions of U.S. Metropolitan Segregation 1960-2000," *Demography* 41 (2004): 37–60.

15. J. R. Logan, D. Oakley, J. Stowell, and B. Stults, *Living Separately: Segregation Rises for Children* (Albany: Lewis Mumford Center, 2001).

16. Jargowsky, "Stunning Progress, Hidden Problems: The Dramatic Decline of Concentrated Poverty in the 1990s"; G. T. Kingsley and P. L. S. Pettit, *Concentrated Poverty: A Change in Course* (Washington: The Urban Institute, 2003).

17. Jargowsky, *Poverty and Place.*

18. Wilson, *The Truly Disadvantaged*, 58.

19. K. Crowder and S. J. South, "Race, Class, and Changing Patterns of Migration between Poor and Nonpoor Neighborhoods," *American Journal of Sociology* 110 (2005): 1715–1763; L. J. Krivo, R. D. Peterson, H. Rizzo, and J. R. Reynolds, "Race, Segregation, and the Concentration of Disadvantage: 1980–1990," *Social Problems* 45 (1998): 61–80; Massey and Denton, *American Apartheid*; and L. Quillian, "Migration Patterns and the Growth of High-Poverty Neighborhoods, 1970–1990," *American Journal of Sociology* 105 (1999): 1–37.

20. Jargowsky and Bane, "Ghetto Poverty in the United States, 1970–1980"; Jargowsky, *Poverty and Place* and "Stunning Progress, Hidden Problems: the Dramatic Decline of Concentrated Poverty in the 1990s"; and Kingsley and Petit, *Concentrated Poverty.*

21. High poverty neighborhoods have generally been defined as neighborhoods in which 40 percent or more of the population are living in poverty.

22. Jargowsky, *Poverty and Place.*

23. Ibid.

24. Jargowsky, "Stunning Progress, Hidden Problems: the Dramatic Decline of Concentrated Poverty in the 1990s"; and Kingsley and Petit, *Concentrated Poverty.*

25. Kingsley and Petit, *Concentrated Poverty.*

26. Ibid.

27 C. DeNavas-Walt, B. D. Proctor, and C. H. Lee, "Income, Poverty, and Health Insurance Coverage in the United States: 2004."

28. Logan et al., *Living Separately.*

29. Fischer et al., "Distinguishing the Geographic Levels and Social Dimensions of U.S. Metropolitan Segregation 1960–2000."

30. Logan et al., *Living Separately.*

31. Wilson, *The Truly Disadvantaged.*

32. F. Echenique and R. Fryer, "On the Measurement of Segregation," (Cambridge: National Bureau of Economic Research, 2005).

33. Anderson, *Codes of the Street*; Massey and Denton, *American Apartheid*; and Wilson, *The Truly Disadvantaged.*

34. Jargowsky and Bane, "Ghetto Poverty in the United States, 1970–1980"; and Jargowsky, *Poverty and Place.*

35. Tracts where more than 40 percent of the population in any year resided in group quarters were deleted in order to remove tracts dominated by prisons, military bases, colleges, and universities and other formal institutions.

36. Less than 30 percent of the tracts in this sample of metropolitan areas do not change boundaries between 1970 and 2000.

37. Jargowsky, *Poverty and Place* and "Stunning Progress, Hidden Problems: The Dramatic Decline of Concentrated Poverty in the 1990s"; Massey and Eggers, "The Ecology of Inequality"; Quillian, "The Decline of Male Employment in Low-Income Black Neighborhoods, 1950-1990"; M. J. White, *American Neighborhoods and Residential Differentiation* (New York: Russell Sage Foundation, 1987).

38. D. S. Massey and N. A. Denton, "Trends in the Residential Segregation of Blacks, Hispanics, and Asians: 1970–1980," *American Sociological Review* 52 (1987): 802–825; D. S. Massey and N. A. Denton, "The Dimensions of Residential Segregation," *Social Forces* 67 (1988): 281–315; D. S. Massey and N. A. Denton, "Hypersegregation in U.S. Metropolitan Areas: Black and Hispanic Segregation along Five Dimensions," *Demography* 26 (1989): 378–379; and Massey and Denton, *American Apartheid.*

39. The mean tract population declines from over 4,300 in 2000 to fewer than 3,200 in 1970. The inclusion of these tracts does not influence the conclusions presented in this paper.

40. While it might be preferable to apply more recent metropolitan area boundaries to earlier decades in order to account for spatial expansion and contraction since 1970, this is not possible since few areas outside of metropolitan areas were tracted prior to 1980.

41. Jargowsky, *Poverty and Place* and "Stunning Progress, Hidden Problems: the Dramatic Decline of Concentrated Poverty in the 1990s"; and Kingsley and Petit, *Concentrated Poverty.*

42. Jargowsky, *Poverty and Place;* Massey and Denton, *American Apartheid.*

43. J. Brooks-Gunn and L. B. Markman, "The Contribution of Parenting to Ethnic and Racial Gaps in School Readiness," *The Future of Children* 15 (2005): 139–168; J. Currie, "Health Disparities and Gaps in School Readiness," *The Future of Children* 15 (2005): 117–138; W. T. Dickens, "Genetic Differences and School Readiness." *The Future of Children* 15 (2005): 55–69; G. J. Duncan and K. A. Magnuson, "Can Family Socioeconomic Resources Account for Racial and Ethnic Test Score Gaps?" *The Future of Children* 15 (2005): 35–54; K. G. Noble, N. Tottenham, and B. J. Casey, "Neuroscience Perspectives on Disparities in School Readiness and Cognitive Achievement," *The Future of Children* 15 (2005): 71–89; and N. E. Reichman, "Low Birth Weight and School Readiness," *The Future of Children* 15 (2005): 91–116.

44. J. P. Greene, *High School Graduation Rates in the United States. Revised,* (New York: Manhattan Institute for Policy Research, 2001); J. P. Greene and M. A. Winters, *Public School Graduation Rates in the United States. Civic Report* (New York: Manhattan Institute for Policy Research, 2002); and R. Haveman and B. Wolfe, *Succeeding Generations: On the Effects of Investments in Children* (New York: Russell Sage Foundation, 1995).

45. T. Cross and R. B. Slater, "The Troublesome Decline in African-American College Student Graduation Rates," *Journal of Blacks in Higher Education* 33 (2001): 102–109.

46. R. B. Freeman and H. J. Holzer, eds., *The Black Youth Employment Crisis* (Chicago: University of Chicago Press, 1986); Haveman and Wolfe, *Succeeding Generations.*

47. Freeman and Holzer, *The Black Youth Employment Crisis*; M. Morris, A. D. Bernhardt and M. S. Handcock, "Economic Inequality: New Methods for Trends," *American Sociological Review* 59 (1994): 205–219; and E. O. Wright and R. Dwyer, "The American Jobs Machine: Is the New Economy Creating Good Jobs?" *Boston Review* 25 (2000): 6.

48. B. Western, *Punishment and Inequality* (New York: Russell Sage Foundation, 2006).

49. Haveman and Wolfe, *Succeeding Generations*; B. Wolfe and L. L. Wu, eds., *Out of Wedlock: Causes and Consequences of Nonmarital Fertility* (New York: Russell Sage Foundation, 2001).

50. Aber et al., *Neighborhood Poverty*; J. Brooks-Gunn, G. Duncan, and J. L. Aber, eds., *Neighborhood Poverty: Context and Consequences for Development* (New York: Russell Sage Foundation, 1997); Clark, "Neighborhood Effects on Dropping Out of School among Teenage Boys"; Connell and Halpern-Felsher, *Neighborhood Poverty*; Duncan, Brooks-Gunn, and Klebanov, "Economic Deprivation and Early Childhood Development"; Garner and Raudenbush,

"Neighborhood Effects on Educational Attainment"; Hogan and Kitagawa, "The Impact of Social Status, Family Structure, and Neighborhood on the Fertility of Black Adolescents"; Klebanov et al., "The Contribution of Neighborhood and Family Income to Developmental Test Scores over the First Three Years of Life"; and Ramirez-Valles, Zimmerman, and Newcomb, "Sexual Risk Behavior among Youth."

# CHAPTER 11

# CHILDHOOD VICTIMIZATION AS A PRECURSOR TO VIOLENCE AMONG ADULT HOMELESS WOMEN*

## *Jana L. Jasinski, Jennifer K. Wesely, Elizabeth Ehrhardt Mustaine, and James D. Wright*

### THE FOUR-CITY FLORIDA SURVEY

Prior to the Florida Four-City Survey analyzed here, studies with samples of homeless women and samples of victims of domestic violence existed, but no study evaluating homeless women's experience with violence, including domestic violence *and* using a large sample has ever been conducted. The Florida Four-City Survey, therefore, marks the first study to examine victimization among homeless women using standardized measurements to make comparisons with other research using samples of housed women possible. In addition, the study was designed to gain a more complete picture of what these women lived through prior to becoming homeless.

Development of the Florida study began in 2002 with a focus group involving six homeless women. From this focus group and a review of the literature, a questionnaire was developed to obtain detailed information about the experience of violence in the lives of homeless women. The questionnaire was designed to help us understand more fully the lifetime experiences of homeless women. We conducted survey interviews with about 200 women at shelters in each of four cities (Tampa, Orlando, Jacksonville, and Miami), for a total sample size just under 800. The scale and geographic range of the study design meant that we would need multiple individuals to conduct the interviews over the course of at least 6 months. Consequently, interviewers in each site were recruited from among existing shelter staff—case managers, intake workers, counselors, etc. All our interviewers were highly experienced in dealing with homeless women and their problems, and all took on their interviewing jobs as a supplement to their normal work roles. Our interviewers were largely case managers, who came into contact with issues of victimization on a daily basis. As such, they were already screened, trained, and provided with resources to deal appropriately with participants.

In addition to the survey, more qualitative in-depth interviews were conducted with about 20 homeless women in Orlando. Women who took part in the qualitative study were recruited by case managers at the Orlando Coalition for the Homeless who had participated in interviewer training. They were asked to identify women at the center who experienced some form of violence. The first 20 women who fit this criterion and agreed to participate were the interviewees for this part of the study. Interviews were arranged by case managers, who set up mutually convenient meetings between one of the study coprincipals and the participant in a private conference or sitting room on site at the homeless shelter.

Altogether, 737 women were surveyed. In Orlando, 199 women were interviewed at the Coalition for the Homeless of Central Florida. In Tampa, 200 women were surveyed at the Metropolitan Ministries facilities. At the I.M. Sulzbacher Center for the Homeless in Jacksonville, 146 women were surveyed and in Miami 192 women were surveyed at the Community Partnership for Homeless Inc. Each of the four facilities provides shelter and other services to some hundreds of homeless people daily, men and women alike. All of the shelters where respondents were solicited are general-purpose homeless facilities, not battered-women's facilities and not special-purpose facilities devoted exclusively to teens, to the addicted, or to the mentally ill.

Existing literature about violence and homelessness is a hodge-podge of results. One reason for this is the general avoidance of standardized, validated measuring instruments in favor of various *ad hoc* measures. Our strategy was to use standardized instrumentation wherever possible, modified as necessary and appropriate given our population and hypotheses:

The *Conflict Tactics Scale (CTS)*[1], as modified by Tjaden and Thoennes,[2,3] was used to measure the occurrence of "major violence" episodes among homeless women (and a parallel sample of about a hundred homeless men). The modifications of the scale by Tjaden and Thoennes make it equally useful in measuring violence committed by intimates or strangers (i.e., both domestic and street violence perpetrated against these women). The modified scale also asks about violence experienced both as child and as adult, inquires about the consequences of each episode, and records details on the reporting of each episode and what happened after the event was reported.

In essence, these modifications transform the CTS into a survey instrument similar to that used in the National Victimization Surveys. These modifications not only make the scale more useful in investigating our study hypotheses but also allow comparisons to a national sample of women.[2] One small modification of the Tjaden-Thoennes victimization items was necessary, namely, follow-ups for the most recent "major violence" episode (or episodes) that ask about mood or behavioral changes in the weeks and months immediately subsequent to the victimization, which allows us to test hypotheses about the consequences of violence in the lives of these women. The CTS has demonstrated reliability and validity.[4,5]

The *Personal History Form (PHF)* is a standardized instrument widely used in studies of homeless people to record family and background characteristics, housing and homelessness histories, recent residential information, lifetime homeless episodes, most recent homeless episode, and the like. The only significant modifications required for present purposes, other than the deletion of some irrelevant items, were (1) to substitute the Tjaden-Thoennes childhood abuse sequence for the one contained in the PHF (the former is far more detailed and informative); and (2) to expand the allowable responses to the questions about "the reasons people have for leaving their residences" (in all the sequences about why the respondent is homeless) to specifically include intimate partner violence as one possible reason.

The *Addiction Severity Index (ASI)*[6] is a widely used instrument that obtains detailed information on respondent's medical status, employment and support, drug and alcohol use, legal status, family history and conflict, and psychiatric status. Again, we have extensive experience administering the ASI and have published on its methodological properties in research on homeless substance abusers.[7] Much of the ASI is redundant with items from the PHF and modified CTS and any redundant items were eliminated. Also, not all sections of the ASI are equally relevant to the aims of this research. From the legal status sequence, for example, our only interest is in the items asking about prior convictions (to test the hypothesis that homeless women with criminal records experience more violence than those without). Very little from the medical status sequence is relevant; moreover, most of the items in the section on employment and support that deal with "survival strategies" needed to be supplemented with additional items. (Note: the modifications to the ASI that we implemented make it impossible to compute so-called "ASI Scores" for our respondents.)

## WHO WERE THE WOMEN THAT TOOK PART IN THE FLORIDA FOUR-CITY STUDY?

Virtually every study of homeless people undertaken in the past three decades has reported that the homeless are "surprisingly" well educated, and our study is no exception. Nearly two-thirds of the women in the sample had at least a high school degree (or better) and more than a third had some education beyond high school. And while these numbers lag behind the Florida population as a whole (among whom in the 2000 Census 79.9 percent had a high school degree or better and 51.2 percent had some education beyond high school), the level of educational attainment is still "surprisingly" high considering the level of impoverishment characteristic of the group.

Almost half of the sample of homeless women identified themselves as African American, with white women comprising one-third of the sample, followed by Hispanic-Latina (14.5%). Please note: In our (and most other) studies, respondents can identify as white, black, or Hispanic; in the US Census, Hispanics can be of any race (i.e., race and Hispanic status are asked as separate questions). Thus, precise comparisons between our results and those of the Census cannot be made. In the 2000 Census, however, only 14.6 percent of Floridians were identified as African American so that group is heavily over-represented in our sample of homeless women, as, indeed, they are in nearly every other study of homelessness ever undertaken.[8–10]

Lack of familial ties and profound estrangement from kith and kin are widely understood to be among the distinguishing marks of homeless people and a principal reason why people become homeless in the first place.[11] Consistent with this understanding, most of the women in our study (79%) had either never married (43%) or were currently divorced or separated from their spouses (36%). Only about one in six was married or cohabiting at the time of the interview. By way of contrast, in 2003, only 24.4 percent of the U.S. adult population had never married; 58.8 percent were currently married, and only 10.2 percent were separated or divorced. So stable, on-going marital relationships are far less common among homeless women than in the population at large.

## HOMELESS HISTORIES

The events that led to being homeless were of particular interest to us . To gain a more complete picture we asked a variety of questions about the women's history of homelessness. The women we interviewed became homeless, for the most part, in their early thirties and had been homeless for an average of 1.6 years by the time we surveyed them. When asked about the longest single period in which they had been homeless, the average was a little over a year. A majority of the women (53%) indicated they were homeless by themselves with the next highest proportion indicating they were homeless with children (24%). This is particularly interesting as only one out of five women indicated they did not have any children. Just over 10 percent were homeless with their partners.

### The Association between Violence and Homelessness

We asked each of the women if they were currently homeless because of violence or abuse committed against them by an adult partner in their last residence. Just about three-quarters of the women told us that violence was not a factor in their homelessness. The remaining quarter indicated that violence was either the main reason (14%) or at least one of the reasons why they were homeless (12%). These findings are generally consistent with the empirical literature, which converges on about one in four or five as the fraction of homeless women who are homeless because of violence. However, these findings are far lower than the one out of two often cited[12–14] with little, if any, empirical evidence to support it. It is obvious that at least *some* women are homeless because they are fleeing abusive domestic situations and that many homeless women were domestic violence victims prior to becoming homeless. Less obvious is whether prior experience with domestic violence is a *major* direct cause of homelessness among women, something that has been asserted far more frequently than it has been researched.

Although many of the women in our study did not identify violence as the primary reason they became homeless, it is clear from their depictions of their childhood that many of these women experienced a variety of negative childhood events, including violence, that certainly have shaped their adult lives in some way. At a minimum these

**Table 11.1**
**Childhood Experiences Among Homeless Women (N = 737)**

|  | Total Sample |
|---|---|
| % experienced childhood psychological aggression | 66.7 |
| % experienced minor childhood violence | 49.8 |
| % experienced severe childhood violence | 49.8 |
| % experienced any childhood violence | 59.4 |
| % parents ever married | 75.3 |
| % parents ever divorced, separated, or widowed | 64.5 |
| Mean number of times parents divorced, SD in ( ) | 1.55 (2.05) |
| % adults yelled at each other | 62.2 |
| % adults hit each other | 39.7 |
| % very unhappy childhood | 14.2 |
| % unhappy childhood | 9.9 |
| % so-so childhood | 30.7 |
| % happy childhood | 26.4 |
| % very happy childhood | 18.8 |

women experienced some family instability, as over two-thirds told us that at some point their families were not intact. Witnessing adults engaging in violent behavior was also common. Most of the women we interviewed told us that the adults in their household yelled at each other and more than one out of three reported that they also hit each other. Perhaps even more telling is that their experiences with violence were not limited only to witnessing adult violence, but also to experiencing violence. More than two-thirds of the women told us that they were victims of childhood psychological aggression including being insulted, sworn at, humiliated, and embarrassed. Even more troubling, however, is that half of the women experienced minor violence (push, shove, grab, pull hair) and half experienced severe violence (threaten to kill, choke, beat up). Even with these negative and sometimes brutal experiences, however, almost half had positive recollections of their childhood. At the same time, half of the women remembered a less than happy childhood.

When we compared the reports of childhood happiness with the women's recollection of negative childhood events (e.g., violence), not surprisingly, we found that women who had experienced any of the negative childhood events (ranging from adults yelling at each other to severe child abuse) were much more likely to report an unhappy to very unhappy childhood. The data follow:

Given the extent of negative childhood experiences, it is not surprising that those experiences influenced these women as adults. For the women in our study, childhood violence was significantly related to their experience of homelessness. Women who experienced childhood minor or severe violence were on average 3 years younger when they first become homeless, and they were homeless more frequently and for longer periods of time. It is apparent that violence did play some role in the experiences of homelessness for these women, even though most did not identify childhood

**Table 11.2**
**Associations between Childhood Happiness and Negative Childhood Events**

|                                                      | Yes  | No   |
|------------------------------------------------------|------|------|
| Adults in HH yelled at each other                    |      |      |
| % Unhappy or very unhappy                            | 33.9 | 8.3  |
| Adults in HH hit each other                          |      |      |
| % Unhappy or very unhappy                            | 42.7 | 12.2 |
| Experienced childhood psychological aggression       |      |      |
| % Unhappy or very unhappy                            | 33.5 | 24.4 |
| Experienced childhood minor violence                 |      |      |
| % Unhappy or very unhappy                            | 41.1 | 7.3  |
| Experienced childhood severe violence                |      |      |
| % Unhappy or very unhappy                            | 40.8 | 7.9  |
| Experienced any childhood violence (minor or severe) |      |      |
| % Unhappy or very unhappy                            | 36.8 | 5.9  |

*Note:* All differences were significant $p$ .001. To clarify the table: Among women who recalled that the adults in their childhood home yelled at one another, 33.9% said that their childhoods had been "unhappy" or "very unhappy." In contrast, among those who did not recall adults yelling at one another, only 8.3% reported unhappy or very unhappy childhoods.

experiences with violence as one of the reasons they were homeless. This information comes primarily from an open-ended question in the survey instrument where we asked the women to tell us some of the reasons they left home the first time they became homeless. Women who experienced childhood violence were also one and a half times more likely to use alcohol and almost twice as likely to use drugs as adults than women who did not experience such violence.

Childhood experiences were also important as they shaped the worldview of these women. In-depth interviews with the women revealed that experiences in childhood provided certain messages about women's sexuality, relationships, men, and violence. These messages had real effects as the women matured into adulthood. For the women interviewed in the qualitative study, childhood and adulthood experiences of violence and abuse played a major role in their development of low self-esteem; many actually used this phrase verbatim. Dee, for instance, said that the result of her child abuse was "low self-esteem. It took me a while to let my husband touch me." Diane, who was called "worthless and no good" and told she would "never amount to anything" by her father, now says, "It's taken me like that last few years to get my self-esteem back." Mo recalls, "I absolutely hated myself." She felt her mother did not want her, and her father continually "threw that up in my face." From childhood, Natalie felt she was "ugly and unloved." Marion says she had "no self value."

As children, many saw women brutalized, abused, and degraded. Often, the women experiencing this violence were our respondents' mothers. In addition to the trauma of witnessing and enduring abuse, seeing women mistreated in these ways relayed powerful meanings. Tamara succinctly states, "All my life I have seen men beat women." Similarly, Eliza recalls, "I thought that's the way life was. Because in the neighborhood I grew up in, it was nothing to see a woman dragged, knocked down, stomped and beat . . . So many women, including my mother—they stood there and they took it . . . So I took on that generational trait. You were just supposed to take it."

This normalization of violence was gender-specific; the women almost always described seeing violence perpetrated by men against women. This was mapped onto their concept of adult relationships. Ruby describes, "All my relationships I had were very abusive and that's what I thought love was about. I didn't know no better. Any time they would beat me up and—they would beat me up bad and they would tell me later on they loved me. And I'd say, ok. And keep going and going and going that way. And that's like I learned it."

Another component to the messages about relationships and men was specific to sex. From both mothers and fathers, the women recalled hearing about how women were only good for one thing, and that one thing did not count for very much. Eliza's father told her she should have been a boy, saying, "You're gonna grow up and be a whore and have a belly full of babies. And you're not gonna be any good."

Both Ruby and Mo learned that men only wanted women for sex, and that women should therefore use their sexuality to their advantage. Mo remembers seeing her mother with many different men, and reflects on a conversation when her mother told her, "Oh, if you ever want to get a guy's attention, wear this kind of stuff, act this way, do this." Likewise, according to Ruby, "[My mother] taught me to lay up with the mens to get what I want. I was supposed to go to bed with all these different mens to get what I want. I didn't know no better. That's what we were supposed to do. My mom always said we had a money maker." Ruby recalls her mother visiting men, working as a de facto prostitute. She says, "I knew she had a lot of different mens. We was well-known as we was growing up as kids." Through messages like this, the women learned that degrading, exploitive, and abusive treatment was simply their lot in life.

Women in the quantitative part of the study had similar experiences. Childhood violence was one mechanism providing entry into sexually exploitative work. For example, women who experienced minor or severe childhood violence were more than twice as likely to work as prostitutes or strippers, professions that likely increased their risk for violence and further solidified their ideas about men, women, and sexuality.

In the qualitative component of this study, the average age that the women left home for good was about 18. Although it seems reasonable, this number belies the amount of shuffling in and out of residences, the early pregnancies and marriages, and the abuse the women experienced while young. Furthermore, the place they lived as children was often not a "home" in the sense that it provided support, survival, or protection. They often lived in an environment characterized by abuse and violence, poverty, loss and dislocation, parental drug and alcohol use, and illness. These factors led to transience and displacement beginning at a relatively young age.

By the age of 19, Amelia had already been shuttled between numerous "caretakers." She lived with her father until the age of 9, when he died. She then moved in with her brother for a year and a half, and then her grandmother from ages 11–15, who then also died. Amelia finally moved in with her mother, only to be kicked out at age 18 by a new stepfather. It took her less than a year to become homeless. Fully 16 of the 20 women we interviewed recounted some sort of physical or sexual abuse as children, with nearly all identifying emotional abuse or neglect.

Eliza lived with her mother, father, and siblings until she was 7. Because of violence and drinking between her parents, she lived with her uncle for a year. After returning to her parents at age 8, she was removed by the state and sent to a children's home. After a year or two, she was sent back home, where she was molested by her father and physically, verbally, and emotionally abused. She was beaten by her mother when she tried to confide her father's abuse. The parental neglect led her to wander the streets at night looking for food and a little bit of care. The first older man she met at age 13 or 14 who fed her when she was hungry became the father of her first two children. He was both a drug addict and abusive.

The sense one gets from the qualitative interviews is that these early abuse experiences left permanent scars on these women and profoundly warped their sense of what is normal and acceptable in adult relationships with men, and this in turn leads to a hypothesis that women who experience the most abuse as children will continue to be abused in later life. These results were mirrored by the quantitative portion of the study as many of the women who reported childhood victimization also reported adult victimization. Specifically, 86 percent of the women who experienced physical violence as a child also experienced physical victimization as an adult ($P < .001$). By comparison 52 percent of the women who did not experience childhood physical violence experienced adult physical victimization. Women who were victimized as children also experienced on average four more victimizations compared to women who were not victimized.

The effects of early experiences with violence linger into adulthood and adult relationships. We asked the women in our study a series of questions about their current or most recent partner to gain a sense of the quality of their intimate relationships. These questions asked about the controlling, isolating, and abusive behaviors of their intimate partners. Women who were childhood victims of violence identified more negative behaviors in their partners than did women who were not victimized. In addition, they also indicated that these negative behaviors occurred more frequently. Although our cross-sectional data do not allow us to presume causality, it is obvious that childhood experiences do influence adult relationships.

One of the mechanisms through which childhood victimization may increase the risk for entering into unhealthy adult relationships is its relationship to self-esteem and depression. In our study, childhood victimization was not significantly associated with adult self-esteem. It was, however, associated with depression. Women who were victims of childhood abuse were more than twice as likely as women who reported no abuse to feel that the term depressed described them very well. Furthermore, depression was significantly associated with adult victimization (stalking, sexual, or physical assault). It is important to note that the measure of depression in these analyses is a subjective assessment by the women themselves rather than a clinical diagnosis. Again, although causal ordering cannot be conclusively established, the association between childhood negative events, depression, and adult victimization cannot be ignored.

Childhood victimization was also significantly related to other types of victimization as well. Women who had experienced minor or severe abuse as children were more likely to be robbed, pick-pocketed, have things stolen from them, have been seriously beat up, stabbed or cut with a knife, and shot at with a gun.

Although there have been many suppositions about the relationship between homelessness and violence, there is only limited empirical evidence looking at factors that may increase the risk for victimization among this vulnerable population. Furthermore, much of this evidence only tackles one aspect of this complex relationship at a time. The Florida Four-City Study was able to provide, for the first time, a more complete picture of the myriad of risk factors that influence victimization using a large multisite sample.

In the Florida Four-City Study, we combined all types of victimization into one dependent variable that represented any adult victimization and find several factors that did emerge as important risk markers for this type of victimization. A common theme throughout the discussion of the results of this study is the impact of childhood experiences on a plethora of behaviors and attitudes. The results of the multivariate analysis indicated that childhood violence significantly increased the risk for adult victimization net of all other factors in the model. In addition, current alcohol use, being divorced or separated, and a greater number of children also increased victimization risk. Women from Miami were at less of a risk of victimization compared to the reference group of women in Orlando. The only characteristic of homelessness, per se, that was significantly associated with victimization was number of times homeless. Women who were homeless more frequently were at a greater risk for victimization. Finally, women who described themselves as depressed were more likely to be victims.

What these analyses tell us is that homeless women are a vulnerable population with childhood violence at the crux of this vulnerability. Minor and severe violence experienced as a child increased the risk of many of factors (including homelessness) that then were associated with a greater risk for adult victimization. At a minimum, these results suggest that that more attention should be paid to the treatment of child victimization and a greater effort should be made to prevent child maltreatment. The women in our qualitative study spoke of childhoods filled with violence that led many to leave their childhood homes and many others ill prepared to develop healthy relationships. Homeless shelters are focused on the most pressing and immediate needs, like a place to sleep for the night. Rarely are they equipped to handle the myriad of problems with which these women and men struggle. They may not be prepared to delve deep into the childhood experiences of the women that arrive at their facilities. Consequently these men and women are in danger of repeating a cycle of homelessness and victimization.

## CONCLUSIONS

The Florida Four-City Survey marks the first large sample study evaluating homeless women's experience with violence, including domestic violence. In addition, our

**Table 11.3**
**"Would You Say Your Adult Partner . . ."**

| | No Childhood Violence | Experienced Childhood Violence |
|---|---|---|
| Has a hard time seeing things from your viewpoint? | 2.32[a] | 2.63 |
| Is jealous or possessive? | 2.16 | 2.68 |
| Tries to provoke arguments? | 1.86 | 2.29 |
| Tries to limit your contact with family or friends? | 1.75 | 2.00 |
| Insists on knowing who you are with at all times? | 2.05 | 2.54 |
| Calls you names or puts you down in front of others? | 1.59 | 2.01 |
| Makes you feel inadequate? | 1.73 | 2.16 |
| Is frightened of you? | 3.69 | 3.61[b] |
| Shouts or swears at you? | 1.71 | 2.21 |
| Frightens you? | 1.61 | 2.02 |
| Prevents you from knowing about or having access to money even when you ask? | 1.54 | 1.85 |
| Prevents you from working? | 1.30 | 1.60 |
| Insists on changing where you are living even when you don't need or want to? | 1.28 | 1.73 |
| Threatens you with the safety of your children? | 1.17 | 1.35 |
| Threatens you with the safety of your animals? | 1.08 | 1.16 |
| Threatens you with the safety of your friends? | 1.14 | 1.40 |
| Insists on you having sex without a condom? | 1.55 | 2.07 |
| Prevents you from seeking medical attention? | 1.19 | 1.38 |
| Disappears for a day or days at a time? | 1.41 | 1.71 |
| Leaves you alone without food, money, or supplies? | 1.22 | 1.55 |
| Steals from you? | 1.25 | 1.50 |
| "Borrows" your credit card or money and does not pay you back? | 1.22 | 1.52 |

[a] Numbers are mean scores. Responses for all questions ranged from 4 (Almost always) to 1 (Never). A higher score indicates the behavior occurred more often.
[b] All analyses with the exception of this are statistically significant.

use of standardized measurements allows us to make comparisons with other research using samples of housed women. Much of what we found mirrors research using housed populations and differs only to the extent that these women experienced greater levels of victimization. Although the women we surveyed were staying in a homeless shelter, Wright and Devine[11] argue that "street homeless and sheltered homeless are not distinct populations; nearly all the homeless people in this sample spend at least an occasional night in an emergency shelter and nearly all of them also occasionally sleep out of doors. Which homeless people are considered "sheltered homeless" depends a great deal on who makes it to the shelter line first. Limitations aside, we now know a great deal more about the experience of violence in the lives of homeless women than was known before our study was conducted.

**Table 11.4**

**Logistic Regression Analysis Predicting Adult Victimization (Physical or Sexual Assault or Stalking) ($N = 632$)**

| Variable | B | S.E. | Odds Ratio | $P$ Value |
|---|---|---|---|---|
| Experienced childhood violence | 1.43 | .23 | 4.19 | .000 |
| Current alcohol use | .76 | .26 | 2.15 | .003 |
| Current drug use | 0.7 | .31 | 1.07 | .827 |
| Marital status | | | | |
|   Cohabitating | .25 | .78 | 1.29 | .748 |
|   Divorced | 1.02 | .42 | 2.77 | .016 |
|   Separated | 1.34 | .58 | 3.81 | .020 |
|   Widowed | .82 | .74 | 2.26 | .268 |
|   Single | .02 | .39 | 1.02 | .964 |
| Race | | | | |
|   African American | −.28 | .27 | .76 | .302 |
|   Hispanic | −.52 | .36 | .59 | .147 |
|   Other racial group | −.01 | .67 | .99 | .987 |
| City of interview | | | | |
|   Miami | −.68 | .31 | .51 | .030 |
|   Jacksonville | −.26 | .33 | .77 | .419 |
|   Tampa | −.08 | .33 | .92 | .801 |
|   Who homeless with | | | | |
|   Homeless with adult | .04 | .42 | 1.04 | .925 |
|   Homeless with kids | .02 | .31 | 1.02 | .955 |
|   Homeless with kids & adults | −.21 | .45 | .81 | .641 |
| Age first homeless | −.01 | .01 | .99 | .294 |
| # of times homeless | .28 | .11 | 1.32 | .012 |
| Total amount of time homeless | .06 | .08 | 1.06 | .499 |
| # of children | .18 | .07 | 1.19 | .010 |
| Depressed | .40 | .17 | 1.50 | .018 |
| Constant | −.99 | .75 | .37 | .183 |

*Note:* The reference groups for dummy variables are as follows: for marital status, married; for race, White; for city, Orlando; and for who are you homeless with, by themselves. Model Chi-square 200.406, $P$ .001; Nagelkerke $R$ square = .401.

A common theme in the victimization literature is the relationship between childhood victimization experiences and later adult victimization, perpetration, and other negative outcomes. These relationships also exist among the homeless women in the Florida Four City Study. As we have seen, abuse of all sorts was common in the young lives of these women. This was poignantly illustrated by the qualitative interviews, in which sixteen of the 20 participants recalled physical or sexual abuse, and all were neglected or emotionally abused in some way. The effects of this abuse were far-reaching, setting the women up for social, emotional, and behavioral deficits that bled into later life decisions and choices.

One significant consequence of being abused as a child is that it led some of the women to "early independence" or a premature departure from the childhood home at a younger-than-average age. This is consistent with research that finds that among homeless and runaway youth, a substantial proportion experienced child abuse.[15–18] In 8 of the 20 cases, the women left home in their teens by way of marriage or pregnancy, and 6 of the women were kicked out or ran away. Others thought they were starting over by leaving the childhood home for some other living situation, only to find their new situation as abusive and unsatisfactory as the old. Consider Cammie, who left home and got married at 18 and tried to "use" her first marriage to start a new family blueprint: "Because I was very much in love with the guy that I was marrying and I had it in my head that I was going to be able to show my parents that you could have a marriage and make it work and you know, children, and not have alcohol and drugs in the middle of it and do things right. And I mean, I looked at it in a very positive light . . . My thought was, I'm going to show everybody in my family, especially my parents that you can have a family and you can do it right."

Cammie then endured years of mental and physical abuse from her husband. In contrast, Eliza, at 13, did not pursue a relationship with an older man, but drifted into it while wandering the streets hungry, looking to stay away from her parents' abuse. "He said, 'What's your name?' He was real nice; he had a pocket full of money, wallet full of money. It was a summer night and I got in his car and I felt safe. And we rode over to where we ate. And he actually fed me and I was actually full . . . He would feed me. I would be hungry. And I would still go home and act like this kid I was. But I'd get hungry. And sometimes there wasn't a pot of beans or some bread in the oven and I'd go find it. And he'd say, 'You eat?' And I'd say, 'no' And he'd say, 'Let's go get something to eat.' He fed me . . . But again, it was a nightmare. It was a daydream, waking up from a nightmare, because I thought he was just so nice, and then after I gave up my virginity and the babies started coming, he wasn't so nice anymore . . . I couldn't go tell my mother because I always see her get beat up, her head split open, or her throwing a frying pan and splitting my father's head, so it was kind of [one] abuse upon another."

Women who grew up in household where adults were yelling or hitting each other were not as happy as women who grew up in households where these events did not happen. For some of these women, these negative childhood experiences led them to leave home early, setting the stage for later victimization. In addition, women who experienced childhood violence were more likely to report unhappy childhoods compared to women who were not victimized as children. Childhood violence also appears to be related to homelessness as these women were first homeless at a younger age, were homeless more frequently and for longer periods of time. Finally, childhood experiences of violence appear to be associated with adult negative outcomes as well.

As these women have described, the path to homelessness is fraught with peril and frequently begins early in life. Childhood violence often provides an unstable foundation upon which to build a life and sets the stage for later unhealthy relationships and behaviors. By the time homeless women arrive at a shelter, their cumulative negative experiences have shaped their view of the world and the chances of obtaining a "normal" life may be beyond reach. Shelters and shelter workers are prepared to deal with the external issues of being homeless such as food, clothing, and shelter, but it is likely they are ill prepared for the complex internal issues resulting from years of violent terror and betrayal. The barriers to self-sufficiency for these women, who have endured years of psychological, physical, and sexual abuse, are massive. They cannot be overcome by simply being provided with a place to sleep.

In recent years, homelessness has faded from prominence as a national political issue. There seems to be a widespread sense among both policy makers and the public that the programs of assistance enacted in the 1980s, while perhaps imperfect, have done as much as can or should be done to address this problem and that homeless people, like poor people in general, need to work themselves out of their condition. As we have seen, however, many of the processes that work to put homeless people out on the streets can be traced to events, experiences, victimizations, and misfortunes that began in early childhood. And certainly, the experience of violence would be high on this list of misfortunes. That many homeless women are homeless because of violence, and many more victims of more violence in a year than many people can expect to experience in their entire lifetimes, does not make homelessness any easier to resolve, but it does, we think, make the resolution all that more urgent.

## NOTES

* Research reported here was supported by a grant from the National Institute of Justice. The views are those of the authors and do not purport to reflect the position of the National Institute of Justice or the United States Department of Justice.

1. Murray Straus, "Measuring Intrafamily Conflict and Violence: The Conflict Tactics Scale," *Journal of Marriage and the Family* 41 (1979): 75.

2. Patricia Tjaden and Nancy Thoennes, "Prevalence, Incidence, and Consequences of Violence Against Women: Findings from the National Violence Against Women Survey," NIJ *Research In Brief* (November, 1998): 1.

3. Patricia Tjaden and Nancy Thoennes "Violence and Threats of Violence Against Women and Men in the United States, 1994–1996." *Inter-University Consortium for Political and Social Research codebook, ICPSR 2566*: 1999.

4. Murray A. Straus, Sherry L. Hamby, Sue Boney-McCoy, and David B. Sugarman, "The Revised Conflict Tactics Scales (CTS2): Development & Preliminary Psychometric Data," *Journal of Family Issues*, 17 (1996): 283.

5. Murry A. Straus, "The Conflict Tactics Scales and Its Critics: An Evaluation and New Data on Validity and Reliability," in *Physical Violence in American Families: Risk Factors and Adaptations to Violence in 8,145 Families*, ed. Murray. A. Straus and Richard. J. Gelles (New Brunswick, NJ: Transaction Publications, 1990), 49–74.

6. Thomas A. McLellan, Harvey Kushner, David Metzger, Roger Peters, Iris Smith, Grant Grissom, Helen Pettinati, and Milton Argeriou, "The Fifth Edition of the Addiction Severity Index," *Journal of Substance Abuse Treatment* 9 (1992): 199.

7. Laurie Joyner, James Wright, and Joel Devine, "Reliability and Validity of the Addiction Severity Index among Homeless Substance Misusers," *Substance Use and Misuse* 31 (1996): 6.

8. Martha Burt, Aron Y. Laudan, Edgar. L., Jesse Valente (eds.),. *Helping America's Homeless: Emergency Shelter or Affordable Housing?* (Washington, DC: Urban Institute Press, 2001).

9. Kim Hopper, *Reckoning with Homelessness* (Ithaca, NY: Cornell University Press, 2003).

10. Kenneth Kusmer, *Down and Out, On the Road* (New York: Oxford University Press, 2001).

11. James Wright, Beth Rubin, and Joel Devine, *Beside the Golden Door: Policy, Politics, and the Homeless* (Hawthorne, NY: Aldine de Gruyter, 1998).

12. Richard Gelles, "Domestic Violence Factoids." Available at http://www.mincava.umn.edu/papers/factoid.htm

13. National Coalition for the Homeless, "Domestic violence and homelessness fact sheet (NCH Fact Sheet #7)." Available at http://www.nationalhomeless.org/publications/facts/domestic.pdf (2006)

14. Joan Zorza, "Woman Battering: A Major Cause of Homelessness," *Clearinghouse Review* 25 (1991).

15. Mark Janus, Arlene McCormack, Ann Burgess, and Carol Hartman, *Adolescent Runaways: Causes and Consequences* (Lexington, MA: Lexington Books, 1987).

16. Mimi Silber and Ayala Pines, "Occupational Hazards of Street Prostitutes," *Criminal Justice and Behavior*, 8 (1981): 395.

17. Kimberly Tyler, Dan. Hoyt, LesWhitbeck, and Ana Marie Cauce, "The Effects of a High-Risk Environment on the Sexual Victimization of Homeless and Runaway Youth," *Violence and Victims* 16 (2001): 441.

18. Les Whitbeck, Dan Hoyt, Kevin Yoder, Ana Marie Cauce, Matt Paradise, "Deviant Behavior and Victimization Among Homeless and Runaway Adolescents," *Journal of Interpersonal Violence*, 16 (2001): 1175.

# INDEX

# ABOUT THE EDITORS AND CONTRIBUTORS

**Barbara A. Arrighi** is associate professor of sociology at Northern Kentucky University. Her research interests include work and family, as well as issues related to race, class, and sexism. Her books include: *America's Shame: Women and Children in Shelter and the Degradation of Family Roles* and *Understanding Inequality: The Intersection of Race/Ethnicity, Class, and Gender*. Professor Arrighi has published in the *Journal of Family Issues and elsewhere*.

**David J. Maume** is professor of sociology, and Director, Kunz Center for the Study of Work and Family, at the University of Cincinnati. His teaching and research interests are in labor market inequality and work-family issues, with recent publications appearing in the *Journal of Marriage and Family, Work and Occupations*, and *Social Problems*. He is currently researching gender differences in providing urgent child care in dual-earner families, gender differences in the effects of supervisor characteristics on subordinates' job attitudes, and the effects of shift work on the work and family lives of retail food workers (funded by the *National Science Foundation*).

**Sandra L. Barnes** is an assistant professor at Purdue University in the Department of Sociology and Anthropology and the African American Studies Research Center. Her research interests include urban sociology, gender/race/class inequality, and the Sociology of Religion.

**Dr. Ruth A. Brandwein** is professor and former dean of the School of Social Welfare. She began her career as a community organizer in Seattle, has taught at Boston University, was Director of the School of Social Work at the University of Iowa, and held a Distinguished Chair at the University of Utah School of Social Work. She also served 4 years as Commissioner of Social Services for Suffolk County, was President of the New York State Chapter of NASW, and a member of the National Advisory Council on Violence Against Women. Dr. Brandwein has published extensively on women and welfare, family violence, feminist theory and practice, and is currently Book Review Editor for *Affilia: Journal of Women and Social Work*.

**Mia Smith Bynum** is an assistant professor at Purdue University in the Department of Psychological Sciences. Her research interests focus on the black family.

**Pamela R. Davidson** is an assistant professor in sociology and public policy at the George Washington University in Washington, DC. Her research interests are in children and poverty, urban policy, and environmental justice. She completed a 2-year postdoctoral fellowship at the University of Wisconsin-Madison in 2004 after receiving her PhD in Sociology from the University of Massachusetts, Amherst in 2002. She received her master's degree from the Ruprecht-Karls-Universitaet in Heidelberg, Germany.

**Josefina Figueira-McDonough**, PhD, is professor emerita of Justice and Social Inquiry and of Social Work at Arizona State University. She was trained in sociology and social work at the University of Michigan and has held positions in both fields at the University of Michigan, Michigan State University, and Vanderbilt University. Her work on social justice, funded by federal, state, and private grants and disseminated in a variety of social science journals, has focused on deviance and control, the ecology of poverty, policy outcomes, community analysis, and curricula. Her most recent books include *Community Analysis and Praxis: Towards a Grounded Civil Society* (2001), *Women at the Margins: Neglect and Punishment and Resistance*, edited with Rosemary Sarri (2003), and *The Welfare State and Social Work; Pursuing Social Justice* (2006).

**Dr. Juanita M. Firestone** is currently a research professor with the Center for Policy Studies and a professor of sociology in the Department of Criminal Justice at the University of Texas at San Antonio. She obtained her PhD in Sociology from the University of Texas at Austin in 1984. She has over 20 years experience in evaluation and survey research, quantitative analysis, and computer applications (both mainframe and microcomputer). She has published extensively in professional journals and chapters in edited books, and has been Principal Investigator or Co-Principal Investigator in 20 community research projects. She has developed and managed all aspects of research projects including initial grant proposal, designing research instruments, selecting analysis techniques, and use of a variety of computer applications to organize, analyze, and report data. During Spring 2002 she was awarded the Fulbright Distinguished Chair in Gender Studies and taught at the University of Klagenfurt in Austria.

Her substantive research specializations encompass issues related to gender inequality, military sociology, health disparities, sexual harassment, and intimate partner abuse. Recent studies include (1) the relationship between strategies used to respond to sexual harassment and perceptions of the success of strategies chosen focusing on DoD data, (2) the impact of the "Don't Ask, Don't Tell, Don't Pursue Policy" on the extent to which individuals in the military experience or observe harassment based on sexuality, (3) occupational change and the gender-based wage gap, and (4) minority health disparities.

**Donna Haig Friedman**, PhD, research associate professor, and 2006–2007 Fulbright Scholar, directs the Center for Social Policy within the University of Massachusetts Boston's McCormack Graduate School of Policy Studies. She is a nationally recognized scholar in the field of poverty, housing policy, and homelessness. Within these fields, she specializes in policy analysis and research on family homelessness. She is the author of *Parenting in Public: Family Shelter and Public Assistance* (Columbia University Press, 2000) and of numerous articles and commissioned reports on homelessness and poverty.

**Jana L. Jasinski** is a faculty member in the Department of Sociology at the University of Central Florida. She is also the associate director of the Institute for Social and Behavioral Sciences. Jasinski received her PhD from the University of New Hampshire in 1996 and publishes in the areas of lethal and nonlethal interpersonal violence (particularly intimate partner violence), substance abuse, the response of the criminal justice system to violence, and the negative consequences of child sexual assault.

**E. Brooke Kelly** is an assistant professor of sociology at the University of North Carolina at Pembroke. Dr. Kelly is a research affiliate of the Rural Policy Research Institute's (RUPRI) Rural Poverty Center and chair of the Poverty, Class, and Inequalities division of the Society for the Study of Social Problems (SSSP). Her research and teaching focuses on inequalities, poverty, gender, work, and family. The article in this volume and other recent research draw from a larger project on the often invisible and taken for granted labors necessary for two groups of rural mothers to get and keep low-wage jobs. Kelly's recent publication in the *Journal of Poverty*, "Leaving and Losing Jobs: Resistance of Rural Low-Income Mothers," examines the importance of working conditions—brittle and unyielding to the needs of parents—in shaping job turnover among a group of low-income mothers in a rural county in the Midwest. Dr. Kelly is also involved in a collaborative research project, Jobs for the Future, assessing the impact of massive job losses in Robeson County, NC, on individuals, families, and communities.

**Joseph Michael** is a PhD student at the University of Cincinnati. His research interests are in racial inequality, class inequality, and family relationships. He is working as a Survey Specialist in the Education department of the National Opinion Research Center in Chicago, IL while he completes his PhD.

**Elizabeth Ehrhardt Mustaine**, PhD, is an associate professor in the Department of Sociology at the University of Central Florida and received her PhD in Sociology from The Ohio State University in 1994. Dr. Mustaine has written numerous journal articles on registered sex offenders and sex offender registries, criminal victimization, violence, violence against women, and stalking. She has also coauthored a book on issues in criminal justice research.

**Diana Pearce** is widely recognized for coining the phrase, "the feminization of poverty." Pearce received her PhD in Sociology and Social Work from the University of Michigan, and has taught at the University of Illinois and American University, and as a Fulbright Professor in Tashkent, Uzbekistan, and Bishkek, Kyrgyzstan. She has testified before Congress and the President's Working Group on Welfare Reform, and has helped found and lead several coalitions, such as the Women, Work and Welfare Coalition. She founded the Women and Poverty Project at Wider Opportunities for Women in Washington, DC, and created the Self-Sufficiency Standard—now calculated for 35 states and cities—and has done related analyses, research and online tools (calculators) that use the Standard. She is currently the faculty at the University of Washington School of Social Work, and is founder and director of the Center for Women's Welfare.

**Ellen K. Scott** is an associate professor of sociology and director of Women's and Gender Studies at the University of Oregon. Her recent research has focused on wage work and care work in low-income families. In collaboration with Andrew London, and with numerous fabulous graduate students at Kent State University, she collected longitudinal, in-depth data over 4 years from interviews with women receiving TANF in 1997 and therefore subjected to welfare reform. They published, and continue to publish, numerous papers from that project. Her current project grew from the research on welfare reform. She is now interviewing families caring for children with disabilities, with a particular focus on low-income, single-parent families, and on racial-ethnic minority families, some of them immigrants, who face particular obstacles in the labor force and in social services. This paper draws only on the data collected in the early phases of the research.

**Jeffrey M. Timberlake** is assistant professor of sociology at the University of Cincinnati. His research focuses on the causes and consequences of urban inequality. He is currently working on projects that estimate children's exposure to neighborhood poverty and affluence, the effects of that exposure on measures of child well-being, and change in urban spatial patterns over time.

**Robert L. Wagmiller, Jr.** is assistant professor of sociology at the University at Buffalo. His research examines the causes and consequences of childhood poverty as well as the social, economic, and historical roots of the urban underclass. Current projects include a study of the effects urban race riots in the 1960s and early 1970s on the spatial concentration of poverty, a study of the short-term and long-term effects of poor parental health on children's exposure to poverty, and a study of the effects of neighborhood disadvantage and segregation on individual's tolerance for risk.

**Dr. Jennifer K. Wesely** is currently with the Department of Criminology and Criminal Justice at the University of North Florida. Jennifer K. Wesely is an assistant professor in the Department of Criminology and Criminal Justice at the University of North Florida, having earned her doctorate from the School of Justice Studies at Arizona State University in May 2001. Her work addresses gender, body, identity, and inequality in contexts that include domestic violence, sex work, sport and the outdoors, and homelessness.

**James D. Wright** is an author, educator, and the Provost Distinguished Research Professor in the Department of Sociology at the University of Central Florida. He also serves as the director of the UCF Institute for Social and Behavioral Sciences. Wright received his PhD from the University of Wisconsin in 1973 and is the author or coauthor of 17 books (on topics ranging from guns to poverty to homelessness to NASCAR) and more than 250 journal articles, book chapters, essays, reviews, and polemics.